Authenticities

Also by Peter Kivy

Speaking of Art
*The Seventh Sense: A Study of Francis Hutcheson's Aesthetics and Its Influence
    in Eighteenth-Century Britain*
The Corded Shell: Reflections on Musical Expression
Sound and Semblance: Reflections on Musical Representation
Osmin's Rage: Philosophical Reflections on Opera, Drama, and Text
Music Alone: Philosophical Reflections on the Purely Musical Experience
The Fine Art of Repetition: Essays in the Philosophy of Music

AUTHENTICITIES

⊙

Philosophical

Reflections

on

Musical

Performance

PETER KIVY

Cornell University Press • *Ithaca and London*

First published 1995 by Cornell University Press.

Design and composition by Wilsted & Taylor.

Printed in the United States of America

⊗ The paper in this book meets
the minimum requirements of the
American National Standard
for Information Sciences—
Permanence of Paper for Printed
Library Materials, ANSI Z39.48-1984.

LIBRARY OF CONGRESS CATALOGING-IN-PUBLICATION DATA

Kivy, Peter.
    Authenticities : philosophical reflections on musical performance
/ Peter Kivy.
        p.   cm.
    Includes bibliographical references (p.) and index.
    ISBN 0-8014-3046-1
    1. Performance practice (Music)   2. Music—Philosophy and
aesthetics.   I. Title.
ML457.K58   1995
781.4'3'01—dc20   94-36842

For Ronald Roseman

My last word in performance

It's a bad plan that can't be changed.

—*Publius Syrus*

Contents

Preface

When logical positivism was in its heyday, one of its leading proponents was charged, in a book review, with "fiddling while Rome burns." With World War II just around the corner and Western Civilization at the edge of the abyss, the meaning of the indictment was all too clear. Instead of fulfilling one of its traditional roles, as the reviewer saw it—that of showing us the way—philosophy was in thrall to questions so abstruse, technical, and abstract as to be incomprehensible to the uninitiated, as well as completely irrelevant to their practical and moral concerns. "What is to be done?" was a question that philosophers either would not deign or would not presume to address.

In recent years a radical change in philosophy has taken place. One can now subscribe to a respectable academic journal called *Philosophy and Public Affairs*. On the committee that apportions kidney machines and organs for transplant you are more than likely to find a philosopher as well as a surgeon. Philosophy departments routinely teach courses in such subjects as medical ethics, business ethics, environmental ethics, and even environmental aesthetics, while some of the best philosophers in the business have made substantial contributions not only in the public press but in learned journals and scholarly books to such subjects of immediate concern as abortion, euthanasia, the right to die, the apportionment of scarce medical resources, nuclear war, suicide, the environment, and half a hundred others. What is more, on many of these issues they seem to have had an effect not only on public opinion but on public practice as well.

But anyone who has ever lectured before practicing artists or the "consumers" of art works on the subject of what philosophers call "aesthetics" or "the philosophy of art" can attest that whatever the Rome of art may be perceived as doing at the present time, the philosophers of art are seen as "fiddling." It therefore may come as something of a surprise, particularly to the musical reader, that a philosopher should be interested in anything so palpably "practical" as performance practice. It may be equally surprising for anyone to claim, as indeed I do, that what philosophy has to say about performance has real—which in this case is to say *practical*—implications, whether or not any real practical effect results.

The performance of "classical" music has come increasingly to be influenced, even dominated, by what certain people call "historical authenticity." And what is particularly interesting about this development, at least from a philosopher's point of view, is that many performance practices have begun to command the allegiance both of prominent performers and of the concertgoing public for reasons that are, in large measure, historical rather than, at least initially, the result of what people have heard and liked. I do not mean to imply that these practices have not become liked or are in place for historical reasons in spite of being distasteful to the ear. On the contrary, the historical authenticity movement has popular support in the concert hall and in the record shop, not only because it seems to have persuasive historical arguments in its favor but because people attest to genuinely liking the musical sounds they hear that have the imprimatur of historical musicology.

This much, however, is clear, and puzzling. Historical reasons have begun to overpower what might be called "reasons of the ear" to the extent that it no longer seems intellectually respectable, in musical circles, to adduce reasons of the ear *against* the claims of historical authenticity. In other words, now reasons of the ear, although they have not ceased to be relevant, have become relevant in only one direction. If you like the way authenticity sounds, that may be a reason in its favor; but if you don't, or if you like something else better, that is, from the critical point of view, no reason at all.

This must strike many, myself included, as an "intellectualist" conclusion, somewhat repugnant to musical common sense and sensibility. In response a thorough philosophical critique seems to be in order, of the whole apparatus that has, to some extent haphazardly, been put together to support the practice of historical authenticity in musical performance. That indeed is what I propose to undertake here.

There is, so far as I know, no systematic philosophical defense of historical authenticity in musical performance practice. It is in bits and pieces, here and there. And if it is to undergo a philosophical critique, some system and order must be imposed upon it from above. That is what I have to some extent attempted to do. Even so, something of the informal, *Schusterfleck* quality of the subject has, necessarily, rubbed off on my discussion, which is why, perhaps more than any of my other books on the philosophy of music, *Authenticities* deserves to be described as "philosophical reflections."

The historically authentic performance, when looked at from a philosopher's vantage point, is a philosophically "soft" subject. That is to say, there is little in the literature for the philosopher to engage, either in controversy or in argument and expansion. There is little written about the historically authentic performance that is "philosophy" because the movement is not primarily philosophical but practical. The people involved are mostly performers and musical historians, and their goal is positive knowledge of, and the subsequent production of, musical performances of a certain kind.

For a philosopher, the lack of a philosophical literature poses a problem. Philosophy feeds on philosophy. It was G. E. Moore, as I remember, who said that had he never read philosophy no philosophical problem would ever have occurred to him.

The bookishness of philosophy, if I may so put it, has the effect that whenever a philosopher deals with one of the central questions of the discipline, the high ground is already occupied, the main positions already staked out; the central questions in philosophy all have a history. The contemporary philosopher may reformulate the questions, and their answers, in contemporary terms; but he or she already has hard distinctions and hard positions to work with, and starts not from scratch but from a sturdy foundation. Philosophy does not continually remake itself anew, as some may think, any more than physics or biology does. What it continually remakes anew is its past.

This claim is true even where the layperson might think otherwise. Gilbert Ryle wrote a book that, famously, contains not a single footnote of any kind, nor does it end with the now customary bibliography of works cited, for there are no works cited. But no philosophically sophisticated reader fails to recognize whom Ryle is arguing with, or what the possible options for the philosophy of mind were in 1949. And even in the notorious case of Wittgenstein, who, we were once led to believe, knew no philosophy but Schopenhauer's, the philosophical past with which he was wrestling is always in the background, implicitly present.

It is because of this presence of the philosophical past that the conclusions of philosophers who work in the central areas of the discipline can be clearly delineated. We know the past options: they have all been explored. We therefore can discern, with the aid of this past, what option the contemporary philosopher has taken. Or if we are presented with something new under the sun, we can discern *that* clearly, in the light of past philosophical options.

It is precisely this conversation of philosophy with its past that the present subject must all but lack, for it has no philosophical past except for a small (although distinguished) collection of philosophical articles. But for the most part I have had to "construct" on my own the philosophical positions that I have discussed and, on numerous occasions, from which I have dissented. To a certain extent, then, my philosophical dialogue has had to be the monologue of a divided self.

Furthermore, it is precisely because I have had, for the most part, to construct for myself the implied philosophical foundations of the historical performance movement that I have not been able to quote chapter and verse: there simply is not much chapter and verse of a philosophical kind to quote. But if I have had to "construct" a "philosophy" of the historical performance movement with which to argue and on which to build, I have by no means woven it out of whole cloth. If an "outsider" to the movement should think so, all I can say is "Become an insider"; for it is a practical movement, not a philosophical one, and one can know its nature only by "feel," not by study and precept. And if an "insider" should think so, then all I can say is "Know thyself"—or, at the risk of hubris, "Read this book."

The consequence, for the maker of conclusions, of the philosophically "soft" nature of our subject is that conclusions are hard to come by and difficult to delineate. That is because the background is philosophically blurry, the philosophical options unformed and unexplored. A philosophical writer on any central question in philosophy is perceived, even without making it explicit, either to fall within one of the well-surveyed positions or to be an innovator in contrast to them. A philosophical writer on the peripheries, which the "philosophy of historically authentic performance" must surely be seen to occupy, has none of this preordained clearness and distinctness to aid him in making his conclusions firm and apparent. Were this a ramble over the well-worn paths of analytic aesthetics, the position of its author, at the end of the exercise, would be clear to see. Because the terrain here is philosophically unexplored, there will be no "hard" conclusions.

The conclusions we seek are not merely theoretical but practical ones. Performers are, primarily, doers, not thinkers or knowers (in the theoretical sense). The question is, What should they *do*? More particularly, Should they be *authentic*? But we shall see that being authentic is not being one thing: it is being four things (at least); and, further, we shall learn that one cannot be all of them at once. So our question is far from a simple one. It is, rather, many questions with many answers.

I think the questions and answers, so far as I can ask and answer them, are within my text. The reader, therefore, and for the reasons already adduced, can expect no grand and structured conclusions at the end of this book, tying together the various strands of argument. There are no grand conclusions. There is only the acknowledgment of a plurality of "authentic" performance practices, a plurality of musical payoffs and pitfalls. There is no a priori road to the best performance—only the genius of the performer tested by the listener's ear.

Of conclusions, then, there will be none, if by "conclusions" we mean a systematic philosophy of musical performance, authentic or otherwise. What I hope there will be, rather, is the groundwork for future dialogue, among musicians and philosophers together. I look forward to that, and to being, when it comes, in the thick of things.

. . .

It is a pleasure now to be able to thank three people who have been of invaluable assistance to me in the completion and publication of this work. Susan Feagin refereed the manuscript for Cornell University Press and gave me the most thorough and detailed set of comments that any manuscript of mine has ever received. I am grateful to her for many improvements—too many, in fact, to mention specifically. But two in particular demand notice. I owe to Susan's urgings the clarification of my general purpose and the expansion of the argument on restoration of artworks. The book is immeasurably better for Susan Feagin's patient and penetrating reading.

Lauren Oppenheim has done to my manuscript what is called in the trade "copyediting." That means she has transformed a scholar's convoluted prose into understandable English. And she has done a splendid job of that. But more—she has read my manuscript with intelligence and understanding, providing, at one place, a substantive philosophical suggestion that I have gladly accepted, and is acknowledged in the appropriate place in the text. If this book is readable, Lauren Oppenheim deserves a good deal of the credit.

Finally, I must acknowledge my continued indebtedness to Roger Haydon, editor at Cornell, who has encouraged me in my work, coddled me when I turned grumpy, and, all in all, managed to make me feel that what I was doing was actually worthwhile. This is service above and beyond the call of duty.

Over the years I have just about exhausted the formulae for exonerating those whom one thanks from culpability in the remaining errors. So I think I will leave it at that. If you have a favorite formula, enter it now!

PETER KIVY

New York City

PART ONE

How to Be Authentic

⊙

The Concept of Authenticity

The highest praise one can bestow nowadays on a musical performance, in many influential circles, is to say that it was "authentic." So powerful has the medicine of authenticity become, indeed, that those who find a musical performance to their liking, but unable to pass for authentic according to whatever tests are currently endorsed by those whose imprimatur carries weight in these matters, must reach out for some new or distant sense of the term in order to like what they like without losing their respectability. "Authentic," then, has become or is close to becoming a synonym for "good," while seeming to confer upon a performance some magical property that it did not have before. It is the musical version of the doctrine of the real presence.

In understandable disgust, Richard Taruskin, one of the most intelligent and sensitive writers on this subject, in the musical camp, is forced to conclude: "The word ["authentic"] needs either to be rescued from its purveyors or to be dropped by those who would aspire to the values it properly signifies."[1] The argument behind this conclusion, partly explicit, partly covert, seems to me to be this. Those who have appropriated "au-

[1] Taruskin et al., "The Limits of Authenticity," p. 3.

1

thentic" as the standard epithet of praise, the so-called early music movement, do not by any means always produce consistently satisfying, convincing, pleasurable, satisfactory—in a word, "good"—performances. Yet their performances are alleged, by these practitioners, to be "authentic." But the continual use of "authentic" by such persons has had an effect on musical discourse that is so profound as to have made it apparently unthinkable for a performance to be inauthentic and good, or authentic and bad. Because, however, there are those who find both bad in so-called authentic performances and good in the inauthentic ones, such dissenters from the orthodox authenticity must wrest the term from its present owners by somehow demonstrating that they use the term incorrectly, for only authentic performances are good, and many performances are either bad in the dissenters' eyes but authentic in the eyes of the orthodox, or inauthentic in the eyes of the orthodox and good in the eyes of the dissenters.

Although well intentioned, this argument is a bad one because it gets two important things drastically wrong. First of all, the dissenter from the authenticity orthodoxy has too willingly acquiesced in the underlying notion that authenticity is self-justifying, that there is no need to give reasons why authenticity, however understood, should be a good thing for musical performances to achieve. It has not, I should add, always been thus. The authenticity movement used to justify itself with arguments. But success seems to have changed all that: authenticity has become so widely accepted that *why* it should be accepted has become an unasked, indeed, a forgotten question among the converted. There was a time, in the age of proselytizing, when the benefits of authenticity were loudly and enthusiastically argued. Now evangelism is over, and the good news is established doctrine. In such a stage foundations cease to be argued for and harden into faith. The time has certainly come to reexamine that faith, as others besides myself have come to believe; and such a reexamination, from the philosopher's viewpoint, is undertaken in the second part of this book.

The second mistake, I think, that the dissenters from the orthodoxy of authenticity make is in claiming that the faithful are misusing the term. On the contrary, it is my view that the "purveyors" (as Taruskin calls them) are applying "authentic" in some of its perfectly correct, canonical senses and that, in fact, the dissenters are applying it, often, in attenuated

The Concept of Authenticity

or metaphorical ways, out of quite understandable frustration. If you do not dissent from the notion that the "authentic" must be "good" and vice versa, then all that remains, if what others call "authentic" you call "bad," and what you call "good" others call "inauthentic," is to claim that you, not they, are applying "authentic" authentically. But a bad argument cannot be defeated by another bad argument. And it seems to me that if the argument is to turn on who is using the word "authentic" correctly, the wrong side is going to win. Semantical "me too–ism" will get us nowhere; yet at this point it seems if not to dominate the discussion then at least to obscure it all too frequently.

Such a situation is not intellectually healthy and suggests that the first step in a philosophical critique of authenticity in musical performance must be lexicographical. So in the spirit of a recent philosophical movement, I begin with the *Oxford English Dictionary*.[2]

The *OED* lists five meanings for "authentic" that seem to bear some relevance to our topic:

1. Of authority, authoritative. (Possessing original or inherent authority.)

2. Original, firsthand, prototypical. (Opposed to copied.)

3. Really proceeding from its reputed source or author: of undisputed origin, genuine. (Opposed to counterfeit, forged.)

4. Belonging to himself, own, proper.

5. Acting of itself, self-originated, automatic. (The spontaneous or authentic motions of a clockwork.)

It seems clear that the first meaning of "authentic"—that is, "authoritative, possessing original or inherent authority"—covers the (as I see it) three basic kinds of performance that the authenticity crowd separately cite as being the hallmark of a "historically authentic" musical perfor-

[2] I am not the first writer on this topic to turn to the *OED* for solace. Cf. Will Crutchfield, "Fashion, Conviction, and Performance Style in an Age of Revivals," in Kenyon, *Authenticity and Early Music*, p. 23. I shall be far more dogged in my lexicographical adventure than Crutchfield; but the fact that another besides myself feels the need to be reacquainted with what the word "authentic" *authentically* means suggests to me that the need is real and not merely my own aberration.

The Concept of Authenticity

mance: adhering faithfully to the composer's performance intentions, conforming to the performance practice of the composer's historical period, producing sounds very similar or identical to those produced in a performance during the composer's lifetime. For each of these "authenticities" might seem, at least on first reflection, to possess some kind of authority and to be reaching back to an original source. The reaching back is true enough and, as it stands here, uncontentious. Whether this reaching back bestows any "authority" on the result, whether it demands our approval, is, of course, another matter and is, as we will have occasion to see, by no means uncontentious or obviously true.

The second meaning of "authentic" seems best suited to the notion that an authentic performance reproduces either the *way* music was performed in the composer's lifetime or the way it *sounded*. For in both cases we have the analogue of the relation of original to copy that obtains in, say, the art of painting. It is not quite the same thing, of course, but close enough to pass muster. There is, to take painting, only one authentic, original *Nightwatch*, although there may be many inauthentic ones, namely copies and forgeries. But in the present sense of "authentic," there could be many authentic performances of, say, the "Goldberg" Variations, namely all those performances that are tokens of the type "performance in the manner of a contemporary one" or "performance that produces the same sounds that would have been produced during the composer's lifetime." Thus, although we do not have in musical performance, as in painting, one authentic object and many copies, we do have the sense of there being an authentic "object," which is to say, any authentic performance in either of the two senses of "authentic" now being considered, and an inauthentic "object," which is to say, any performance that does not fulfill the criteria for authenticity in either of these two senses. The concept, then, of an authentic original and inauthentic copies does indeed, in clearly recognizable form, exist both in the notion of authentic musical performance as performance in the manner of the composer's period and as performance reproducing the sounds of the composer's period. So we can, with regard to both these notions of authenticity in performance, put aside the charge that those who defend either of these authenticities are misusing the word "authentic." The *OED* is on their side; and there can be no appeal from that unimpeachable source.

The Concept of Authenticity

But what of the notion of the authentic performance as the one faithful to the composer's intentions, by far the most frequently appealed to in the literature? How will it fare under lexicographical scrutiny? Just as well as the other two, it turns out. For the third of our *OED* entries clearly enfranchises it.

The third of our definitions of "authentic" makes a connection not with "authority," as the first one does, but with the other obvious correlative, "author." The authentic version of a text is the one "really proceeding from its reputed source or author." According to this definition, the authentic *Messiah* is the one proceeding from Handel, not Handel as revised by Mozart. All this is clear enough, and trivial. But the performance, one might say, no less than the score, may be authentic or inauthentic in this very sense; it may "issue" from the composer, fulfilling his intentions or not, as the case may be. The manner of performance, one might say, no less than the score—the sound relationships that the score lays down— are the composer's "creations." And departure from them in performance renders it not "really proceeding from its reputed source or author," namely the composer. So, again, in a perfectly bona fide sense of "authentic," sanctioned by the *OED*, a performance of a musical work is correctly called "authentic" if it follows the intentions, wishes, and instructions with regard to the performance of that work that the composer has made known to us, or that we infer, "inauthentic" if it does not. With regard to the intentional understanding of authenticity in performance, then, no less than with regard to the others, the charge that the supporters of authentic performance are misusing the term to their own purposes is quite unfounded.

.   .   .

I have, so far, canvassed the first three of our dictionary definitions of "authentic," which, as we have seen, all have fairly obvious application to the three versions of historical authenticity in musical performance that dominate the historical performance literature. What of the other two? Interestingly enough, they both have application to exactly the kind of performance that the orthodox of the historical performance movement have turned their backs on—what, for want of a better term, and because it is already in the literature, I shall call "mainstream" performance practice; that is to say, the performance practice of the performer on modern instruments, who sees him- or herself as part of a tradition of playing that is transmitted by a laying-on of hands rather than acquired by historical research. (Needless to say, the two are intimately intermingled, and no one can pursue either exclusively.)

What could it mean to say of Vladimir Horowitz, for example (whom I once heard say that he plays Mozart like Chopin and Chopin like Mozart), that his performance of a Mozart piano concerto is "authentic"? It is perfectly clear what we might mean by calling it inauthentic—namely, that it is not true to the performance practice of Mozart's time, does not produce the sounds of that period, does not accurately enough reflect Mozart's intentions for the performance of his works. But how "authentic"? Well, clearly, if one meaning of "authentic" is, according to the *OED*, "belonging to himself," his "own," then what we are saying is that Horowitz's performance is uniquely his; it is his original creation, not derivative, not a copy or imitation of someone else's way of playing Mozart. And something of the same thing is suggested by our final definition of "authentic"—"acting of itself, self-originating"—even though the *OED* gives a mechanical rather than a human example: the "authentic" works of a clock. In other words, a performance so described is being characterized as autonomous, sincere, self-originating, original, an expression of the performer rather than of someone whom the performer is aping.

It should also be clear that when we call a performance "authentic" in these two senses we intend to be praising the performance and paying the performer a compliment. And it should be clear, furthermore, that this sense of "authentic" meshes nicely with the venerable notion of the performer as an "artist," a "performing artist." For it is just this kind of authenticity—originality, not slavish imitation; sincerity and truth to oneself, not false consciousness—that we tend to think the artist should have. Thus there is nothing foreign to our thinking on these subjects in connecting to them authenticity of the kind our fourth and fifth definitions are displaying. Quite to the contrary: they are quite congruent with the old notion that the musical performer is an artist, the performance his or her creation or "artwork."

· · ·

As can be inferred from the preceding remarks, it is my opinion that there are (at least) four notions of authenticity meaningfully applicable to musical performance practice. These are the notions of (1) faithfulness to the composer's performance intentions; (2) faithfulness to the performance

The Concept of Authenticity

practice of the composer's lifetime; (3) faithfulness to the sound of a performance during the composer's lifetime; and (4) faithfulness to the performer's own self, original, not derivative or an aping of someone else's way of playing.

Two things are to be noticed straightaway about these four notions of authenticity. To begin with, only the first three are *obviously* examples of what is called in the trade *historical authenticity*. And it is historical authenticity with which this book is mainly concerned. Nevertheless, appearances here may very well be deceiving, so we will be giving the fourth notion of authentic performance a careful look, even though appearances may be against it as an example of *historical* authenticity.

Furthermore, it may not be clear to the reader, on first reflection, that the first three notions of historical authenticity in performance are, indeed, distinct in practice, even though they may be in principle. For, it might be suggested, if one fulfilled the composer's performance intentions, one would, ipso facto, perform his or her work in the manner of its period and, in so doing, would, ipso facto, produce the sound of a period performance. Thus, it might seem that the composer's performance intentions, period performance, and period sound all converge on one performance or, at least, on one class of similar performances. Such, indeed, seems to be the assumption underlying a lot of the literature on this subject, a conclusion that can be inferred from the fact that these three concepts of authenticity are frequently used interchangeably, as if they all really amounted to the same thing.

It will become clear, however, as this book progresses, that we do really have three distinct notions of historical authenticity here, not one notion under three different descriptions. These notions do not—cannot—converge, either in practice or in principle.

That said, it is now possible to state the general plan of this book. In the first part, I shall be concerned exclusively with stating as clearly as I can each of these four notions of authentic performance and examining the philosophical problems that surround them. This will be as completely a nonnormative account as can be achieved, given the human condition. In other words, I shall make no attempt in the first part of this book to suggest why or whether any of these "authentic" ways of performing music might be desirable or undesirable.

The normative question (or, rather, questions) will be broached in Part

II. There I shall examine the arguments that have been given (or, in some cases, that should have been given) for and against these four approaches to authentic performance, with a critical and evaluative eye. This, of course, is a delicate matter, for it may seem that a philosopher of art has no more business giving advice to performing artists—which is what it might seem I am doing—than a philosopher of science has giving advice to biologists. I hope it will be clear, when we come to these considerations, that it is not advice I am offering but, rather, philosophical analysis. Although as a member of the musical audience as well, I suppose I am as entitled as anyone else of that class to make value judgments. For performance is, after all, for the benefit of an audience, not merely for that of the performer (or so, at least, I have been taught). And an audience, I daresay, has its rights of rejection and approval—so if I sometimes clap my hands or boo, I feel I am entitled.

⊙

A u t h e n t i c i t y   a s   I n t e n t i o n

By far the most frequently cited measure of historical authenticity in musical performance is faithfulness to the composer's intentions. And no one has expressed this criterion more clearly than Stephen Davies, whom I quote as an exemplary instance rather than a typical one: "A performance of X is more rather than less authentic the more faithful it is to the intentions publicly expressed in the score by the composer (where those intentions are determinate and not merely recommendatory of performance practice). . . . As a commendatory term 'authentic' is used to acknowledge the creative role of the performer in realizing faithfully the composer's specifications."[1]

As clear as Davies's expression is, problems immediately suggest themselves. To begin with, Davies has apparently committed himself in this passage to only those intentions of the composer explicitly stated. But this certainly seems unduly restrictive, if not unintentional, and not in conformity with historically authentic performance practice as its practitioners usually understand it. I take it that we claim to know many intentions of the composer not by "what has been publicly expressed in the

[1] Davies, "Authenticity in Musical Performance," p. 39.

9

score" but by making inferences from what we know, or what we think we know, about the performance practice of the composer's period, or anything else of that kind. Thus, to instance an obvious case in point, devotees of the authentic performance movement may claim to know that the trills in Handel's *Messiah* were intended by the composer to start on the upper note not because it is so stated or notated in the score of the work but because treatises and other descriptions of baroque performance practice tell them that this is the way trills were performed during the period: the inference depending, obviously, on the assumption, in the absence of evidence to the contrary, that Handel acquiesced in this practice.

It is important to note here that we may seem to have already crossed the border between two different authenticities: *authenticity as intention* and *authenticity as contemporary practice*. But this is not the case. For contemporary practice is being appealed to here not as the criterion for authenticity but as evidence for intention, which is itself the criterion for authenticity. There is no doubt that in the musicological literature, the issues are not always so nicely distinguished. Outlines get blurred, and the boundaries between authenticity as intention, authenticity as contemporary practice, and authenticity as contemporary performance sound are crossed over and back to such an extent that it is often difficult, in the individual instance, to know which is being appealed to as evidence for the other, and which as criterion for authenticity. But in each of the chapters of this book devoted, respectively, to authenticity as intention, authenticity as contemporary performance sound, and authenticity as contemporary performance practice, the inferences will go in one direction only. And in this chapter they go from contemporary performance sound, or contemporary performance practice, to the composer's performance intention, and only from there to authenticity.

·   ·   ·

A second problem with the passage quoted from Davies is not unique to it but universal to the subject. Davies, like the rest of us, has inherited the word "intention" itself from a context and a tradition importantly unlike the present one, in which performance practice is the issue. That is the context and tradition of literary interpretation and the so-called intentional fallacy connected with it as a result of the highly influential article of the same name by William Wimsatt and Monroe Beardsley. I am not saying that the word "intention" was never used to refer to the composer's attitudes toward performance before the publication of Wimsatt and Beardsley's essay. But after that it became entrenched in the literature in a way that makes it extremely difficult to dislodge, if not impossible, and with some undesirable results.

For one thing, it doesn't seem, at first blush, to make sense to say that someone intended that something be performed in such and such a way. I can urge you to play my piece allegro, or I can leave instructions that it should be played that way; I can wish it to be played that way, and you may be able to infer my wishes even though I may never have explicitly stated them. I can strongly or tentatively suggest a particular way of performing my music. But I can no more intend that you play my piece allegro, it would seem, than I can intend that you do anything else. I can intend to go for a walk. I cannot intend that you go for a walk, except in the sense of "intend" that expresses, simply, my command, as in "the general intends the seventh regiment to advance."

This is simply a point about the "logic" of "intend," as I understand that word. But it is not merely a logical quibble. For if it makes no sense to say that a composer intends his piece to be played allegro, in the way it makes sense to say that a person intends to take a walk or to ride a bicycle, then, I suggest, the sense that is always implicitly understood when we talk about composers' performing intentions is the sense in which the general intends the seventh regiment to advance. And that means that an important question has been surreptitiously begged from the very start, by use of the word "intention." The begged question is to the effect that the composer's wishes, desires, hypotheses, instructions, and suggestions about performance always have the strength of commands or, short of that, desires or wishes at the strongest possible level of intensity. The composer's performance instructions, whether expressed or inferred, take on, implicitly, by our calling them performance *intentions*, the status of stentorian admonitions, no matter what the circumstances.

The result is that composers' performing intentions—even though they may far more properly be called wishes or suggestions, provisional instructions, or tentative recommendations—by that very naming take on an authority that the composers perhaps never "intended" them to have. But, as I have said, it is probably too late to dislodge the usage. So I will acquiesce in this use of the term "intention" when I have to, and where

Authenticity as Intention

the writings I discuss force it upon me. I will try my utmost, nevertheless, to introduce some clarity into the subject by avoiding the term where I can, except when I mean specifically to refer to those wishes of composers that really are intentions in the proper sense of "commands." So far as I am concerned, then, the word "intention," when used to refer to the various wishes and instructions and suggestions of composers with regard to how their works are to be performed, is frequently a misnomer, because it implies a force that not all these possess. And when I use the term "intention" in this regard it will be used as a term of art to mean any of the composer's performance wishes, no matter how weak or tentative they may be. For, as I have been arguing, not all a composer's performing "intentions" are really *intentions*.

One further observation concerning the quotation from Davies, relevant to the point made earlier, about intentions, is in order here before we go on to other matters. It is of some significance that Davies defines authenticity in performance as adherence to "those intentions [that] are determinate and not merely recommendatory of performance practice." For, of course, it is a very nice question which of a composer's performance intentions are "determinate" and which are "merely recommendatory." As I have been arguing, the use of the term "intention" in the first place tends to plant the unconscious thought in the mind of the unwary that all the composer's expressed or inferred wishes concerning performance are of the former kind, because it suggests that all are of the strength of "intention" in "the general intends the seventh regiment to advance"—that is to say, incontrovertible orders.

Davies, as can be seen by his parenthetical qualification, is not one of the unwary and does recognize that composers' performance "intentions"—"wishes," as I would prefer to call them—are of varying strengths and not all determinate of an authentic performance. Were it not too late to do so, it would have been useful to reserve the term "intention" for just those performance wishes of the composer's that are determinate; for that usage would coincide with the ordinary usage in which "intention" has the force of command. But failing that, it is at least salutary to point out that Davies does, where most do not, make a careful distinction between the varying strengths of whatever instructions, explicit and implicit, that composers have left us as regards the performance of their works. (I shall have more to say about this later on.)

·   ·   ·

With some understanding of the vagaries of the term "intention"—and there is more to come in that regard—we can now go on to a serious objection that has been brought against the whole program of achieving the composer's performing intentions: an objection, interestingly enough, originating not from the external vantage point of philosophy of art but from within the musicological community itself. It is, indeed, suggested by Richard Taruskin that the intentions of composers are simply inaccessible to us in the first place and, further, that, at least with regard to the *kinds* of performing intention that those in quest of historical authenticity are seeking, composers don't really have them at all. Thus, the argument is that composers don't have the sought-for performing intentions, and, even if they did, we would not be able to know what they are. In Taruskin's words, "I will not rehearse here the familiar epistemological impediments to learning what the composer's intentions were. . . . I wish to go a bit further and suggest that in many if not most instances composers do not even have the intentions we would like to ascertain."[2]

A puzzling point to be noticed straightaway about Taruskin's double-edged skepticism with regard to composers' intentions is that it seems blatantly self-contradictory: self-refuting at least. For Taruskin claims to know that composers did not have certain intentions. And I cannot see how he is entitled to know this if there are indeed epistemological impediments to learning what composers' intentions were, because one would think that knowing the negative and knowing the positive are here on the same epistemological footing: that is to say, if I know that composer A did not have intentions of kind K, I know that he did not intend K_1, K_2, . . . K_n; and to know what composer A did not intend is to know his "intentions." But if I know his intentions, then there cannot be epistemological impediments to knowing what composers have intended; and if there are, then I cannot know what they did not intend, any more than I can know what they did intend.

But we cannot let the matter rest with merely pointing out an apparent inconsistency. For it is important that we determine whether either of

[2] Taruskin, "On Letting the Music Speak for Itself," p. 340.

Authenticity   as   Intention

these apparently inconsistent claims is true, because both are equally destructive of the quest for performance authenticity as conformity with the
composer's performing intentions. If there are insurmountable epistemic
barriers to our having access to the composer's performance intentions,
then of course we can have no rational method of seeking access to
them and no rational procedure for verifying what must needs be our
purely accidental success in divining them. In short, we can never know
whether or not we have achieved authenticity. And if there are no such
intentions in the first place, there can be no authenticity at all for us ever
to blindly seek or accidently achieve.

·   ·   ·

Let us first ask what "the familiar epistemological impediments" might be
that Taruskin thinks make the composer's intentions impenetrable. There
are, it seems to me, two plausible ones that one might venture. The first is
that because there is reference in close proximity to the previously quoted
remarks of Taruskin's to Wimsatt and Beardsley, Taruskin might be thinking of the familiar assertion from "The Intentional Fallacy": "the design
or intention of the author is neither available nor desirable as a standard
for judging the success of a work of literary art. . . ."[3]

Wimsatt and Beardsley's assertion must be taken in context, however;
and when it is, it has no implications at all of a skeptical kind about the
accessibility of the author's or anyone else's intentions. We are, to begin
with, ignoring the question of intentions as a "desirable standard" and
confining ourselves to the question of their availability. And what Wimsatt and Beardsley are responding to, in their assertion, is the kind of "romantic" criticism (*their* term) that seeks for the author's intentions in bio-
graphical (and other) documents external to the work itself. These
documents, they claim, seldom, as a matter of empirical fact, give evidence of what the author intended; and indeed, again a matter of empirical fact, the best evidence we can have of the author's intentions is to be
found in the work itself: "One must ask how a critic expects to get an answer to the question about intention. How is he to find out what the poet
tried to do? If the poet succeeded in doing it, then the poem itself shows
what he was trying to do. And if the poet did not succeed, then the poem
is not adequate evidence, and the critic must go outside the poem—for

[3] Wimsatt and Beardsley, "The Intentional Fallacy," in Tillman and Cahn, *Philosophy of
Art and Aesthetics*, p. 647.

Authenticity   as   Intention

evidence of an intention that did not become effective in the poem."[4] But if one goes outside the poem, then what Wimsatt and Beardsley are saying, as I read them, is that the evidence out there is paltry. So, taken in context, what they mean by saying that intention is not available is that it is seldom available *outside the poem*. Far from denying that authors' intentions are accessible, for some deep reasons of epistemic debility, they are merely telling us, rightly or wrongly, where the most reliable evidence for such intentions is to be found, if we want to find it—namely, in the literary work itself, as we interpret it.

The second conjecture I would venture with regard to Taruskin's (and others') epistemic suspicions as to performance intentions is that the source may lie in reverberations from the philosophical problem of other minds, and the resultant epistemic suspicions as to our knowledge of mental states *tout court*. Gary Tomlinson, another musicologist who has written on this subject, thinks that Taruskin's "familiar epistemological impediments" are the unfortunate result of "a by-now outmoded historical theory."[5] But whether or not that is the proximate cause, the ultimate cause, the very source of such historical skepticism, as Gilbert Ryle so incisively pointed out in *The Concept of Mind*, is the solipsistic fallout from the Cartesian mind-body problem: "Adhering without question to the dogma of the ghost in the machine, these philosophers were naturally perplexed by the pretensions of historians to interpret the actions and words of historic personages as expressions of their actual thoughts, feelings and intentions. For if minds are impenetrable to one another, how can historians penetrate the minds of their heroes?"[6]

In a word, Taruskin's "familiar epistemological impediments" seem to be impediments born of the egocentric predicament to the knowledge of any states of mind whatever, except those of the introspector himself. Nor is this a paranoia only of Taruskin; and nor is it directed only against performance intentions. To illustrate the widespread contagion, I quote from Robert Marshall, engaged in examining what one would have thought to be some of the most intention-laden of all musical documents, the composer's working manuscripts. Marshall warns us in this regard that

[4] Ibid., p. 658.
[5] Tomlinson, "The Historian, the Performer, and Authentic Meaning in Music," in Kenyon, *Authenticity and Early Music*, p. 117.
[6] Ryle, *The Concept of Mind*, p. 56.

A u t h e n t i c i t y   a s   I n t e n t i o n

it should be emphasized that when, in speculating about the meaning of the autograph corrections of Bach—or of any creative artist, for that matter—we attribute to the artist certain reasons for writing this or changing that, we only seem guilty of some form of the "intentional fallacy." It is more than obvious that we can never in fact know what went on in Bach's mind at the moment he wrote down or corrected any symbol. Such phrases as "Bach changed *x* to *y* because . . ." or "the A♭ was rejected for the following reasons . . ." are expressions of convenience which really mean "the observable effects or consequences of this reading or that correction are the following. . . ." The composer may well have been totally unaware in any verbally conscious sense of these "reasons"—as they are perceived by the observer.[7]

What seems so puzzling to the outsider about many such passages in the musicological literature—the quotation from Marshall being merely a case in point and far from rare—is that Wimsatt's and Beardsley's "intentional fallacy" has been transformed from the fallacy, as they understood it, of inferring an author's meaning *from* his or her intentions to a universal interdict against inferring *to* a composer's intentions from any evidence whatever. And aside from turning the intentional fallacy on its head in this manner, the notion that we cannot know about composers' states of mind seems utterly false, not to say completely destructive of the whole musicological enterprise.

The philosopher's eye falls here inevitably on the word "know" in such statements as Marshall's "It is more than obvious that we can never in fact *know* what went on in Bach's mind at the moment he wrote down or corrected any symbol." If one means by "know" anything like "have justified true belief," then it seems to me more than obvious that Marshall, in his careful and ingenious examination of Bach's composing scores, has gained and imparted to us considerable knowledge about what went on in Bach's mind. And if the opposite seems obvious to Marshall, then it strongly suggests that he is placing on "know" the burden of *certainty*, or else the philosophical skepticism born of the problem of other minds, neither of which is justified or relevant in the present instance.

Knowledge as certainty can be dismissed straightaway in both of the

[7] Marshall, *The Music of Johann Sebastian Bach*, p. 145.

Authenticity   as   Intention

most obvious ways that "certainty" might be construed. To start with, I take it that no one expects the certainty of logical rigor—of logical possibility and impossibility—in any form of empirical inquiry, including history. If that is what Marshall is denying us in our attempts to ascertain composers' mental states, he is denying us nothing any sensible scholar would claim and certainly not denying us *knowledge* in any current understanding of the concept.

Perhaps, though, we are merely being warned that states of mind tend to be less accessible—more difficult to find out about—than, for example, the physical world of historical artifacts and events. This may indeed be so: a simple empirical truth. I think I *am* more certain about what took place at the battle of Antietam than about what McClellan and Lee and the rest thought and felt. And if the former is historical certainty, then the latter may be something less. But I cannot see that admitting this commits one to denying the possibility of *knowledge* of the latter, in the sense of justified true belief. We are justly warned to be cautious, but not to be skeptics.

The possibility that strongly suggests itself, then, is that Marshall is indeed raising the specter of skepticism with regard to other minds—a ghost that, if it has not been laid to rest within the philosophical community, certainly need not haunt the historian without. For it seems to me obvious that the level of skepticism required to call into question whether we can have any knowledge at all about what people of the past wished, intended, felt, and thought—which is nothing less than the level required to generate the egocentric predicament—would render what Marshall thinks the historian of music cannot do impossible, but, alas, would render what he thinks *can* be done impossible as well. We need assume no more, in thinking that we can have *some* knowledge—which is to say, justified true belief—about what went on in Bach's mind when he made a correction than we *must* assume to know even that it is a correction we are talking about in the first place, or, for that matter, to treat what is before us as a score and not merely a piece of white paper with black smudges on it.

That something like the "privacy" problem is nagging at Marshall is strongly suggested, I think, by his observation that when he ascribes "reasons" to Bach for the corrections in the composing scores, "The composer may well have been totally unaware in any verbally conscious sense of these 'reasons'—as they are perceived by the observer." What Marshall seems to be worried about is that if we claim to "know" that Bach "had in mind" achieving such and such effect by, say, changing the A to A♭, then we must be claiming to have some direct acquaintance with exactly what specific conscious states succeeded one another in Bach's mind, as if, in order to "know" that you have a toothache, I must be feeling your toothache, which, of course, *is* impossible in some very deep sense of impossibility that is hard to state but universally felt. For if I do not "know" what your toothache feels like by feeling it, or what conscious states succeeded one another in Bach's mind when he changed the A to A♭, how can I really "know" that what you are feeling when you say "I have a toothache" is what I am feeling when I have one, or what was really "on Bach's mind," what his reasons really were, when he changed that A to A♭? Thus, I cannot *really* "know" in the "true" sense of "know" that you have a toothache or that Bach *intended* such and such when he changed the A to A♭.

But, of course, there is absolutely no need to satisfy such severe, perhaps even unintelligible constraints on knowledge to be able to say, with assurance, that you *know* I have a toothache or that Bach had on his mind—that he intended—such and such when he changed the A to A♭. No one should expect that a composer of the eighteenth century and a musicologist of the twentieth should have the same conscious states when they both reason to the conclusion that the A should be or was changed to an A♭ for such and such a reason: clearly what Bach "knew" instinctively the musicologist "knows" by analysis; and there are many other differences in their conscious states as well, no doubt. None of this, however, makes it impossible for the musicologist to know, to have justified true belief about, what the composer's intention was in changing the A to A♭—what the composer "had in his mind"; and the same argument applies, pari passu, to knowledge of what a composer may have intended or wished with regard to the performance of his or her music.

The conclusion I want to draw from these considerations of the accessibility of composers' intentions, desires, and other states of mind with regard to the performance of their works, then, is that there are no special epistemic barriers to our gaining knowledge of them. That it is hard work to discover these things goes without saying. It is hard work to find out anything interesting. But that historians in general, or musical historians

Authenticity   as   Intention

in particular, must abstain from making conclusions about the states of mind of historical figures because there is some metaphysical or epistemic impediment to doing so is simply false in all particulars. Knowledge of composers' states of mind is not only possible but, indeed, actual. And *if* composers have intentions about how their works are to be performed, then authenticity of performance, defined as the realization of intentions, is a possible object of knowledge, even if, in the event, it may be impossible or undesirable to realize in practice.

But I expressed this conclusion as a hypothetical—I said *if* composers have performing intentions—because, as we have seen, this seemingly obvious fact about composers has been denied by Taruskin. And before we can rest content with the conclusion that authenticity of performance as the realization of the composer's performing intentions is a bona fide object of knowledge, we must satisfy ourselves that Taruskin is mistaken, or at least confused—perhaps a little bit of both—and that the obvious is true: composers really have had intentions about how their works were and are to be performed. To that question I now turn.

· · ·

To understand exactly what it is about performing intentions that Taruskin is denying we must first understand what motivates his denying it. I have, to begin with, overstated the case. Taruskin is not, of course, denying that composers have had performing intentions. What he is denying is that composers have had, as he puts it, "the intentions we would like to ascertain." And what might those intentions be? Clearly, the ones that Davies has described as "determinate and not merely recommendatory of performance practice": what I have argued are performing *intentions* properly so called, not merely performance wishes or suggestions or tentative recommendations. In other words, Taruskin is denying that composers have performing intentions that are in some sense inviolable, like the general's intention that the seventh regiment advance.

What motivates this denial of "determinate" performing intentions? I suggest that it is the quite understandable and, in my view, fully justified impatience with the dogged pedantry driving the authentic performance movement. Like the attempt, discussed in the previous chapter, to wrest the very concept itself of authenticity from the true believers, the present attempt to do the same for the kind of intentions Taruskin sees the movement as requiring derives from the perception that slavishly following

Authenticity as Intention

"authenticity," in whatever form the "authenticity" takes—whether as intention or as practice or as sound—is destructive of the spirit of musical performance. And if one can show that the only performance intentions demanding of such slavish allegiance—namely, those with the force of the general's command—were never really entertained by the composers of the past at all, then one has, at least to that degree, loosened the stranglehold of authenticity. A general's commands one must obey. A general's requests one may take under advisement.

But what we must notice, straightaway, is that all the argument Taruskin can muster for his denial of strong performance intentions to composers is anecdotal evidence derived from the statements and behavior of *a few*; and it is quite easy to adduce evidence to the contrary from the statements and behavior of others. For every Debussy Taruskin can come up with who "was in his own eyes only one interpreter [of his own music] among others,"[8] there is a Handel who, so the stories go, snatched the violin out of Corelli's hands in a fit of anger to show how he *intended* a passage to be executed, and nearly defenestrated a singer to the same end.

Nor is such "mixed" evidence anything but what one would expect, given the varieties of human temperament and musical style. Taruskin's conclusion is that "in many if not most instances composers do not have the intentions we would like to ascertain." The "if not" seems to me ambiguous between denial and affirmation of the "most." If Taruskin's conclusion is that many but *not* most composers have lacked strong performance intentions, I agree with it, for it is compatible with the belief, for which there is adequate evidence, that many also did possess such strong intentions. But if his conclusion is that most composers did indeed lack strong performance intentions, the argument he offers for it, in the form merely of rather meager anecdotal evidence, is surely not strong enough to sustain it; and there is, as well, anecdotal evidence for the opposite conclusion.

It appears to me, then, that attempts like Taruskin's to discredit the concept of authenticity as the realizing of the composer's strong performing intentions, by attempting to show either their inaccessibility or their nonexistence, must come to nothing, well-intentioned though they may be. And, indeed, the position seems to be at least halfway self-refuting, for in

[8]Taruskin, "On Letting the Music Speak for Itself," p. 341.

Authenticity   as   Intention

proving the latter claim true one would be proving the former false. I see no grounds for believing that the seekers after authenticity in the performance intentions of composers are aiming either for a nonexistent goal or for a goal unachievable by dogged, imaginative historical research. Such authenticity is intelligible as a concept and viable, within the limits of human capabilities, as a research program. This conclusion brings us to an important juncture in the argument; and we must pause at this point to take stock before we will know in what direction to go on.

·   ·   ·

If, as I have argued, the quest for intentional authenticity is both an intelligible and epistemically possible enterprise, and if, further, it leads to a performance practice that seems overly slavish in its adherence to authority, overly pedantic in its interpretations of what that authority "commands," substituting historical judgment for musical taste, emulation for creativity, we are faced with an unpalatable choice between equally unappealing alternatives. We can reject intentional authenticity altogether, as an acceptable model or program for musical performance, simply on grounds of *taste*. Or we can swallow it, hook, line, and sinker, with the inevitable result that it will continue to offend our sense of taste and to frustrate our desire for "spontaneity" in performance. Let me expatiate on these alternatives briefly.

The attempt to discredit the authenticity of intention program as either a quest for the nonexistent or one doomed to failure would have been, had it worked, a quick and easy way with all those baleful effects of the authenticity movement in performance that the intentional interpretation of authenticity bestows. For it would have rendered the concept of strong performance intentions utterly impotent as a guide to performance practice. As things in fact lie, however, strong performance intentions are both there and available. So if we want to reject them as a guide, it would seem that we must reject them not for any intrinsic defect in the concept of strong performance intention itself but on the basis of our aesthetic judgment, our musical taste—in other words, not on the basis of its intelligibility as a standard but on that of its *desirability* as one.

We are not yet in a position to raise the normative question of desirability. That will be our concern in the second part of this book. But it will be well to observe, at this point, that the pull of the composer's wishes, instructions, intentions, and the like with regard to performance is very strong indeed on the conscience of the performer in the twentieth century, among not merely those in the authentic performance movement but those in the mainstream as well. And to grab the horn of our dilemma that seems to say "Taste is all, intentions be damned" is to reach for an extreme as unpalatable as that slavish surrender to intention that it was meant to replace. We seem to be going from tyranny to anarchy.

But the other horn of the dilemma *is* tyranny, it would seem—the tyranny of ever more detailed knowledge of what composers have, by precept and by implication, revealed to us about their notions of performance. Are we really hostage to these mind-sets, formed so many generations ago, in times and circumstances so unlike our own? Surely the exercise of taste is a necessary palliative; and so we are in danger of being thrown back into the other, recently vacated horn of our dilemma.

Of course there can be no escape from the necessity of *justifying* intention as a guide to performance practice—it is not *self*-justifying. Nor can there be an escape from musical taste as part of that ultimate justification. Suppose, though, we could somehow show, *prior* to our invocation of taste, creativity, spontaneity, and other such, that the embrace of the composer's intentions need not be the straitjacket it has come to seem? Suppose it could be shown that a great deal of the inflexible pedantry that has resulted from appeal to the composer's intentions is due not to the concept of intention itself but to a systematic misunderstanding of it by the musical scholars and practitioners? That indeed is what I shall argue in the second half of this chapter. Wishes, suggestions, intentions, commands—all are part of our daily lives and common-sense psychology. What we must do is recapture the sense of what they really mean and how they are really assessed, which has been lost in the process of musicological debate over performance practice. With common usage and common sense regained, I think we will see that we can have authenticity of intention, in the true sense of that concept, without the baggage of pedantry or surrender of musical judgment that it has come to some of us to represent.

•   •   •

What does Wanda want? She said that she wants to be a nurse. But is that what she *really* wants? Well, if she could, she would *really* like to be a doctor.

Authenticity   as   Intention

Such a question-and-answer sequence is a familiar part of our everyday lives. And we are all aware, at least implicitly, of what such a sequence implies about the concept of wanting or (pari passu) intending.

The first thing to notice is that wanting is always a matter of *choosing*;
and choosing is always among *the available possibilities*.

Wanda says she wants to be a nurse. But, of course, her wanting is not
some contextless, disembodied mental state. Her wanting to be a nurse is,
to begin with, a selection. She could be a sales clerk, or a schoolteacher,
or a beautician. But her parents cannot afford to send her to medical
school, and so she chooses to be a nurse. That is what she wants.

Is that what she *really* wants? Well, yes and no. Wanda really wants to
be a nurse rather than a sales clerk or a schoolteacher or a beautician. But
if she had her druthers, what she *really* would like to be is a doctor. Her
circumstances being what they are, however, Wanda *really* wants to be a
nurse.

It might be interjected here that, after all, one *can* really "want" *anything*, even though one cannot "intend" *anything*. It makes no sense,
clearly, for me to say "I *intend* to be X," where X is flat-out impossible for
me, whereas it may seem, anyway, to make sense for me to say "I want to
be X." (Contrast, for example, a person who does not know how to play
the piano at all saying "I *intend* to play the *Hammerklavier* Sonata faultlessly in six weeks" with her saying "I want to play the *Hammerklavier* Sonata faultlessly in six weeks.") Cannot one want the impossible? Isn't it
an unfortunate fact of the human condition that we frequently, alas, *do*
want the impossible? I think not.

G.E.M. Anscombe, I think, has it exactly right when she contrasts, in
this regard, wants with idle wishes.

> It is a familiar doctrine that people can want anything; that is, that
> in "A wants X," "X" ranges over all desirable objects or states of
> affairs. This is untenable. . . . We are not concerned here with idle
> wishes. A chief mark of an idle wish is that a man does nothing—
> whether he could or no—towards the fulfilment of the wish.
> Perhaps the familiar doctrine I have mentioned can be made
> correct by being restricted to wishing.[9]

[9] Anscombe, *Intention*, p. 67.

Authenticity as Intention

It may be laid down, in the light of this distinction, as a cautionary note that we are dealing here, in the case of Wanda, and others, with "wanting," not "wishing"; with "wants," not idle "wishes." Wanda can "wish" for the moon; she cannot "want" it.

Now, as a matter of fact, Wanda's parents want her to be a schoolteacher. But, being generous and sympathetic, they fully intend to gratify their daughter's desires in this matter. Fate takes a hand, however, in the form of an unexpected bequest from a long-lost uncle in Argentina, enabling Wanda's parents now to send her through medical school. Anyone, I am sure, would say that to give Wanda what she *really* wants, under the altered circumstances, her parents should pay for her medical education. For, given the change in their fortunes, the answer to the question, What does Wanda *really* want? is not, She wants to be a nurse rather than a sales clerk or schoolteacher or beautician, but instead, She wants to be a doctor rather than a nurse. And it would be absurd for her parents to reply, But Wanda always *said* she wanted to be a nurse, and because we want to grant her wish, a nurse she shall be. Of course, Wanda never *said* she wanted to be a doctor. What would have been the point? She couldn't be one. So she always said she wanted to be a nurse. However, any reasonably intelligent person who knows Wanda's capabilities and personality, has observed her behavior over the years, and knows how much more gratifying her life would be, in the healing arts, as a doctor rather than a nurse can infer from all this, *pace* what Wanda has been saying all these years, that Wanda, under present circumstances, wants to be a doctor rather than a nurse.

One further point, before I get off Wanda's case. According to this story, Wanda's family was, in fact, left a substantial sum of money by the long-lost uncle in Argentina. But suppose they hadn't been so lucky. We still can, nevertheless, express in a counterfactual conditional what Wanda *would have* wanted had her family inherited enough money to facilitate her going to medical school. And what Wanda *really* wants is, in part, a function of such counterfactuals. Wanda really wants to be a nurse, given that her possible choices are nurse, sales clerk, schoolteacher, beautician. But she really wants to be a doctor rather than a nurse, given the counterfactual, If her family's financial condition were to improve sufficiently, Wanda would prefer medicine to nursing.

So the moral of this story is that in order to know what someone *really*

wants, you must know what alternatives are open to the person in question, and you must make your inferences not only from what that person
says but from a host of other things you may know about the person, his
or her behavior, and the circumstances in which the person lives. Further,
you must make inferences not only from what is the case but from what
might be or might have been. All this is part and parcel of what ordinary
people ordinarily mean when they talk about someone's wishes, desires,
intentions, and the like.

·   ·   ·

Such considerations are complicated by the introduction of temporality
into the equation. And to understand this, let us move on to another case.

What does William really want? William was born in Bristol, England,
in 1769 and chose to go to sea rather than apprentice to a harness maker.
He wanted to be a sailor and to see the world, given that his choices were
limited to that or a life at the workbench.

William did *not* want, then, to be a harness maker. We can say that with
assurance. But if our only grounds for saying it were that he didn't decide
to become a harness maker, then I suppose we can say with assurance
that William did *not* want to be an aviator or a computer programmer,
either. He did not decide to pursue these occupations and entertained no
desire to do so.

But there is something that must strike us as very odd about saying that
William did not want to be an aviator or a computer programmer. That is
because, as we saw in the case of Wanda, we project wants, desires, intentions against a background of envisaged alternatives about which one can
deliberate, and choose or reject, on the basis of preference and practical
possibility, as Wanda did with regard to the professions of nurse, sales
clerk, schoolteacher, beautician, and doctor. William, however, cannot
even *contemplate* the career of aviator or computer programmer, let alone
reject them, because, of course, they are unthought-of possibilities of an
age and state of society far removed from William's in time, customs, and
technical development. It sounds odd, then, to describe William as not
wanting to be an aviator or a computer programmer even though in one
sense of those words it is literally true, because they suggest, in the more
usual sense, that the alternatives were available, thought about, and rejected; and that cannot be the case: they cannot be rejected because they
cannot even be thought about.

A u t h e n t i c i t y   a s   I n t e n t i o n

Nevertheless, in the case of William, one might, I think, at least frame intelligible counterfactuals, such as, Had William been born in 1969 rather than 1769, he would have wanted to be an aviator rather than a harness maker, sailor, or computer programmer; whereas I think it is probably bordering on the unintelligible to say that about one of the artists of the Lascaux caves. In the case of William, we perceive characteristics—his lack of patience with sedentary occupations, his sense of adventure, his love for the technically innovative forms of travel rather than settled and developed ones, say—that have recognizable counterparts in a contemporary young person, even though life in eighteenth-century England was so different in many ways from life in twentieth-century America. Enough is comparable to make the thought experiment possible. But we don't quite know what to imagine in a thought experiment that puts Cro-Magnon in contemporary Akron. Not enough is comparable for us quite to know what would satisfy the conditions. Where, however, we can make such a *Gedankenexperiment*, we certainly can intelligibly ask, and possibly answer, questions about what a long-dead individual would have wanted had the conditions of his or her wanting been those of twentieth-century America rather than of eighteenth-century Austria or fifteenth-century Italy.

The most obvious causal factor in rendering counterfactuals concerning wishes and intentions unintelligible is, of course, the sheer passage of time. The more remote in time a person is from us, the more difficult it is for us to imagine that person making choices under our conditions of life. But the simple passage of time is not the only parameter. Two others are clearly relevant.

To begin with, because the passage of time is not itself what makes the kinds of counterfactuals we are talking about unintelligible, it being merely a sign of cultural disparity, we can well imagine societies closer in time to our own being more culturally remote than societies more remote in time. Thus, I daresay it might be far easier for us to imagine what a citizen of Periclean Athens might want if transported to twentieth-century America than a peasant in a medieval village.

Furthermore, there are unique characteristics of individual human beings that distinguish them from their contemporaries in particular ways, making certain questions about their counterfactual wishes and intentions in contemporary society far more intelligible than those same

A u t h e n t i c i t y   a s   I n t e n t i o n

questions asked of their contemporaries or persons closer in time and culture to us than to them. If one thinks, for example, of contemporary science and technology, then Roger Bacon seems to me far less remote from
us in intellect than David Hume, and certainly far less remote than his
contemporaries.

Thus, although time, culture, and personality may make certain questions about certain counterfactual wishes and intentions of certain historical personages impossible of determination, to the point of unintelligibil-
ity, such questions are by no means either unintelligible or, at least within
certain limits, unanswerable in all cases. It is a problem for the historian,
in any given instance, to investigate the possibility of answering such
questions about counterfactual wishes and intentions, and to answer
them, where possible. And it is part of our everyday notion of wishes and
intentions that such questions sometimes make sense and sometimes
have answers. For we ask, and try to answer, questions about the counterfactual wishes and intentions not only of great historical figures in the
remote past but of our own departed friends and relatives as well, which
we may want to ascertain for legal or other less pressing reasons.

.   .   .

Two further points to notice about wishes and intentions are that they
tend to be hierarchical and that there may be wishes or intentions concerning what happens after the death of the wisher or intender.

That wishes and intentions customarily are embedded in hierarchical
structures can easily be seen by briefly returning to the case of Wanda.
She wanted to be, you will recall, a nurse or (if circumstances allowed) a
doctor. We might generalize from that to the conclusion that Wanda
really wanted to be in the health services profession rather than, say, in
business or education. Looking at things this way, we see that her wish to
be a doctor or a nurse is a means of accomplishing her higher-order intention to be in health services. And if other professions should become relevant to medicine—electronics, for example—then Wanda might satisfy
her first-order intention to be in health services not only by being a doctor
or a nurse but by being as well an expert in the vast array of electronic
gadgets that are currently available to the medical community. Contrariwise, there are professions that, at other times, would have served her
purposes but no longer do: for example, astrology, or magic, or leech-
gathering. And so, if Wanda had been born in the ninth century A.D., she

Authenticity as Intention

might have wished to be a magician or astrologer or that other loathsome thing for the same reason—a higher-order wish to serve a suffering humanity—that now impels her to study nursing or medicine. Which of course means that, given her higher-order wish, we would best gratify her *real* desires today not by enabling her to study astrology or magic or leech-gathering but by enabling her to study nursing or medicine or electronics; for the former disciplines (if they can be so called) are no longer seen to accomplish her higher-order wish, whereas the latter are seen to do so preeminently.

As to wishes and intentions that have posthumous objects, for most ordinary mortals, these have to do with descendants, particularly children, and are, of course, customarily expressed in wills and other such legal documents. Needless to say, the wishes and intentions of composers as to the performance of their works are also, quite as a matter of course, taken by performers and musicologists as having been meant to survive the composers' deaths (although for how long is a nice question). And the time has now come to apply the conceptual lessons we have here learned, about wishes and intentions, to these posthumous examples.

. . .

As I suggested earlier in this chapter, it is no good talking about the performance "intentions" of composers as if they were all of a piece as regards strength of purpose (if I may so put it). Indeed, to the extent that "intention" already begs the question in favor of strong as opposed to weak purpose—"the general *intends* the seventh regiment to advance" as opposed to, say, "the general thinks it might be advisable for the seventh regiment to advance, given what he currently knows"—it is a damaging misnomer to call all the instructions, either explicit or implicit, left behind by the composer for the performance of his or her works expressions of "intention." And it is, of course, a historical question—a question, one assumes, for musicologists—which performance indications are to be understood as expressions of intention properly so called, and which expressions of something weaker, all the way down to mere suggestions, with no real force of authority behind them.

I emphasize that determining the strength of a composer's performance attitudes is a job for specialists, for historians of music, to avoid haggling over the illustrations I am about to give here of what I am talking about. It does not matter if what I adduce as something weaker than a performance intention really is or is not or, similarly, whether something I adduce as a performance intention really is or is not. What matters for the argument is the conceptual point at issue—namely, that there are varying degrees of strength attached to the instructions that composers explicitly give, or that can be inferred, concerning the performance of their music; and to take something weaker than an intention (as I am now using that word) for an intention is not to be faithful to the composer's intentions (as others use the word) but, on the contrary, to be unfaithful to them.

A pair of examples will help here. Both are pretty familiar ones. I have reference to two well-known "facts" of musical history. The first fact is that Bach transcribed one of the movements from Cantata 140, *Wachet auf, ruft uns die Stimme*, for organ as one of the "Schübler" chorale preludes; and it has also been transcribed, in the twentieth century, for modern symphony orchestra. The second fact is simply that Beethoven, after the invention of the metronome, put metronome markings to various of his works, most notably (and controversially) his symphonies. I put the question now quite baldly: are the modern transcription of the Bach chorale movement and performances of Beethoven's symphonies that do not observe his metronome markings historically inauthentic, in the present sense of not in accordance with the composers' performing intentions?

I suppose one wants immediately to say that the question is not just baldly put but bordering on the absurd. Could there be any clearer examples on earth of historical inauthenticity—for which, read: flying in the face of authorial intention—than to play a composition by Bach on instruments other than the ones he specifically prescribed, some of which have changed so much since his time that he would scarcely recognize them, others not even invented until long after his death? Or playing Beethoven's symphonies at tempos different from those the composer took care to indicate, not just vaguely but with numerical precision?

But if what I have said before is taken into consideration, it becomes immediately apparent that the question is not in the least bit absurd and the obvious answer quite possibly incorrect.

First of all, in the sense of intention expressed by "the general intends the seventh regiment to advance," it is not at all clear and must be argued for on historical and perhaps psychological grounds whether or not Bach and Beethoven have expressed their *intentions* at all in these two instances. One might argue, for example, that the very fact of there being

Authenticity as Intention

two such radically different scorings for the Bach chorale as one for a chorus of tenors, a section of violins, and basso continuo on the one hand
and one for a single keyboard instrument on the other, without singer or
text, both authorized by the composer, might suggest that Bach's "intentions" as to what forces were appropriate for a performance of this work
were far from *intentions* in the strong sense of commands, and more like
suggestions: the general thinks it advisable under the circumstances . . .
But, contrariwise, it might be argued that, given what we know of Beethoven's somewhat imperious attitude toward his work—the "grand mo-
gul," you will recall, was the way Haydn described him—and the fact that
he did choose to express his decisions about tempos with the most exact
means at his disposal, they were perhaps *intentions* in the full-blooded
sense of *commands*.

But the crucial point here is not whether Bach's or Beethoven's "intentions" were *intentions*. The crucial point is that the question can be raised
in the first place and that the answer is not forthcoming without historical research. What is remarkable about this seemingly obvious observation that the strengths of composers' attitudes toward their own performing instructions might vary in intensity and, in particular, that they might
in some instances fall far short of the strength of intention, in the sense of
the general's command, is not that it has gone unnoticed; for it has been
remarked upon willy-nilly in the literature. What is remarkable is that no
one seems to have realized the deep systematic significance of what is
usually cited in the form of anecdotes, from which no conclusion, or the
wrong conclusion, is drawn. There are many stories abroad of composers
approving performances that go contrary to their instructions. Many a
composer has praised a performer for revealing an unthought-of and successful way of performing his or her work. And such anecdotal evidence
is indeed used quite rightly, as Taruskin, for example, has done, as an antidote to the carving of performance instructions into the tables of the
law. But to draw from this anecdotal evidence the general conclusion that
all composers have such a pragmatic approach to the performance of their
works, and performance intention in the sense of the general's command
is a musicologist's myth, is obviously unwarranted by the evidence. Nor
have I ever come across the right conclusion being drawn—which is, it
appears to me, that it ought to be a research program, in music history, to
determine by all available means, not excluding psychological specula-

A u t h e n t i c i t y   a s   I n t e n t i o n

tion, as well as good old "imaginative reconstruction of the past," what the individual composer's attitude toward performance might have been. A composer is a flesh-and-blood embodiment of will and personality, not a historical artifact; and if one really wants to know whether the marks on the paper are an expression of intent or suggestion or anything in between, one cannot shrink from the speculative leap.

Now, at this point one can well imagine the historian replying in this wise. Look here. Historians write history, not historical novels. And history must stay within the confines of the hard evidence. The black marks on the score are "♩ = 60." That is all we have. *Perhaps* they are mere suggestions, open to the performer's judgment and possible revision. And *perhaps* they are strong intentions: the general's command. *Which* they are, in the absence of further evidence, is pure speculation, and the historian must withhold judgment either way. The safest course, therefore, for the performer, and the only one warranted by the historical evidence—the black marks on the page—is to play ♩ = 60.

But this is a serious misunderstanding of what the available evidence in the given case does and does not sanction.

If I *unswervingly* obey the performing instructions, the black marks on the page, while admitting that they may be mere suggestions, open to revision, I am indeed on safe historical ground. However, I would be on equally safe historical ground if I revised them in light of my musical judgment, after trying them out in performance, while admitting that they may be expressions of strong intention. In the former case I am treating the instructions *as if* they are expressive of strong intentions, while not committing myself to the fact; whereas in the latter case I am treating them *as if* they are mere suggestions, while not committing myself to *that* as a fact. And the black marks on the page, in conjunction with the assumed present state of my historical knowledge, sanction both courses of action equally. In the absence of evidence and interpretation, the black marks are simply "black marks."

This seemingly meager conclusion about intentions—that, strictly speaking, many of the composer's expressed wishes and intentions concerning performance may not be *intentions* at all but merely suggestions or conjectures, fully open to the performer's discretionary judgment—has, I want to urge, implications of far from meager significance both for theory and for practice. For theory it implies that we cannot simply go on calling

Authenticity as Intention

every attitude toward the performance of his or her work that a composer has expressed, either explicitly or implicitly, an intention in the strong sense of the general's command, as, it seems to me, is now usually done; rather, we must institute research programs that, if need be, go beyond what the "positivist" historian is willing to risk, in order to determine, within the limits of certainty that the question allows, what the strengths of the composer's performance "expressions" really are. To put it another way, when confronted with a composer's expression, whether explicit or implicit, of how his or her music is to be performed, it is the musicologist's task to determine not merely its propositional content but its *illocutionary force* as well.

The immediate practical implication of recognizing the various kinds of illocutionary force that an expression of performance "intention" may have is to render suspect the distinction between historically authentic and inauthentic performance, whenever that distinction involves the "violation" on the performer's part of one of the composer's expressed performing "intentions." I am told in a recent article on Pablo Casals's performance (on record) of the Saraband from Bach's D-minor Suite for Cello: "Although Bach's autograph copy of the suites is not extant, in its absence we assume that the Anna-Magdalena Bach, Kellner, and Westphal manuscripts can reveal sufficient evidence of Bach's intent to warrant performance."[10] Yet nowhere in this article do I find any attempt to evaluate the illocutionary force of the enormous variety of "expressions" the author finds in these autographs of what he so complacently calls Bach's "intent." Again, the author laconically remarks that "we assume that Bach's notation reflects his intents."[11] Well, it certainly reflects, we must assume, *something* about Bach's states of mind. But does it *all* reflect his *intentions* in the strict sense of that term? No argument is forthcoming to tell us.

Is Casals's performance historically authentic? Well, as the author painstakingly points out, Casals takes great liberties with Bach's rhythm, for example, *as notated*. But what are we to infer about the taking of liberties? If the notation, in the respects in question, reflects Bach's *intentions*, then the performance is historically inauthentic, in respect of its vi-

[10] Planer, "Sentimentality in the Performance of Absolute Music," p. 241.
[11] Ibid.

Authenticity as Intention

olating them. If, however, the notation reflects a given range of *suggestions* for performance, with the tacit understanding the word "suggestion" carries, that these matters are discretionary and that the performer might find a better way, Casals's performance may be as historically authentic as the most punctilious performance of the musicological purist. Whether it is a better performance or a worse one is not the point at issue now. The issue is whether it is historically authentic. And to the extent that Bach's instructions for performance, whether they are in the form of words or in that of notation, are expressive of suggestions or conjectures rather than of commands, to that same extent deviation from them is as authentic as strict observance. Indeed, deviation *is* observance.

Even at this early point in our analysis of composers' "intentions," then, we can begin to conclude—and the conclusion will grow stronger as the argument wears on—that a good deal of what is today cried down in "mainstream" performance practice by the adherents to historical authenticity as "historically inauthentic" may well be full-bloodedly authentic in the very sense of that word as employed by the critics. For deviation from the composer's instructions, no matter how conveyed, is historically inauthentic, in the sense of betraying those instructions, only if the instructions are expressions, literally, of *intentions*—the general's command. But it is more than just a good guess that not all are that. And, furthermore, we are entitled in every case to a determination of what the force of these instructions is—a duty of the musical historian that, in my experience, is seldom if ever discharged.

But even if all performance instructions were expressive of intention, in the strongest possible sense, with the force of the general's command, they would still not possess the kind of inviolable status that they seem to have in the eyes of those who subscribe to the historical authenticity movement in performance, which mandates literal observance. Or, to put it in another, more accurate way, far more of what the mainstream performer does that may appear to deviate from composers' intentions does not so deviate, and is just as historically authentic, in that respect, as a great deal of what the self-described "historically authentic" performer does that is defended as being scrupulously in accordance with intentions. This will be the real musical payoff of the conceptual analysis of wishes and intentions previously undertaken. I turn to that now.

Authenticity   as   Intention

From the most strongly felt intention to the most tentatively entertained inclination, what we discovered about them all, and what we can safely say about them all, is that they make no sense except in relation to some context or other, some understood set of conditions. And this applies, of course, pari passu, to composers' intentions, wishes, inclinations, conjectures—about the performance of their works. If it does not, then I do not know what we are talking about.

We might, then, begin by reviewing, in the form of a list, what the contextual variables are that govern the concepts of intending and wanting and the like:

1. Wanting or intending is always a matter of choosing among available possibilities.

2. What one *really* wants or intends can only be understood relative to the available choices; and if the range of choices should change, then what one *really* wants or intends must be relative to the new set of choices.

3. What one *really* wants or intends is relative not merely to an actual set of choices but to possible sets of choices ("circumstances," for short) as well. And so what one *really* wants or intends is expressible as a counterfactual: if circumstances were C_2, he or she would want (or intend) W_2, given that the circumstances are C_1, and he or she wants (or intends) W_1.

4. The most interesting and relevant counterfactuals, for our purposes, are those that are projected from some past time to the present. That is to say, given that he or she wanted (or intended) W_1 at time T_1, where conditions C_1 obtained, what would he or she want (or intend) now, given conditions C_2?

5. What one did *not* want or intend in the past is complicated by an ambiguity. William did *not* want to be a harness maker, and he did *not* want to be an aviator. But the former is a career choice he considered and rejected, whereas the latter is a career choice he could not possibly have considered in the eighteenth century and so was not wanted by default (as it were). But it does make sense to ask whether, were he alive today, William would want to be an aviator;

and if the answer is affirmative, then that *is* what he really wants, whereas harness making is not.

6. Not all counterfactual questions projected over time in the manner here being described are intelligible. This depends on three interrelated variables: the length of time elapsed between the actual wants or intentions and the projected, counterfactual ones; the cultural disparity between the wanter's (or intender's) circumstances then and now; and the particular intellectual and psychological makeup of the wanter (or intender). But where such temporally projected counterfactual questions are intelligible, they may indeed be answerable, within certain evidential limits, and, if so, cannot be passed over in determining what someone in the past *really* wanted or intended.

7. Wishes and intentions are not single spies but come in battalions. They form systems, as do beliefs. And that being the case, they tend to be hierarchical, sometimes in the relation of means to ends.

It remains for us now to run through this list, with musical performance intentions as examples, to see what we can determine about historical authenticity in performance considered as the realization of the composer's *real* wishes or intentions.

· · ·

Composers' wishes concerning the performance of their compositions, like any other human wishes, are contextual. In a document well known to Bach scholars, the composer submitted to the Leipzig Town Council his specifications for the instrumental forces he apparently thought minimally necessary for the performance of his sacred music—his want-list, so to speak, certainly modest by modern standards.[12] Assuming that the human condition, in such matters, has not changed much since Bach's day, I would guess that Bach asked for more than he thought he could get, under the circumstances, less than he really wanted, and less than he would have asked for had his circumstances been more favorable. Thus, the question, What does Bach *really* want?—like the question, What does Wanda *really* want?—can be asked and answered only relative to the circumstances. And it would be just as absurd to insist implacably that Bach

[12] David and Mendel, *The Bach Reader*, pp. 120–24.

Authenticity as Intention

really wanted "2 or even 3 for the *Violino 1*" because that is the number he explicitly stated, without reference to the circumstances that gave rise to that explicit statement, as it would be for Wanda's parents, under improved financial circumstances, to insist implacably that Wanda really wanted to be a nurse because that is the only thing she explicitly stated she wanted to be, when it is perfectly obvious that that was a desire relative to a set of circumstances that has now been replaced by a more favorable set, under which what she really wants to be is a surgeon.

As in the case of Wanda, we must observe that Bach's statement of what he wanted was the expression of a choice among available alternatives. And, also as in the case of Wanda, we can raise questions, expressed counterfactually, about what Bach would have wanted under conditions different from the ones in which he found himself, and among alternatives other than those that in fact offered themselves up for his consideration. And I would remind the reader that in framing such hypotheticals, we are not departing from the question of what Bach really, in point of fact, wished or intended but, on the contrary, are pursuing that very question. For Bach's actual wishes and intentions concerning the performance of his works, like anyone else's actual wishes and intentions concerning anything whatever, are determined not merely by what they implicitly or explicitly convey, relative to the circumstances in which they actually find themselves, but by what they would explicitly or implicitly convey concerning their wishes and intentions in other possible circumstances.

Now, I am moving very slowly, even pedantically, here, to be sure, and probably have not said anything yet with which anyone would not readily agree. But I do have a reason for being so deliberate. I want to move so gradually as to leave no suspicion in the reader's mind about my having skipped any steps or said anything about composers' performing wishes or intentions not true of wishes and intentions *tout court*. That being the case, when I begin to say things about performing wishes and intentions contrary to received opinion in historical authenticity circles, it will be readily seen that they follow directly from the perfectly ordinary, presystematic concepts of "wish" and "intention" themselves, not from some dissenting aesthetic premises of my own about how music is to be performed. And it is incumbent upon those who make use of these concepts to use them in the ordinary, accepted senses or else make clear that, and how, they are being departed from—it being obvious, I think, that

Authenticity as Intention

36

departing from the senses in which "wish" and "intention" are ordinarily used compromises any claim to be accurately reflecting, in performance, the wishes and intentions of composers.

The next step is to observe that what we are particularly interested in, of course, in formulating counterfactual questions about composers' performing intentions under circumstances other than those in which they found themselves when they framed them, is projection through time to actual conditions currently obtaining. That is to say, since we want to perform their music *now*, we want to ask questions about what their performing intentions would be, given the conditions under which their music would *now* be performed, not under the conditions *then* prevailing. This, I take it, is common sense and in need of no argument.

But it makes little sense to talk about conditions now obtaining, as if there were only one such relevant set of conditions to consider, when deciding what a composer's performance intentions and wishes might be. So let us begin with a question specific enough to suggest at least the possibility of an answer. Suppose we were to ask, What instrumental and vocal forces would Bach have wished for a performance of his *St. John Passion* in New York's Philharmonic Hall on Good Friday, 1990? (And for the sake of the argument, let us mean by performing forces the number of performers and the nature of the instruments.) We have a pretty good idea of the forces for which he wrote in Leipzig's Thomaskirche; but if what we have learned about *all* wishes and intentions so far is reasonable, the performance wishes and intentions that those forces *may* represent cannot, without further argument, be considered the whole description of Bach's performance wishes and intentions in this regard. For any description of wishes and intentions must give us the conditions, the circumstances under which those wishes and intentions are or were formulated. Various documents and physical evidence tell us what Bach's intentions and wishes were, given the choices open to him, and the conditions obtaining in Leipzig during his career there. But they cannot tell us, without further argument and evidence, documentation and conjecture, what his intentions and wishes would have been for a performance, given the choices open to him and the conditions obtaining in Philharmonic Hall, New York City, on Good Friday, 1990.

One rather amusing possibility is that Bach would have been horrified at the prospect of his work being performed as "public entertainment" at all and insisted that he would not wish his great religious utterance to be heard outside of the Lutheran service for which he wrote it. If one could present a good argument for that response, then *any performance* of the *St. John Passion*—in the concert hall, in the recording studio, on record or disc, or even in church—would, if it were merely a "performance," be contrary to Bach's wishes and intentions and hence historically inauthentic, no matter how it might be musically realized.

This conclusion is possible, of course intolerable, and, I hasten to add, entirely avoidable. We are, after all, in asking counterfactual questions here, creating a "hypothetical Bach," so to speak, and are free to alter our hypothetical Bach to meet our needs. So we can force the issue by replacing our first Bach, who himself was, after all, only hypothetical, with a more tractable one who is like the historical Bach in every relevant respect in which it is possible for us to determine but who will acquiesce in modern "performances" of his *Passion* and answer our question—Given, Herr Bach, that your *St. John Passion* is to be performed for an audience of American music lovers on Good Friday, 1990, in Philharmonic Hall, New York City, what are your wishes with regard to performing forces? We want to be authentic to your wishes.

Would the most likely answer of our hypothetical Bach be, Under the given circumstances I would wish my *Passion* to be performed as closely as possible with regard to instrumental and vocal forces to the way it was performed by me in Leipzig on Good Friday, 1724? I don't think anyone really knows. And I think an equally likely answer might be, Given the nature of Philharmonic Hall, the nature of twentieth-century life in America, and the nature of a twentieth-century American audience, I would like my *Passion* performed on modern instruments with a larger chorus than was available to me in Leipzig.

It is the obvious conclusion of this line of reasoning that the performance of Bach's *St. John Passion* in a modern concert hall with performing forces modeled closely on those Bach intended for a performance in the Thomaskirche under his direction might be contrary to the composer's performing intentions, and a performance on modern instruments, with larger forces, might be in accordance with them. And it must be a music-historical question whether this is the case or not.

Furthermore, this conclusion is generalizable for *any* aspect of performance: phrasing, dynamics, ornamentation, "expression," and so on. Some may be more "relative" to circumstances than others. But in every case, one must ask not only, What did Bach intend, given the choices open to him, and the circumstances obtaining in Leipzig in 1724? but also, What would Bach intend, given the choices open to him in 1990 in New York City? And, needless to say, the conclusion is generalizable for any composer at all and for any of his or her compositions.

This indeed is the conclusion that the present chapter has been aiming at all along—the conclusion that a composer's performing intentions and wishes cannot be stated *sans phrase*. They must be stated relative to choices available, and reigning circumstances. There is no single set of a composer's performing intentions, certainly not the set of those consciously framed during the composer's lifetime for the performance of his or her works amid those time-dependent choices and in those time-dependent circumstances. But this is not by any means a transparent conclusion: it has complications that must be worked out and possible objections that must be answered.

·   ·   ·

You will recall that one complication with regard to expressed wishes and intentions—the fifth item in our summary list—was with regard to the question of what the composer did *not* wish or intend. Bach did not wish the aria "Ich folge dir . . ." to be accompanied by oboe or violin or another instrument, for he expressly stated that it should be accompanied by two transverse flutes in unison. He also did not wish it to be played on modern silver, gold, or platinum flutes with modern Boehm keywork but instead on a wooden one-keyed instrument. It is the second negative intention that provides the complication because, of course, the "did not wish" in the first case suggests the possibility of considered alternatives; whereas in the second case it does not because Bach could not have contemplated the choice of an instrument that had not yet been invented. But this should no more bother us than does the case of William, who did not wish to be an aviator, in the obvious sense that, being a citizen of eighteenth-century England, he could not even contemplate the notion, because there were no flying machines or, a fortiori, people to pursue the profession of piloting them. It is, of course, part of our counterfactual framing of wishes and intentions in terms of future possibilities that we can ask, Were William alive today, would he have wanted to be an aviator? and, similarly, Were Bach alive today, would he have wanted "Ich folge dir . . ." to be performed on modern flutes or period instruments?

But this leads us directly to the more serious complication—the sixth item in the summary list—as to whether it is in fact intelligible at all to ask, and expect to answer, these kinds of hypothetical questions. Certainly some such questions do seem to be bordering on the amusing absurdity of the parlor game in which one member of a group assumes the character of a famous personage and the others try to guess the name by asking questions like "If you were a cheese, what kind of cheese would you be?" "If Napoleon were a cheese, what kind of cheese would he be?" is not, it appears to me, an intelligible question with a real, determinable answer. And if all questions of the form, If composer X were alive today . . . ? were of that level of absurdity, surely the view being put forward here could be dismissed out of hand. It is indeed quite easy to think up such imponderable questions with regard to musical performance. If Ion the rhapsode, with whom Socrates had a famous conversation, in the dialogue of the same name, were alive today, would he want his "rhapsodies" accompanied by a "modern" instrument or an "ancient" one? No one can hope to answer such a question because of the unbridgeable gap between Ion's performing world and our own. We hardly have the remotest idea what it was that he "performed."

But I scarcely think such an unbridgeable gap exists between our performing world and Bach's, or Ockeghem's even, or even yet that of the Notre Dame School of polyphony; although, I readily grant, it may be easier to conjecture about Bach's reaction to the twentieth century than about Leonin's. There have, after all, been historians who have given us intimate glimpses of what it might have been like to live in the middle ages, for example—glimpses that are the product not of fictional fantasy but of the *historical* imagination. And if the conjunction of "historical" with "imagination" strikes a reader as an oxymoron, I daresay so also ought the pair "scientific" and "imagination," in which case I do not think the reader really has a grasp of what constitutes the creative intellect in any area of research.

I am not, to be sure, suggesting that musicologists give up facts for imagination, any more than did the author of *Medieval People*.[13] I love a

[13] Power, *Medieval People*. Power's book was first published in 1924.

Authenticity as Intention

fact as much as the next person; and I admire someone with a talent for establishing them, which, as anyone knows, requires its own kind of imaginative leap. But "hard evidence" is not the sum total of historical research in general or of music-historical research in particular. And there are those with a talent for the imaginative leap from the physical artifact to the mind that made it. That too is history, not fiction—the kind of history that can give us the insight we need to answer such questions as it is necessary to raise if we are to have a full-blooded notion of what the composer really wished or intended with regard to performance.

.   .   .

At this point the hard-nosed, "positivistic" historian may still have a powerful response, even having granted the intelligibility and tractability of counterfactual questions about performing intentions. Look here, I imagine the positivist saying: granted that intelligible conjectures, at some level of probability, can be made about how a composer like Bach would have wished or intended his music to be performed, given twentieth-century possibilities and conditions, conjectures they will remain, with little hope of our making them anything like firm conclusions. But we *do* have hard evidence that can lead to one set of firm conclusions about Bach's performing intentions, and these conclusions tell us how Bach *in fact* intended his music to be played in his lifetime. Those are the only performing wishes and intentions of Bach's that we have firmly in our grasp. The evidence for those is greater than the evidence ever can be for any hypothesis with regard to how Bach would have wanted his music to be performed if he had open to him present-day choices and had to perform his music under present-day conditions. Therefore, if we want to play Bach in accordance with his wishes and intentions (to achieve historical authenticity), it is Bach's wishes and intentions expressed implicitly or explicitly in his lifetime, about how his music then and there was to be performed, that we must realize in our performances. These are the only ones for which the evidence is really compelling.

But such a response is in fact a non sequitur. For if we understand historical authenticity in performance, as we have been doing, as the realizing of the composer's performing wishes and intentions with regard to *the performance we are now giving*, then we are not, ipso facto, realizing those wishes and intentions by realizing the wishes and intentions with regard to a performance that took place during the composer's lifetime, *unless* it

Authenticity   as   Intention

is also the case that the composer would have sanctioned those same wishes and intentions for the present performance. And that is just the kind of counterfactual conjecture the response is framed to avoid, the conjecture lacking, as it must, "hard" evidence, and depending, as it must, on imaginative reconstruction.

Suppose, however, that the "positivist" insists that it is the composer's actual intentions and wishes for performance in his own lifetime that constitute the favored ones: those alone whose realization would warrant the title of "historically authentic performance"? (After all, those are the "old" ones.) Is there any justification for such a position? I do not see that there is.

Recall the definition of "authentic" from the *OED*, adduced in Chapter 1, on which our very concept of authenticity is based in the present chapter. According to this definition, the authentic version of a text is the one "really proceeding from its reputed source or author." But if our "text" is a musical performance, then, in the present instance, if we want to know whether the performance—the "text"—of Bach's *St. John Passion* on Good Friday, 1990, is authentic, we have to know if *that* very performance, *that* very "text," is "really proceeding from its source or author." And to know that, of course, is to know whether it conforms to Bach's performing wishes and intentions for a performance in 1990, not to those for one in 1724. So we are right back where the positivist does not want us to be, and where common sense about wishes and intentions tells us we must be—namely with how Bach would have wished or intended his *St. John Passion* to be performed, given the choices open to him in the twentieth century and given the circumstances under which, in the twentieth century, the work will be performed. That is authenticity as we are construing it in the present chapter. And it is, let me emphasize, *historical* authenticity. For historical authenticity, understood intentionally, is the authenticity of performance with the composer's intentions as its source, rather than some unhistorical set of performing intentions as, for example, those of a modern editor or conductor. With that concluded, we can leave the positivist sulking in his tent and go on to other matters.

The final, seventh item in our summary list of conclusions about wishes and intentions in general is the observation that wishes and intentions usually are not isolated but exist in hierarchical systems, some related as means to ends. The same surely is true of composers' performing wishes

Authenticity as Intention

and intentions, as has been insightfully brought to our attention by Randall R. Dipert, in one of the most valuable contributions to date, by a philosopher, to the present debate.[14] The direct relevance to the discussion at hand of this fact about intentions and wishes in general, and composers' in particular, is that in order to determine what Bach's wishes and intentions would be for a performance of his *St. John Passion* in Philharmonic Hall, Good Friday, 1990, we must have some idea of, among other things, what the rank ordering of his intentions and wishes were for a performance in his lifetime. For the nub of the matter is that reinterpreting wishes and intentions under *changing* conditions will reveal new possibilities to the composer (in whose mind we are trying to place ourselves as his or her surrogates) and new conditions under which his music is to be performed and heard. That being the case, a *system* of performing wishes and intentions that may have been more or less consistent in 1724 may not be today; and, furthermore, a *system* of performing wishes and intentions that may have been less than consistent in 1724, and may have produced a less than satisfactory result, might today, with new possibilities available, be modified to produce a better overall result with regard to some of those wishes and intentions at the expense of others, resulting in a more consistent system than heretofore possible. What would Bach choose to do, under the altered conditions? One necessary condition for answering this question is knowledge of the rank ordering of the original, 1724 wishes and intentions. An example, somewhat simpler than that of the *St. John Passion*, will help here.

The *concertino* of Bach's Second Brandenburg Concerto comprises trumpet, recorder, oboe, and violin. My *interpretation* of this aspect of the work—and I emphasize "interpretation" because it will become apparent in a moment how important that is—is that Bach wanted to play with these particular tone colors in his concerto, and he wanted them in perfect dynamic balance, because each instrument sings an equal, independent voice in the ensemble.

My experience has been that if one performs the concerto as scored, using period instruments, the balance of trumpet, oboe, and violin is good; but the recorder, most particularly in its low register, is almost completely overpowered. If it is played on a modern "Bach" trumpet with valves, a modern, metal transverse flute, a modern oboe, and a modern violin, the

[14] Dipert, "The Composer's Intentions."

Authenticity   as   Intention

balance is much better; but, of course, all the tone colors have been altered to *some* extent. Years ago, before trumpet players had rediscovered
the art of playing Bach's stratospheric trumpet parts and special "Bach"
trumpets were not yet available, the trumpet part of the Second Brandenburg was simply unplayable on the trumpet as written and was frequently
played on a clarinet or saxophone instead, with modern flute, oboe, and
violin. The balance was excellent, but, of course, the tone color even more
seriously compromised. I am going to assume, for the sake of argument,
that the balance, in the solo instruments, as I have laid out my example,
is in rank order, proceeding from worst to best, and the tone color, in rank
order, proceeding from best to worst. And I now want to ask, Which of
these three ways of performing his concerto would Bach have wished or
intended for a performance in 1990?

The first point to notice here is that we are now dealing with two kinds
of wishes and intentions: those having to do with the aesthetic effect that
Bach wanted his concerto to have, namely (among other things), the play
of those particular tone colors, and a perfect balance of the four instrumental lines; and those, the performing wishes and intentions, which
were directed toward making that aesthetic effect audible. Dipert calls
these, respectively, "high-level" and "low-level" intentions;[15] and he correctly concludes with regard to them that "we should follow first and primarily his [i.e., any composer's] high-level intentions. To do otherwise is
to follow the letter and not the spirit of his intentions."[16]

Thus Dipert recognizes a hierarchy of wishes and intentions, in which
the ones regarding performance are subservient to the ones regarding the
aesthetic payoff. But we must mark also, as Dipert does not in his article,
a hierarchy of wishes and intentions, wherever they may be incompatible
among the high-order, aesthetic wishes and intentions as well. In the
present case, we must ask ourselves whether tone color or equal dynamic
balance has priority for Bach, in the *concertino* of the Second Brandenburg. For they cannot, under the circumstances given, both be fully realized. If we decide that the structural property of dynamically balanced
lines has very high priority, for Bach, over the coloristic property of instrumental timbre, then, *ceteris paribus*, we might conclude that Bach
would have wanted the solo parts (*horribile dictu*) to be played on saxo-

[15] Ibid., pp. 206–8.
[16] Ibid., p. 208.

Authenticity   as   Intention

44

phone or clarinet, modern silver flute, modern French oboe, and modern violin. If, however, we decide that equality of parts was a priority for Bach but not an overpowering one, we might conclude that he would have wanted a performance, *ceteris paribus*, on modern "Bach" trumpet, modern silver flute, modern French oboe, and modern violin. And if, finally, we decide that tone color had priority in his aesthetic intentions over equality of voicing, we might then conclude that he would have wanted, *ceteris paribus*, a performance on "period" instruments.

Now, the general conclusion we can draw from this example is that, in any case whatever, we must map out the hierarchy of Bach's high-order intentions and wishes before we can make reasonable conclusions about his low-order wishes and intentions with regard to performance. And that mapping of high-order, aesthetic wishes and intentions is part of what I called, earlier, an *interpretation* of the music. In short, an interpretation of the music is prerequisite for deciding what manner of performance would most closely coincide with the composer's wishes and intentions—which is to say, what manner of performance would, under the present understanding, be historically authentic. And because a musical interpretation is, at least in part, a judgment of the musical ear, it follows that historical authenticity of performance cannot be determined apart from such musical—that is, aesthetic—judgments: judgments of taste.

·   ·   ·

It has been my main purpose in this chapter to try to shake ourselves loose from the notion that realizing a deceased composer's performing intentions or wishes in a present-day performance is a matter of following—to the letter—instructions, whether explicit or implicit, that were given for a performance at a time long past under conditions vastly different in relevant respects from those that exist today. Indeed, it is *not* following them to the letter at all, because in order to follow *literally* someone's wishes and intentions, whether musical or any other kind, one must interpret them, and to interpret them one must reunderstand them relative to the conditions under which they are now to be realized. To do otherwise would be like thinking you can bring to pass today Napoleon's grand design for the unification of Europe by restaging the battle of Waterloo in original costumes.

In concluding this chapter I want to emphasize two points. The first is that what I have been indulging in here is purely theoretical speculation.

What I have presented is an analysis of the concept of historical authenticity in performance, under the assumption that what is meant by "historically authentic" is "conforming to the performing wishes and intentions of the composer." This is meant to be a value-free inquiry. That is to say, I have not raised at all the normative question of whether historically authentic musical performances, in the sense defined, would be a good thing or a bad thing to produce. Nor have I gone into the matter of how such a question might be answered. That normative inquiry is reserved for the second part of this book.

Nevertheless—and this is the second point I want to emphasize—the purely conceptual conclusions reached in this chapter already have, it appears to me, profound practical implications for current performance practices and the discussion surrounding them. To put the matter bluntly, a performer who plays Bach, say, on a modern instrument, with phrasing and dynamics that depart from the *Urtext*, may very well be closer to the composer's wishes and intentions in those very respects, and therefore more historically authentic than the performer who plays Bach on a baroque instrument with the *Urtext*'s phrasing and dynamics as sacred writ. It is an open question, in every individual case—or, at least, with every individual composer—whether "mainstream" or "historically reconstructed" performance practice conforms more closely to authorial wishes or intentions. Nor is this a logician's trick. It is simply the result of using words in their proper senses.

Nevertheless, there is bound to be some residual feeling in the musicologically oriented reader that *something* about playing music on a period instrument, in a manner consciously envisioned by the composer, is "historically authentic" in a sense in which playing it on an instrument invented after the composer's death in a manner the composer could not possibly have had in mind is not. And although authenticity as realization of the composer's wishes and intentions does not capture that intuition, perhaps one of our other historical "authenticities" does. These are, it will be recalled, authenticity as reproduction of contemporary sound, and authenticity as reproduction of contemporary performance practice. I shall turn to the former now.

Authenticity   as   Intention

⊙

Authenticity as Sound

I suppose that anyone who has ever been the least bit interested in the history of musical performance has, at one time or another, wished that he or she could have been present at some past musical event: the first playing of the *Eroica*, say, an organ recital by Bach, or perhaps a Verdi opening night. And I suppose further that that particular *Gedankenexperiment* provides the standard against which one might want to measure the historical authenticity of a performance heard today of the *Eroica*, a Bach organ fugue, or *La forza del destino*, if the historical authenticity one is pursuing is that of "how the music sounded then," as opposed to "what the composer intended" or "how the music was played." Our idea here is that sound is, after all, a physical phenomenon, musical sound a special case of it. So the sounds Bach produced by playing an organ fugue in the Thomaskirche are, so to speak, an "objective" physical fact: perturbations of a physical medium, determinately measurable, at least in principle. And we can imagine having a recording of a performance by Bach, as we have of performances that took place in the early twentieth century, that could reproduce (within the physical limits of the recording device) the physical sounds of Bach's performance.

Now, if we had such a recording of Bach, we could measure any present-day performance against it to determine, in this particular sense of "authenticity," whether that performance was historically "authentic" or not, or in what degree, by listening to the performance (or a recording of *it*) and the recording of Bach, and comparing them. Let us call the concept of authenticity that this *Gedankenexperiment* embodies "sonic" authenticity. A present-day performance of a Bach fugue, then, is sonically authentic if it is sonically identical with a performance that Bach might have given. And, of course, we can generalize this concept of authenticity to cover any case. We can say that a present-day performance of any composition you like is historically authentic, in the sense of sonic authenticity, if it is close to or identical with the physical sound sequence of some past performance that, for whatever reason, we have chosen as our measure of historical authenticity.

·　　·　　·

Sonic authenticity is uncomplicated to conceptualize although, of course, not at all easy to achieve or to be reasonably convinced that one has achieved. But there is another kind of authenticity that might also be called "sonic" that is far more problematic, far more interesting, and not always clearly distinguished in the literature from what I am calling "sonic authenticity." An example will be useful in introducing it.

Early Music is a rather glitzy periodical that seems to serve the dual function of a learned journal on historical performance practice and a trade magazine with advertisements for the latest thing (or should I say the earliest thing) in rebecs, curved cornettos, and citoles (to name but a few of the esoteric offerings). But what particularly caught my eye in an issue of this periodical that came into my possession recently is a full-color advertisement, occupying the full back cover, for the "Roland C-50 Classic Harpsichord," which is, its manufacturer assures us, "a product of the latest digital technology."[1] The instrument is, in other words, an electronic harpsichord.

What particularly fascinates me about the Roland C-50 is that it includes, among its many features, the ability to reproduce not only the distinctive plucked harpsichord tone but, its maker says, "the characteristic click of the jacks resetting," which, of course, because the machine possesses neither jacks nor strings, must, like the plucked tone, be repro-

[1] *Early Music* 17, no. 3 (August 1989): back cover.

duced electronically. In other words, the modern electronic harpsichord maker has bent every effort to construct an instrument that can make a "noise" the early harpsichord maker was bending every effort *not* to make (and of which Charles Burney, I seem to remember, complained in his European travels when, he said, he heard "more wood than wire"). Our triumph is their failure.

This seemed to me, at the time I first read it, a case of historical authenticity run amok. But I didn't realize quite how interesting a case it was until I put to myself the absurdity of trying to reproduce, in a musical performance, what was not music at all but the inevitable and undesirable noise that always accompanies its production, and that musicians, as well as the makers of their instruments, try to eradicate. For the realization that it was noise, when it finally sank in, reminded me that as perceivers we tend to filter out noise—to become unaware of it when it is something always with us, but in the background of our attention and interest. As a city boy, I am always reminded of this phenomenon when I retire to the country for the summer. I become, my first few nights, acutely aware of the *silence*; of the absence of city noises that, in the city, I have ceased to hear. Or, to take another example, "Since the sound of engines is life to an airplane, their heavy rhythmic beat became not a sound but like the action of breathing, only a noise to be heard when the mind desired."[2] And if the click of harpsichord jacks resetting is noise, then one has good reason to assume baroque audiences ceased to hear it, the way I have ceased to hear traffic noises, and the pilot the noise of engines. Thus, in a perfectly obvious sense of "hear," if I want to hear what a seventeenth-century audience heard at a harpsichord recital, I should leave the "clicking" stop of my Roland C-50 *off*, but if I want a seventeenth-century audience, *per impossible*, to hear my Roland C-50 the way they hear their own instruments, I should leave it on. For if I left it off for a seventeenth-century audience, they would hear the silence, just like a city boy in the country.

We have, then, two different senses of "hear." Sometimes when I say that I want to reproduce what someone heard, I mean that I want to reproduce *what was there to be heard*—the physical perturbations of the medium that reached that person's physical sense. But there is another sense of "hear" intended when I say that I don't hear the noises of the city any-

[2] Gann, *Island in the Sky*, p. 70.

A u t h e n t i c i t y   a s   S o u n d

more, or that seventeenth-century music lovers were so accustomed to the clicks of harpsichord jacks resetting that they ceased to hear them. Here we mean "hear" in the sense of what is present to one's conscious perception. The noises of the city are there to be heard, but they no longer hold my attention; they are not present to my listening consciousness: I don't "hear" them.

But as there are these two senses of "hear," there must be two senses of "historical authenticity" relevant to the reproduction of what an audience of the past "heard": the historical authenticity of physical sound, or sonic authenticity; and the authenticity of what was consciously heard, which I shall call "sensible authenticity," for want of a better name. Actually there is a better name for it: "intentional authenticity," the authenticity that reproduces what contemporary philosophy would call the "intentional object" of listening. But this usage would lead to confusing the present authenticity with the authenticity of following the composer's performance intentions. So it cannot be adopted here, although the concept of the intentional object will be a useful one to have, and when an unambiguous situation arises, I shall occasionally use the phrase "intentional authenticity" in this manner.

·　　·　　·

I have used a (to me) rather trivial example to introduce what I am calling "sensible authenticity"—namely, what most of us would consider a non-musical noise, not a proper part of the sound of the *music*. But it is well to point out, before we go on, that the distinction between "music" and "noise" is bound to be contentious. In fact, even the click of the jacks resetting elicited an argument when I broached the subject to a harpsichordist, who immediately sat down and played the opening of a Scarlatti sonata that had, he pointed out, a particularly Spanish flavor. "You can hear the sound of castanets in the clicking of the jacks resetting" was his point.

Now, personally I consider this an "off the wall" interpretation of the Scarlatti sonata; and I think I could adduce some pretty good arguments for the view that the clicks of the jacks resetting are not part of the music of any composition written before the twentieth century, although there is no good reason why such sounds could not figure musically in a composition *today*. I recently heard a piece for saxophone with a movement in which the performer didn't blow the instrument at all but merely slapped

Authenticity as Sound

50

his fingers on the keys (which actually does make a percussive tone). As Arthur Danto would say of such doings, I imagine, the art world must be ready for the clicks of the jacks resetting, and the like, to be considered music rather than noise in order for them to be music rather than noise. And demonstrably, I would suggest, Scarlatti's art world was not conceptually ready for such sounds to be heard as music. (That is John Cage territory.) Again, to make use of Danto's terminology, the clicking of jacks resetting was a "commonplace" not yet "transfigured."[3]

Another case that came up in my discussion of the noise question with musicians will help nail down the point and has, as well, some interesting perplexities of its own to contribute. A player of the baroque flute essentially gave me an argument for what I would have confidently called, before I spoke with her, playing (regrettably) with slightly bad intonation—that is to say, with a particular kind of unwanted "noise," endemic to wind instruments without modern key systems.

In order to play sharps and flats, performers on keyless, "period" woodwinds must employ what are called in the trade "forked fingerings"—fingerings in which a hole is left open between two closed holes. These fingerings do not, alas, produce perfect intonation; and the farther one gets from the basic scale of the instrument, the more pronounced, by simple addition, these intonation problems become. Thus, a keyless flute or oboe will sound better, have a more evenly tempered scale, playing in C than playing in A♭ or E.

But these instruments do have a distinctive tone, different from that of their modern counterparts; and for reasons that we will get into when we get to the normative part of our discussion, many people think it is preferable—indeed imperative—to play Bach, for example, on period flutes and oboes because their tone and dynamics are better suited to the music that, they emphatically point out, was after all written specifically with those instruments in mind. Now, I have always looked at this as a kind of trade-off. If you want optimal intonation, temperament, evenness of scale, then use modern flutes and oboes. But you pay the price for it in loss of the distinctive tone color of the period instruments, if that is what you fancy. On the other hand, the price you must pay for that distinctive period tone is some palpable loss in temperament, intonation, evenness of scale.

[3] See Danto, *The Transfiguration of the Commonplace.*

A u t h e n t i c i t y   a s   S o u n d

I was brought up sharply in my thinking on this regard, however, by the aforementioned player of the baroque flute, who explained to me that the gamy intonation, far from being an undesirable by-product of keyless woodwinds, was indeed, on her view, one of their much-to-be-prized, musically expressive qualities. Here is the example she adduced to make her case.

In Bach's *St. John Passion*, there is an "anguished" aria in F minor, "Zerfliesse, mein Herze," scored for two flutes (in unison), two oboes da caccia (in unison), and basso continuo. The somewhat doubtful quality of the intonation of Bach's keyless flutes and oboes, playing in that key, the flutist insisted, adds to the expression of anguish; and this was surely a musical part of what Bach's audience heard. The flaws in intonation are not "noise" but part of the "expression" of these instruments.

Now whatever else one might think is wrong, even slightly "crazy," about this argument, the unexamined assumption that Bach's audiences heard the flaws in intonation of their woodwinds in just the way we do must give us pause for at least one obvious reason. The musical ear is generously "forgiving." It makes charitable adjustments, hears what it wants and expects. If it didn't, *all* music would sound "bad." It is well to remember that Bach's contemporaries did not have our modern flutes and oboes as a comparison class against which to measure the intonation of theirs. Their standard was the best of their instruments; so it seems plausible to assume that they heard the best of their flutes and oboes to be more perfect in intonation than we do, who compare them with the best of ours.

Thus we have another example here of "sonic authenticity" and "sensible authenticity" clearly not coinciding. I do achieve sonic authenticity of intonation when I perform the Bach aria on period flutes and oboes, and I do not if I perform it on modern ones. But given the charitable ear, I do not achieve sensible authenticity of intonation with the former. Furthermore, if we really want to allow that the gamy intonation of the period flutes and oboes contributes to the expressiveness of the aria, making it more anguished in performance than when executed on modern woodwinds, we do not achieve sensible authenticity of *expression*, either, with a period performance. For if Bach's audiences did not hear their flutes and oboes with the gamy intonation that we perceive in them, then they did not hear that "extra" anguish that we do when we hear a performance on period woodwinds. We are making our performance more sensibly anguished than Bach's. So if we want to get sensible authenticity of expression in our performances of this aria, we might better achieve it by using modern rather than period woodwinds.

So far I have merely tried to introduce the distinction between sonic and sensible authenticity with some obvious examples. But we need to know more about sensible authenticity than we so far do. In particular, we want to know what role our musical *beliefs* play in how we hear. For far more interesting and controversial cases arise when we consider the considerable influence that our musical beliefs have on the way we hear and on the way audiences of the past have heard. To that complex question I now turn.

.   .   .

Without delving into the dark secrets of aesthetic metaphysics, let me introduce two fairly obvious kinds of aesthetic properties that a work of music might have. They are both consequences of the fact that music has a history and that we do not appreciate music ahistorically.

In general, the size of the performing ensemble has increased considerably since the time of Bach. Furthermore, the noise level of our environment must be orders of magnitude higher than that of eighteenth-century Leipzig. If you put these two obvious facts together, the conclusion must be that when Bach's audience heard the opening movement of the *St. Matthew Passion*, even with the (from our viewpoint) modest numbers at the composer's disposal, the massed forces of double chorus and double orchestra must have had an impressive, almost overwhelming effect on them, much like the effect Berlioz's Requiem still has on us. And why not? Bach was representing in the opening chorus of the *Passion* the wailing and shouting of a crowd. But if our paradigm of "large" music is Berlioz's Requiem, or the *Carmina Burana*, then the opening chorus of the *St. Matthew Passion*, with the numbers available to Bach, far from sounding like massed forces, is going to have a rather modest, almost chamber music–like sound. So if we want sensible authenticity in this regard, we cannot achieve it by performing this chorus in Bach-like size: doing so will merely give us sonic authenticity.

Many such examples come to mind. And there are two ways to describe them. We might say that a new aesthetic property is imparted to the music by history, in this case the intimate or modest sound that the opening chorus of the *St. Matthew Passion* now has for us, when performed with sonic authenticity. Or, looked at from the negative point of view, we might say that an original aesthetic property is destroyed in the music by history, in this case the massive, noisy musical sound that the opening chorus had for Bach's audiences. We need a name for these kinds of aesthetic properties, and I propose to call them *historically imparted* properties (if looked at from the positive point of view) and *historically voided* properties (from the negative).

.   .   .

But there is another kind of property that might well be described as "historical," far more philosophically interesting and problematic. I shall call them, for reasons that will become obvious in a moment, *historically embedded*. Here are two examples.

The slow introduction to the first movement of Beethoven's Symphony no. 1 in C is somewhat revolutionary, or at least significantly innovative, and certainly would have been perceived as such by its early audiences. For the slow introductions to symphonic first movements before Beethoven's Op. 21—of which Haydn's are the most prominent examples—always begin by firmly establishing the tonic key in the opening gesture. Whereas Beethoven begins with the dominant seventh chord of F—the subdominant of C. So not only does the work start in the wrong key but it doesn't even start on the tonic chord of that key. (Beethoven, in this period, experimented with the same trick in the slow introduction to the *Creatures of Prometheus* Overture, also in C, and is even more daring in that instance, the opening chord being not only the dominant seventh of the wrong key but in third inversion as well.)

Now, it is fair to say that this "syntactically" innovative beginning to Op. 21 is a very significant aesthetic property of the work and was clearly intended as such by Beethoven. And it is also clear that it is a property of the work that has as a necessary condition for its existence at least the recent previous history of classical style in general and the history of the symphony in particular. It is a *historically embedded* property. In order to perceive it the listener must be situated in a particular place in that history. But further, in order for it to be a property of the work, the work must be in the history of such works and their styles. Let this stand for a paradigmatic case of a *historically embedded* property.

But consider now a twentieth-century listener to the opening of Beethoven's First Symphony. As one recent writer has put the point,

Authenticity as Sound

we know that when Beethoven's First Symphony was originally performed, many people were surprised by its beginning on a dissonance, and one, moreover, that was foreign to the home key (it is the dominant seventh of the subdominant). In finding this opening surprising such people must have been consciously or unconsciously comparing it with the openings of other contemporary symphonies, and their ability to do so will have depended not on formalized study of the genre but simply on familiarity with a sufficient number of examples of it.

However, he goes on: "Nobody today will find its opening surprising, as contemporary audiences did, in consequence of simple enculturation," for "[t]he frequent use of dissonant and tonally oblique openings in music written since Beethoven's time" has made Beethoven's daring stroke completely familiar and syntactically unsurprising.[4]

The moral of this little story is, of course, that historically embedded properties, like historically imparted and historically voided ones, are hostage to the course of events and one's place in that course. But the story is not quite finished. For we have looked only at a historically embedded property that a work, through the passage of time, has lost. Before we go on, though, we should look also at one that, through the passage of time, has been acquired.

It is a well-known cliché in writing about music, or about any of the other arts in fact, to observe "anticipations": "romantic" harmonies in Bach, premonitions of atonality in *Verklärte Nacht*, the daring modern experiments of Ives coming "before their time," and so on. We are, in our listening, the products of music history. And when we—that is to say, present-day audiences—hear music, we hear it in its history. We cannot help it; and if we can, it is only by effort. (More of that presently.)

Each time a listener hears an "anticipation," he or she hears a musical property that could not have been heard by audiences contemporary with the work. It is, I suppose, a nice question in metaphysics whether Bach's music (to take but one example) acquired romantic harmonies or always had them, in some timeless sense; but it is a question I shall not try to answer here. Certain it is, however, that listeners could not hear these harmonies in their intentional objects, nor could the intentional objects

---

[4] Cook, *Music, Imagination, and Culture*, pp. 146–47.

Authenticity   as   Sound

possess them until the time one could frame the concept of romantic harmony in the first place.

It is also a nice question whether such historically embedded properties as Bach's romantic harmonies are "artistic" properties of the music—that is to say, properties the perception of which we consider a proper part of our musical experience. That it is a nontrivial question can be demonstrated directly merely by pointing out that such properties could not possibly have been intended to belong to the works that possess them by their composers. Of course, Bach intended those harmonies we call "romantic" to be in his music—but not under that description, because he could have had no concept of romanticism a hundred or more years before that movement came into being, and, a fortiori, no intention of composing harmonies that might prefigure those for which the movement became known. And because there are those who believe, not without at least some prima facie plausibility on their side, that intention is a necessary condition for a property's properly belonging to a work of art, there is at least a prima facie case for historically embedded properties of the "retrospective" kind—that is to say, those that by hindsight "anticipate" some movement, style, or technique—being rejected as "artistic," rejected as allowably to be savored in our musical appreciation.

In order to discuss this question further, it is first necessary to get some terminological business out of the way. It concerns that nasty word "aesthetic," which I have so far avoided here in favor of "artistic." Sometimes the phrase "aesthetic appreciation" is used to mean, roughly, in regard to works of art, appreciation of those properties or aspects of works of art that are proper to the appreciation of art *qua* art. To take an uncontroversial pair of examples, I am appreciating my Cézanne aesthetically when I am enjoying the contemplation of the wonderful balance of the composition, but not when I am enjoying the contemplation of its considerable monetary worth. But sometimes aesthetic appreciation is taken in such a way as to get the result that I am aesthetically appreciating my Cézanne when I am enjoying the contemplation of the wonderful balance of the composition but not when I am enjoying its representational properties. When used in this way (as Clive Bell and Roger Fry were likely to), aesthetic appreciation is being preempted as the name for the enjoyment of only the formal and sensual qualities of artworks favored by "formalists" and others of that stripe. And if one thinks, as I certainly do, that other properties of artworks besides the formal and sensual are proper objects of appreciation, one might like to introduce the phrase "artistic appreciation" to cover the enjoyment of all the properties of artworks, *qua* art, reserving the phrase "aesthetic appreciation" for the enjoyment of only that subset of "artistic properties" that consists in the formal and sensual ones. Adopting such a terminology, it would then turn out that when I am enjoying the contemplation of the wonderful balance of the composition in my Cézanne, I am appreciating it aesthetically (and artistically); when I am enjoying the contemplation of its wonderful representational qualities, I am appreciating it artistically (but not aesthetially); and when I am enjoying the contemplation of its considerable monetary value, I am appreciating it neither artistically nor aesthetically. (It is well to point out that for formalists, aesthetic appreciation, so conceived, and artistic appreciation are coextensive.)

Now, in certain discussions, it is crucial to have the extra clarity that the preceding distinction between aesthetic and artistic appreciation affords. But one pays the price in adopting this refined terminology of going against the grain of ordinary speech habits. For use of the term "aesthetic," among those untainted by philosophy, tends to be broad rather than narrow, "aesthetic appreciation" usually doing duty for the enjoyment of anything in a work of art that might seem relevant to its "arthood"—including, needless to say, representational features. And because there is no particular need in the discussion that follows for the additional distinction between aesthetic and artistic appreciation, I shall forgo it in the interest of plain speech. So from now on I shall be treating aesthetic appreciation and artistic appreciation as co-extensive and interchangeable, roughly to mean the enjoyment of contemplating those features of works of art that ordinary people think are just the ones that works of art exist for the purpose of displaying for our pleasure. The question is, Are Bach's romantic harmonies, and other historically embedded features of that kind—that is, the "retrospective" ones—aesthetic, artistic features: proper objects of aesthetic, artistic appreciation?

. . .

In the heyday of the New Criticism and the Intentional Fallacy, we would have been very clear about whether the romantic harmonies in Bach

Authenticity as Sound

were or were not aesthetic features of the works. The harmonies, under some description or other, would, of course, have been considered un-qualifiedly *echt*. But under the description "romantic harmonies" they would have been dismissed as artifacts of art history, not of art. To appreciate them as romantic harmonies rather than merely functional harmonies in some historically neutral sense would have been to appreciate the audacity and prescience of Bach, or perhaps the extraordinary position of these harmonies in the history of music, but it would not have been to appreciate them artistically.

Of course there might be a perfectly benign sense of "romantic," applicable to Bach from the ahistorical point of view. If, for example, one were using the word merely to capture some phenomenological quality of the harmonies that a contemporary of Bach's might also have recognized and described as, say, *empfindlich*, there would be nothing about "romantic" of historical significance except that you would not have had the use of that particular word to describe those particular harmonies before the historical period in which it was made available to talk about the harmonies in question. One would, in such a case, no more be talking about music history or about Bach's place in it than if one were to use the word "saccharine" to refer to some harmonies in Meyerbeer that his contemporaries might have described as "sugary."

What might motivate one to deny that historically embedded qualities of the retrospective kind are aesthetic qualities of the work? Mention of the New Criticism and the attendant Intentional Fallacy suggests an obvious answer. The denial must be theory-driven. In order to reach the conclusion that historically embedded qualities such as the romantic harmonies in Bach are not aesthetic qualities, one needs a theory "from above" that implies it. And the theory would have to be a pretty powerful one, at that. Such theories are hard to come by.

Why one would need a theory to disallow historically embedded properties of the retrospective kind, it seems to me, is simply because they are common currency, part of the perfectly ordinary way in which perfectly ordinary people appreciate music. They are the stock-in-trade of program annotators, whose business it is to help lay audiences to appreciate music. Furthermore, it is clear that perfectly ordinary enjoyers of music, with no technical knowledge of it, appreciate these properties as part of their ordinary interactions with music and seem to be enjoying them in much the same way that they enjoy those properties of music that are not of the historically embedded kind. It may take a certain amount of expertise, to be sure, to hear a chord progression in Bach as "an anticipation of the *Tristan* chord" but little, if any, to hear it as "romantic," or "sort of Schuberty." It would seem, then, that historically embedded properties of the retrospective kind have, at the very least, prima facie respectability, and, it would seem, the presumption of innocence. That being the case, an argument is wanted to impugn their credentials: the burden of proof is on the prosecution. But if the argument is against a commonly accepted practice, I cannot see how it can be generated by anything less than some aesthetic theory of a general kind.

The kind of theory that recent philosophy of art has frequently marshaled against what I have been calling historically embedded retrospective qualities is characterized by Gregory Currie as a form of empiricism, and penetratingly described as follows:

> Empiricism finds its natural expression in aesthetics in the view that a work—a painting, for instance—is a "sensory surface." What is aesthetically valuable in a painting can be detected by looking at it. Features that cannot be so detected are not properly aesthetic ones. . . .
>
> The idea is in various ways extendable to the other arts that we are considering here. Thus it is said that the limits of musical appreciation are the limits of what can be heard in the work. Properties of the work that we cannot come to know simply by listening to it are not aesthetic properties.[5]

Currie himself seems to treat historical properties of art, of which my historically embedded retrospective properties are a special case, as a given, their existence clearly a *reductio ad absurdum* of aesthetic empiricism. His answer to aesthetic empiricism is an ingeniously worked-out ontology of art founded on the precept that "aesthetic appreciation is indissolubly linked to a very detailed understanding of the work's history of production."[6] For what we appreciate, on Currie's view, when we enjoy a

[5] Currie, *An Ontology of Art*, p. 17.
[6] Ibid., p. 39.

A u t h e n t i c i t y   a s   S o u n d

work of art, is a "performance," of which the artwork is an inseparable part: a performance that "must be seen as integral to the work itself."[7] More specifically, a painting, for example,

> is the outcome of an experiment, and . . . when we judge it we are weighing the evidence that it provides concerning what we should say about the artist's performance, taking "performance" in that wide sense which includes not merely his actions in applying paint to canvas but also his path to the conception and execution of the work, an understanding of which involves an analysis of the conventions and technical limitations that constrain his actions.[8]

It can readily be seen how, on a view like Currie's, the romantic harmonies in Bach are to be appreciated and why they would be appreciated differently—valued less highly—if, say, it were revealed that the composition in which they occurred, previously thought to be by Bach, turned out to be an imitation or forgery of Bach by a nineteenth-century composer. (Remember the "antique" compositions of Fritz Kreisler!) For what in Bach would have been an extraordinary and daring series of harmonies would in a nineteenth-century imitator be quite ordinary and unremarkable, because Bach's "performance," in composing them, would have been extraordinarily difficult and daring, and the "performance" by the nineteenth-century hack easily brought off and lacking in interest.

I present Currie's way of dealing with the kind of properties I am talking about here neither to endorse nor to refute it. Such a task would have to be undertaken in a book very different from this one. My point is simply to leave the very strong suggestion in the reader's mind that what I have been calling historically embedded retrospective qualities are respectable not only in lay circles but increasingly in philosophical circles as well, however one wishes to analyze them philosophically.

Within the boundaries of this book, however, which confine me to the specific subject of musical aesthetics rather than the broader one of aesthetics in general, I have another strategy to pursue to the end of both strengthening the claims of historically embedded retrospective properties and further clarifying their importance to the whole notion of histor-

[7] Ibid., p. 42.
[8] Ibid.

Authenticity as Sound

ically authentic sound. Indeed, as we shall see, there is something slightly paradoxical here that has not, so far as I know, been taken notice of before.

· · ·

But before I get to this "paradox" I must guard against a possible objection to what I have said so far, coming from the direction of aesthetic metaphysics. I have spoken of properties being voided and imparted by the history of music; and the notion, particularly, of imparting properties to artworks of the past seems to invoke an extremely suspect concept. For me here and now to cause something to happen yesterday is a paradigm of "backward causation," and an out-and-out metaphysical impossibility. And for the romantic movement to have caused a passage by Bach to possess romantic harmonies when it could not possibly have possessed them before seems to be a case of the selfsame backward causation and, hence, the selfsame impossibility. If one is to believe, as seems reasonable, that a work of art completed in 1726 was indeed *completed*, in the sense of possessing *then and there* all its artistically relevant properties, then because, by hypothesis, having romantic harmonies—in other words, "presaging" romanticism—*is* an artistically relevant property, and something that happened in the nineteenth century caused a 1726 artwork, complete in all its relevant respects in 1726, to possess romantic harmonies, to presage the romantic movement *then and there*, we seem to have backward causation with all its sins upon its head.[9]

The question of whether or not artworks can gain relevant properties over time is a vigorously debated one in current aesthetic discussions; and I do not think this is the place to get deeply into it. What can be done is to point out that at least a large number of what I have referred to as historically imparted properties can with equal propriety and no loss be called historically *revealed* properties instead. That is to say, what appears an instance of history's imparting some property to an artwork it did not theretofore possess might, in many cases and perhaps all, be redescribed as an instance of history's simply revealing some property that the artwork had all along but that could not be descried until some movement or other made us able to do so.

Such a position is taken by Jerrold Levinson:

[9] I am grateful to Noel Carroll for calling my attention, in this regard, to the problem of backward causation.

Authenticity as Sound

It is not *artworks* that, in the crucial sense, change over time, it is rather *us*. We think more, experience more, create more—and as a result, are able to find more in artworks than we could previously. But these works are what they are, and remain, from the art-content point of view, what they always were. It is not their content that changes over time, but only our access to the full extent of that content, in virtue of our and the world's subsequent evolution.[10]

Thus, where we tend, perhaps for "pragmatic" reasons, to describe a work of art as acquiring an art-relevant property in the course of art history, our description is of the "as if" kind and can be translated, with no loss of significance for appreciation, into a description to the effect, rather, that history and our present situation enable us to see in the work a property there all along, waiting, as it were, to be noticed.

An ingenious way of thinking about at least some of the properties I have been talking about here was proposed by Arthur Danto in his influential article entitled "The Artworld."[11] It is a way of thinking that, in *one* of its formulations, does not treat historically imparted or acquired properties as *imparted* or *acquired* at all and hence does not conjure up the bogey of backward causation.

Danto asks us to consider pairs of predicates that he calls "opposites." Opposites are like contradictories in that where they apply, one of each applicable pair must be true and the other false, the difference being that every pair of contradictories applies to every object in the universe, whereas pairs of opposites have limited applicability, something's having to be of a certain kind for it to make sense to apply either of a pair of opposites to it. (Thus, for example, "artwork" and "nonartwork" are contradictories, everything in the universe either being an artwork or not; whereas, to appropriate Noel Carroll's example, "officer" and "nonofficer," opposites, apply to soldiers, and one or the other must be true of each, but they do not apply sensibly to cabbages and kings at all.[12])

The interesting opposites, for present purposes, are such stylistic pred-

[10] Levinson, "Artworks and the Future," in *Music, Art, and Metaphysics*, pp. 180–81.
[11] Whether Danto's position in this regard is consistent with his later and better-known position is a question raised by Noel Carroll in "Danto, Style, and Intention." I am grateful to Carroll both for rekindling my interest in Danto's position in "The Artworld" and for fruitful discussion of it.
[12] Danto, "The Artworld," in Margolis, *Philosophy Looks at the Arts*, pp. 164–65.

A u t h e n t i c i t y   a s   S o u n d

icates as "representational" and "nonrepresentational," "expressionist" and "nonexpressionist," or (to take our own example) "romantic" and "nonromantic." Of such predicates as these Danto writes,

> let F and non-F be an opposite pair of such predicates. Now it might happen that, throughout an entire period of time, every artwork is non-F. But since nothing thus far is both an artwork and F, it might never occur to anyone that non-F is an artistically relevant predicate. The non-F–ness of artworks goes unremarked. By contrast, all works up to a given time might be G, it never occurring to anyone until that time that something might be both an artwork and non-G; indeed, it might have been thought that G was a *defining trait* of artworks when in fact something might first have to be an artwork before G is sensibly predicable of it—in which case non-G might also be predicable of artworks, and G itself then could not have been a defining trait of this class.[13]

So if we consider a seventeenth-century Dutch landscape, it is nonexpressionist and representational. But until the advent of expressionist painting, no one could have noticed that it possessed this negative property, because it could have occurred to no one that a work of art could possess its opposite. Nor could it have occurred to anyone that "nonrepresentational" is a possible feature to ascribe to an artwork, because up to that time nothing was both an artwork and not representational, being representational considered a defining property of artworks.

On Danto's view, then, in the manner thus far stated, artistic movements and revolutions add to the vocabulary of critical language; but they do *not* add to the features of artworks. The paintings of the seventeenth century already possess the negative property of being nonexpressionist. However, it is only after the advent of expressionist painting that they can be noticed to lack that property.

To be sure, Danto is not altogether consistent in the presentation of this view. For in the first statement of it, already quoted earlier, he says, "Throughout an entire period of time, every artwork is non-F," and only after F becomes a property of artworks is the non-F–ness of previous artworks *noticed*; but in a later statement he seems to suggest that the non-

[13] Ibid., p. 165.

Authenticity   as   Sound

F–ness is *acquired* after *F*-ness becomes a feature of artworks. Thus, he writes:

> It is, of course, not easy to see in advance which predicates are going to be added or replaced by their opposites, but suppose an artist determines that *H* shall henceforth be artistically relevant for his paintings. Then, in fact, both *H* and non-*H* become artistically relevant for *all* paintings, and if his is the first and only painting that is *H*, every other painting in existence becomes [N.B.!] non-*H*, and the entire community of paintings is enriched, together with a doubling of the available style opportunities.[14]

Danto, then, seems to have two alternative ways of representing his view: that artworks possess, all along, negative features, which future stylistic movements make evident by making their opposites features of new artworks; or that artworks *acquire* negative features as their opposite, positive counterparts become features of later artworks. In the former formulation, the specter of backward causation is not raised—a formulation, I should add, that Levinson seems to have missed.

Levinson presents numerous examples of cases in which a familiar kind of description in terms of property acquisition through time can be understood, less paradoxically, in terms of property revelation or discovery instead. There is no need for us to canvass them all. But a particular class of cases, those in which a work of art (as in my own example of Bach's "romantic" harmonies) is now seen to presage an artistic movement long after the work in question was created, or, more difficult still, those in which a work of art is seen to have an *influence* on a future artist or artistic movement. It is such cases, more than any others, that seem to demand backward causation; for it seems necessary, in such cases, to describe the situation as one in which an event *after* the creation of the work imparts a property to the work, makes a change in it (and not merely a "Cambridge change").

But even here Levinson gives us at least some plausible grounds for redescribing an apparent case of property acquisition as, rather, a case of property revelation. To do this he makes a "distinction between perspectives and assessments *possible at* a time vs. perspectives and assessments

[14]Ibid., p. 166.

Authenticity as Sound

justified with respect to a time.""[15] Which is to say, we must, again, distinguish between perspectives and assessments that are enabled at a time subsequent to the time in which the artwork was created and assessments that are made valid by a time subsequent to the time in which the artwork was created. And one of Levinson's illustrations of this distinction is precisely to the present purpose: "Beethoven does not become the most important initiator of Romanticism in music only when the nineteenth century, and thus Romanticism, concludes; he is plausibly that as early as the C Minor Piano Trio of 1795. Yet this is compatible with its being impossible for such a judgment to have been intelligibly made at that time."[16]

Closely related to these cases of apparent property acquisition, and perhaps the more difficult, are those in which a work of art is said to have influenced future artists and artistic movements: "Propheticness is thus clearly a property of a work when created, though usually not one that can be justifiably ascribed [at that time]. For a work of art to be influential, though, seems more strongly to presuppose *actual* achievement, accomplishment, or fulfillment. It seems appropriate to withhold the ascription of influentiality until such influence, as it were, *occurs.*"[17]

Levinson's strategy is the same here as with "prophetic" properties, although he acknowledges "the force of such an intuition" in favor of the future *imparting* properties to the object of art:

> Instead of regarding the future as *making*, in progressive steps, the influentiality, seminality, or importance of a work of art, we might equally well think of it as *revealing* or *disclosing* what is already present, though in covert fashion. We can regard the influentiality of a work as given with the work in its historical setting—for surely it is the work's structure and character, appearing in just that setting, that makes it influential if it is—and as something that only becomes *evident* with the passage of time.[18]

And so: "To the question 'Is this an influential work?' or even 'Is this influential now?' asked of a piece created last month, we are not bound to give the answer 'Not yet; it may become so.' We can just be agnostic: 'In-

---

[15] Ibid., p. 207.
[16] Ibid.
[17] Ibid., p. 209.
[18] Ibid.

Authenticity as Sound

fluential?—i.e., affecting in a significant way future developments in the arts?—I don't know; we'll have to wait and see if it is.'"[19]

So we are in a position to conclude, by means of Levinson's arguments, that at least a good many, perhaps most, of what I have been calling historically imparted properties might be described more accurately and less paradoxically as historically revealed properties; and I retain the former appellation merely for "pragmatic" rather than "metaphysical" purposes—to call attention to the fact that *our appreciation of them* is contingent upon the course of history and our place in it. The question of whether they can be legitimately appreciated in the musical cases has already been answered in the affirmative by me. And Levinson is not altogether averse to such an answer, if not quite so liberal as I am. For he himself says of "anticipations," for example, "The question of legitimate vs. illegitimate searches for and uses of anticipations of one artwork by another is a difficult one, and I don't mean to imply that a work's anticipations of a later work can *never* be appreciatively relevant to it."[20]

Be that as it may, there seems no good reason to fear that what I call historically imparted properties are metaphysical monstrosities, with the ogre of backward causation as their progenitor. At least all those properties that are necessary for present purposes can be readily understood as historically *revealed*. With the metaphysical specter of backward causation, and artworks changing over time, out of the way, we can now proceed with what I alluded to as a "paradox" of authentic listening that historically imparted properties might be seen to raise.

·   ·   ·

How did a contemporary of, say, Bach and Handel listen to a cantata by the former or an opera by the latter? One correct answer to that question is "ahistorically." By that I simply mean to call attention to the well-known fact that eighteenth-century musical auditors, and the musicians themselves, had no knowledge of or interest in the history of their art. Unlike poetry, music did not have a past for the audiences of Bach and Handel. If the eighteenth century was to a large extent ahistorical across the board—and this is how intellectual historians usually portray it— then with regard to music it was ahistorical in spades. Ironically, one of the pioneers in the discovery of our musical past, Charles Burney, gives

[19] Ibid., p. 210.
[20] Ibid., p. 298n.

Authenticity   as   Sound

us, in his monumental *History*, as clearly delineated a picture of his century's ahistorical attitude toward musical listening as we are likely to get: "So changeable is taste in Music, and so transient the favour of any particular style, that its history is like that of a ploughed field: such a year it produced wheat, such a year barley, peas, or clover; and such a year it lay fallow. But none of its productions remain, except perhaps a small part of last year's crop, and the corn or weeds that now cover its surface."[21]

We all know that if an opera by Handel ran for two weeks it was a hit, and that Bach had to write a new cantata for every Sunday of the church year. In Bach's case, of course, he was creating a repertory for himself—a well-regulated church music—that he would reuse as the occasion arose. But there is no sign that he had any thought of his repertory outliving him or that the next cantor might not make a repertory of his own. Audiences expected to hear new music, not familiar masterpieces. There *were* no musical masterpieces. How *could* there be? There was no musical history. In music there was only "now": like a plowed field, "none of its productions remain."

Of course, no one can listen to music in the pure present. Music has a "history" for everyone, if only the history of his or her past listenings—the musical experience that initiates one, unself-consciously, into one's musical culture and makes the appreciation of music possible in the first place. But apart from that, the audiences of Bach and Handel—whom I cite simply as familiar examples—heard music ahistorically to a degree far beyond that of even a completely untutored modern concertgoer and beyond that, certainly, of the eighteenth-century reader. In 1757, David Hume formulated an account of critical judgment, based on what we would nowadays call the "test of time," that clearly implies a kind of historically informed literary appreciator. Without going into the intricacies of Hume's theory or dispute over its interpretation, we can observe that Hume operated under the assumption of an enduring literary past, against whose background our present critical judgments are projected.

---

[21] Burney, *A General History of Music*, vol. 2, p. 380. Burney's growing ambivalence to this ahistorical attitude is quite evident in the next sentence: "Purcell, however, was such an excellent cultivator of his farm in Parnassus, that its crops will be long remembered, even after time has devoured them." But note that Burney says Purcell's works will be remembered, not *performed*; and, indeed, time will devour them. On Burney's ambivalence, see my introduction to the reprint of Burney's *An Account of the Musical Performances in Westminster-Abbey*.

Authenticity as Sound

Thus, "The same Homer who pleased at Athens and Rome two thousand years ago, is still admired at Paris and London. All the changes of climate, government, religion, and language, have not been able to obscure his glory."[22] And from this literary immortality we can fairly infer, Hume thought, a uniformity of critical principles:

> It appears, then, that amidst all the variety and caprice of taste, there are certain general principles of approbation or blame, whose influence a careful eye may trace in all operations of the mind. Some particular forms or qualities, from the original structure of the internal fabric are calculated to please, and others to displease; and if they fail in their effect in any particular instance, it is from some apparent defect in the organ.[23]

Needless to say, it is a far cry from this rather limited "historicism" of Hume's, with its severely constrained canon of classical masterpieces, to the modern reader's array of paperbacks, which offer within arm's reach the whole of world literature. But even the limited historical vistas of the educated eighteenth-century reader far outstripped the historical aware-ness of the eighteenth-century musical audience. For the music lover there simply was no historical vista at all. And it was a momentous event in that regard—a historical breakthrough, as it were—when in 1784 the British celebrated the centennial of Handel's birth (a year too early) with a series of concerts in Westminster Abbey, "reviving" the music of a com-poser who had been living in their midst a scant thirty years before and whom many of the participants must have known personally. Handel's music was "old music" to the eighteenth century twenty-five years after his death, as Burney is constantly reminding the audiences at the com-memoration, in his "program notes," where, for instance, he remarks of an aria: "And though the life of a musical composition is in general much shorter than the life of a man, yet this bears its age so well, that instead of fifty-two years old, it seems in all the vigour and bloom of youth."[24] (In the eighteenth century, fifty-two was old for a musical composition as well as for a man.)

[22] Hume, "Of the Standard of Taste," in *Essays*, pp. 237–38.
[23] Ibid., p. 238.
[24] Burney, *An Account of the Musical Performances in Westminster-Abbey*, p. 65.

Authenticity   as   Sound

One obvious conclusion that must be drawn from the fact that, for eighteenth-century audiences, music lacked a past and, by consequence, listening was ahistorical is that they did not hear many of what I have been calling historically embedded qualities at all. They indeed could not hear them; for, in a sense, neither they nor the musical works they listened to were "in" musical history. They could not hear historically embedded retrospective qualities, of course, because these are qualities that music acquires by being heard as pointing to the future. No audience of Bach's, for example, could hear him as the culmination of a tradition in seventeenth-century German music, nor could they hear anticipations of his harmonic language in the music of the early seventeenth century, because the music of even its recent past was a closed book.

But we do, with varying degrees of knowledge and self-consciousness, hear music historically. Our music has been a historical repertoire to some degree at least since the birth of modern musicology in the nineteenth century; and increasingly so since then, until now one has literally at one's fingertips a listening capacity that spans ten centuries.

No one who goes to concerts can escape this musical historicity. Program notes are now for the most part historically oriented, for the people who write them are trained, or have trained themselves, in historical musicology. The same is true of the reviewers. Historical listening is no longer just for *Kenners* but for *Liebhabers* as well. The intentional objects of our musical listening are as embedded with historical properties as those of the eighteenth and previous centuries were barren of them.

But furthermore—and surely there is a bit of irony to be remarked upon here—the culmination of historical listening, its crowning glory and most impressive achievement to date, must be the "historically authentic performance" itself. For in it we become as acutely aware as it is possible to be of the historical setting of the musical experience. We come to hear not only music historically but musical *performance* historically as well. We come to appreciate Bach on his instruments, Mozart on his, and, with the inexorable progress of the historical performance movement, Berlioz on his. (The ophicleide has already made its triumphant return to the concert stage.) We have become acutely aware both of the different physical means by which music has been made in various periods and of the differing manners in which it has been made.

A u t h e n t i c i t y a s S o u n d

The irony, of course, is that here, as elsewhere, historical authenticities can be at cross-purposes. For if we ask, What is the historically authentic sound, say, of Bach? *one* correct answer is, The sound produced by period instruments, with ensembles of the size Bach would have had at his disposal, in a manner consistent with Bach's performance practice, and so on: in other words, *sonic authenticity*. But another answer to the question of how to hear the historically authentic sound of Bach is: *ahistorically*. That is to say, if you want to hear Bach-sound as Bach's audiences heard it—and that is what "historically authentic sound" would be—then you must, as much as is possible, hear your Bach without a twentieth-century historical consciousness. And certainly one way to facilitate ahistorical listening is to perform music just the way it was performed *before* our historical consciousness progressed to the point of the historically authentic performance movement. For the *uniformity* of "mainstream" performance is both a direct expression of the ahistorical listening attitude and a principal way of making us listen ahistorically.

To perform Bach and Handel, Haydn, Mozart and Beethoven, Brahms and Berlioz, Strauss and Mahler, Stravinsky and Berg with the same modern, "state of the art" instruments, and with more or less the same, prevalent performance aesthetic, whatever it might be at a particular time and place, is to remove music from its historical setting and place it in a timeless present. This is just the attitude, for example, that Mozart and Baron van Swieten were evincing in their "up-to-date" performances, with Mozart's orchestrations, of *Messiah* and *Alexander's Feast*, or in the Philharmonic concerts of my youth, where one heard the Third Brandenburg Concerto with the full complement of strings (no continuo, of course), followed by the traipsing-on of the appropriate wind and brass players for a late Haydn symphony, and finally, after intermission, Mahler or Brahms with the whole crew aboard. (In the latter case, of course, the ahistorical nature of performance manner and means were somewhat offset by the clearly chronological structuring of programs: even in 1946 a twelve-year-old was likely to know that Bach was before Haydn, and Haydn before Brahms, and would listen accordingly.)

We have come, then, to the somewhat paradoxical conclusion that the historically authentic performance movement, which is meant to restore to us historically authentic musical sound, does so only at the cost of de-

Authenticity as Sound

stroying historically authentic sound: it gives us sonic authenticity with
one hand and takes away, in the form of ahistorical listening, sensible authenticity with the other. But the "paradox" of the historically authentic
performance is really just a special case of a larger paradox, which might
be called the "paradox of historical musicology." This broader paradox requires further exploration.

· · ·

When I ask myself what the greatest gifts of historical musicology have
been to the musical listener, two readily come to mind: the recovery of
lost or unjustly forgotten masterpieces of former times, indeed whole historical repertoires; and the enlarging of our musical appreciation by way
of "historical listening." The former is obvious enough and requires no
further comment. The latter I wish to pursue.

Many of the historically embedded qualities of music about which I
have been speaking here are revealed in or imparted to music—depending upon your metaphysics—by historical listening. And even historically
embedded qualities of the nonretrospective kind, like the surprise and audacity of the opening of Beethoven's First Symphony, that the progress of
musical history has voided for us can, in a sense, be partially restored by
historical knowledge and historical listening. For although we cannot, for
example, appreciate it *as* surprising and audacious, we can appreciate *that*
it was surprising and audacious by appreciating it in the light of history, in
its historical context—by, in other words, listening to it historically. But
historical listening was made possible for us by the impressive accom-
plishments of historical musicology in the twentieth century.

In discovering to us our musical past, musicology gave us a historical
repertoire; and the result of that was not merely more music for us to hear
but a historical setting in which to hear it. Once music had a past for us,
our listening habits were changed to the extent that we not only listen
now to the music of the distant past but listen in a different way to the music of the recent past and present—which is to say, we hear the standard
repertoire and contemporary music as well as "early" music *historically.*
In what I take to be a quite literal sense, historical musicology has made
available to us more musical qualities for us to appreciate and enjoy, both
in the canon and in contemporary works. I have argued elsewhere that
increased musical knowledge leads to increased musical enjoyment

through the amplifying of the intentional object of musical appreciation.[25] Historical musicology, and the knowledge it imparts, is simply a special case of this general principle; and the historically authentic performance is a special case of the special case.

In other words, in increasing our historical knowledge of music, in enabling us to hear historically, historical musicology has given us musical properties to appreciate and enjoy that we could not have appreciated and enjoyed before, just as music theory and analysis do (on my view); but whereas the properties that theory and analysis reveal may (but needn't necessarily) be ahistorical ones, those revealed or imparted or restored by historical musicology are of necessity what I have been calling historically embedded. Of these historically embedded musical qualities, those appreciated and enjoyed in so-called historically authentic performances—or, more exactly, *certain of those*, not all—are a subclass. The historically authentic performance movement has given us another whole group of historically embedded musical properties to appreciate and enjoy in our musical experience.

But if part of the purpose of historical musicology in general, and the historically authentic performance in particular, has been to get us to hear the music of the past in a historically authentic manner, it has also at the same time gotten us to hear it, for the most part, in a historically *inauthentic* manner in getting us to hear *historically*. For most of the music that historical musicology has given us to hear, and taught us to hear with sonic authenticity, is just the music that was heard by its first audiences ahistorically. And since the inevitable (perhaps desirable) result of this revolution in musical listening habits has made us appreciate and enjoy music historically—how else can one hear, now that historical musicology has given music a past?—the same revolution that has given us sonic authenticity has given us also sensible or intentional inauthenticity in the form of historical listening. In short, in a very deep sense historical musicology has made us hear most of the music it promotes in a historically inauthentic manner, which is to say, *historically*.

Now at this point one can well imagine the historical musicologist replying, "Look here: we have given you the music of your past and the knowledge that enables you to perform it properly, that is, with sonic historical authenticity. What more do you want? The rest is up to you. What

[25] Kivy, *Music Alone*, chap. 6.

you must do is make every effort to listen to this music *ahistorically*. Whether that is entirely possible or not we cannot tell. But to the extent that you can hear preromantic music ahistorically, you will be hearing it with *sensible* authenticity. Historical listening is an undesirable side effect of the historical musicology movement. Like all such side effects it must be combatted to the best of our ability."

This reply I find paradoxical, though not, indeed, formally paradoxical: there is no logical contradiction in practicing the discipline of historical musicology while proselytizing against historical listening. But it would be very odd, to say the least. It would be to urge rejection of one of the greatest legacies of the historical musicology movement. In restoring to us our musical past, in teaching us to listen historically, historical musicology has enormously enriched our musical experience.

I can think of three possible grounds for rejecting historical listening and the historically embedded musical qualities it imparts or discloses or restores to us. Perhaps one can argue that the payoff in musical enjoyment will be greater if one listens ahistorically. Or one can argue, on theoretical grounds, that historically embedded qualities of the kind that historical listening makes available are not genuinely aesthetic, not proper objects of musical appreciation and enjoyment in the first place. Finally, it might be argued that listening ahistorically, being part of a kind of historically authentic performance—namely, the kind that aims at sensible authenticity—may have special virtues that accrue to just that kind of historically authentic performance. We have already explored the second strategy and found it problematic. Nor does the first seem any more promising, and for two reasons.

First of all, there is nothing I can see to suggest that abjuring historical listening will have a greater overall payoff in musical enjoyment. And common sense, anyway, suggests the opposite. Remove possible objects of enjoyment—in this case, the historically embedded musical properties made available by historical listening—and you must, it would seem, reduce enjoyment accordingly: there will just be fewer qualities to enjoy.

In the second place, the notion that we can employ a simple hedonistic calculus to determine, by credit and debit, whether we are or are not better off without historical listening seems to me seriously mistaken. And that is the notion underlying the claim that our musical enjoyment sum would be greater without than with the enjoyment consequent upon his-

torical listening. The musical enjoyment we get by appreciating these historically embedded qualities, made available by historical listening, is a
special enjoyment: it is not just musical enjoyment but *that kind* of musical enjoyment. And the increase, if there would be, of *another* kind of musical enjoyment, upon its removal, does not, ipso facto, answer in the affirmative the question of whether we would be better off without the
enjoyment of the historically embedded musical qualities in question. If I
value variety as well as quantity, I might rationally prefer having three apples and three bananas to having eight apples, even though my "fruit enjoyment sum" is higher in the latter case.

But, likewise, the enjoyment consequent upon *ahistorical* listening is
also a special kind of musical enjoyment, perhaps; and that brings us to
our third possible objection to historical listening: it will deprive us of the
special enjoyment of ahistorical listening. Indeed, there may well be some
truth in this, as there is in the opposite claim that historical listening
brings special musical enjoyment. And this suggests, one would think,
that both kinds of listening, if possible, should be available. However, we
now are already getting involved with normative questions concerning
historical authenticity; and this is not yet the time to do so. For now, I
think, it is time to retrace our steps and take stock of what conclusions we
have reached so far about the historical authenticity of musical sound.

·   ·   ·

I have distinguished in this chapter two very different ways of looking at
the concept of historically authentic musical sound. In the first way, musical sound is taken to be, in effect, a purely physical phenomenon—
sound waves, perturbations of a physical medium. It is what a recording
machine would "copy" if, *per impossibile*, we could transport the thing to
the time of Bach or Josquin. As one recent writer, James O. Young, characterizes this kind of authenticity, "An authentic performance is one
which causes air to vibrate as it would have vibrated at the time of its
composition, under ideal conditions."[26]

The second way of construing historically authentic sound is as an intentional object of musical perception. R. A. Sharpe has, I think, nicely
captured, in capsule, what I have been driving at in this regard, with the
phrase "authentic reception," and his characterization of it as "hear[ing]

[26] Young, "The Concept of Authentic Performance," p. 235.

Authenticity   as   Sound

the music as a decently experienced musician or music-lover contemporaneous with the music's composition would have heard it."[27]

Furthermore, I have emphasized, in my discussion of sensible authenticity, the role of historical listening and the resultant imparting to or discovery in music historically embedded qualities. I am certainly not the first writer to recognize in the context of historically authentic performance practice the distinction between, as Sharpe puts it, "how the music sounded" and "how the music would have sounded to."[28] But the role of historical listening, in relation to the distinction, cannot, it seems to me, be overemphasized and has not, at least in my experience, been given the attention it deserves or ever been recognized with any kind of clarity. It is obviously crucial, as I have argued, to the whole enterprise of historically authentic performance, and somewhat paradoxical at that.

Now, the point of this exercise is not to make philosophical paradoxes or philosophical distinctions of no practical implication for performance. On the contrary, the distinction between sonic and sensible authenticity, and the recognition of just how deeply historical our listening has become, raise serious questions for anyone who wishes or claims to give historically authentic musical performances. If one seriously claims or intends to give the present-day listener the musical experience of an eighteenth- or fifteenth-century one, for whatever reason, he or she must recognize that, in doing the usual things musicians do to achieve "historical authenticity," one does not necessarily achieve it and may, indeed, be helping to achieve just the opposite result.

Now the question may well be raised here as to whether I am goring the wrong ox in admonishing *performers* to recognize, *in practice*, the distinction between sonic and sensible authenticity. Is it a performance matter at all? Sharpe does not think so: "It will be clear that authentic performance and authentic reception are not the same. It is for the performer to aim at the first. He cannot do much about the second *qua* performer; the task of raising the consciousness is up to educators."[29]

A preliminary point here requires comment. It seems to me to beg a rather serious question merely to assume, as Sharpe seems to, that getting

[27] Sharpe, "Authenticity Again," pp. 163–64.
[28] Ibid., p. 163.
[29] Ibid., p. 164.

Authenticity as Sound

people to hear "authentically" is to raise the consciousness. For if, as I have argued, to hear Bach or Josquin authentically is, among other things, to hear them ahistorically, then clearly this species of "authentic reception" arguably lowers the consciousness in at least one particular respect. More generally, it seems reasonable to assume—and not so long ago it was assumed by many—that in many ways we have better listening attitudes toward at least some of the music of the past than its contemporary audiences could have had, who were hearing "strange sounds" for the first time and probably finding them difficult to appreciate for that reason. In any case, this is a question not about the nature of historically authentic performance but about its desirability, and so does not concern us at this point in our deliberations—but will later on.

So, putting aside the question of whether or not achieving what Sharpe calls "authentic reception" is consciousness raising, a good thing to achieve, what we want to ask is whether or not Sharpe is correct to prize it completely apart from the performer's task. I think it can be gathered from my previous remarks that I do not think he is correct. And it is necessary now to make that very plain.

To free our discussion from any premature normative commitment, let us make "consciousness raising" "consciousness changing" instead; and we might add "consciousness sustaining" into the equation as well. For it will certainly be the purpose of various interested parties both to change musical consciousness if they are dissatisfied with it and to sustain it if they find it satisfactory.

There is no gainsaying the fact that those other than musical performers are deeply involved in both changing and sustaining the listener's consciousness; and it is obvious who many of them are. To that extent, of course, Sharpe's point is well taken. But surely one takes too narrow a view—as I think Sharpe does—in claiming that it is exclusively those others, not the performers, whose task it is to mold, one way or the other, both our conscious and our unconscious listening stances and habits.

Why does Sharpe claim for nonperformers exclusive influence over "authentic reception"? He does not explicitly say. But if one were to incline to this view—and I do not say Sharpe does—because those others, the critics, musicologists, program annotators, reviewers, and so on, are engaged in a verbal activity that might on that account be expected to influence people's musical attitudes, whereas performers are engaged in a nonverbal activity that could not be expected to have such an influence, I think that would be a very poor argument. It should be obvious enough, to start with, that in general practice does have an influence on thinking and mind-sets, and that musical performance practice in particular has an influence on musical thinking, affects listening attitudes and habits both immediately and in the long run in its lasting effect and presence as a tradition, at least as long as it remains in place.

I have already adduced, as a case in point, the tendency, at least so I believe, of "mainstream" musical performance, with its uniformity of performance means and performance aesthetic, to encourage ahistorical listening. This is both an immediate effect in the particular performance and a sustaining effect of this kind of performance practice over time. But apart from the general effect that "mainstream" musical performance practice may have to encourage ahistorical listening, or "historically authentic" performance practice may have to encourage historical listening, all kinds of individual performing decisions can and are meant to have direct consequences regarding how a musical event is heard. That is to say, performers manipulate (in a nonpejorative sense) the way their audiences hear what they play. To instance a case in point, already alluded to, a conductor who decides to attempt re-creating something of the surprise and shock that the opening of Beethoven's First Symphony must have produced in its first audiences will devise a different way of performing it from that of a conductor who has other ideas: perhaps he will accentuate the first chord in some arresting way. Or, to suggest another example, a player who wishes her audience to hear the "romantic" harmonies in Bach's Chromatic Fantasy and Fugue will doubtless play them in a characteristically "romantic" way—expressive, mannered tempo changes and that sort of thing—whereas another player, who wishes his audience to hear Bach as of his time and place rather than as a "precursor" of romanticism, will downplay such harmonies by playing the passages "straight." But in all such examples it seems that performers have it as part of their goal, and have it in their power, to influence their audiences' listening attitudes—to change or sustain their consciousness, to mold the intentional objects of their listening.

It also needs pointing out that although performance is, in a very obvious sense, a nonverbal activity, it exists not as a separate entity but,

Authenticity as Sound

rather, as part of a musical institution imbued deeply and throughout with a conceptual, verbal structure. We do not experience a performance without a conceptual framework in which to perceive it, place it, understand it, any more than we do so with the work of art, the musical composition, that the performance instantiates. (Indeed, it is arguable that a performance *is* a work of art in its own right: more of that anon.) And so we must not see a performance, because it is a nonverbal activity, as somehow cut off from our conceptual lives and impotent to influence them.

Thus it seems to me by no means as clear-cut as Sharpe makes it out to be that the division of labor puts sensible authenticity outside of the performer's workshop. On the contrary, it appears to me to make perfectly good sense, and to accord with actual musical practice, to represent performers as, in their efforts to produce historically authentic sound, giving careful consideration not only to the physical sounds themselves but to the intentional objects that human beings make of them. And the conclusion I wish to elicit, in this regard, is that there are two very distinct kinds of historically authentic sound here, not necessarily both achievable in one and the same performance practice.

·   ·   ·

It ought to be apparent at this point that my conclusions about "authenticity as sound" coincide with those about "authenticity as intention" in one very important respect. What we discover is that a certain kind of mindless pedantry, which seems to many of us to infect the authentic performance movement, is banished straightaway, before we even consider whether a "historically authentic performance" of any kind is a desirable goal, merely by examining the concept of historical authenticity itself and realizing that it is not the conceptual straitjacket it is taken to be by the unreflective zealots. In the case of authenticity as intention, we discovered that there is nothing time-bound or, to put it another way, past tense–bound about the performance wishes of the composer: that it is not merely a matter of what was intended but what would have been intended *if* . . . And in the case of authenticity as sound, we now discover that reproducing historical sound in the physical sense of sound—perturbations of a physical medium—does not by any means exhaust the deeper notion of "historical sound": the sound-experience of the past musical listener.

Authenticity   as   Sound

But I do not wish to be misunderstood here. Sonic and sensible authenticity are not two independent, unrelated things. Obviously, a logical first step in reproducing the musical experience of a past age may very well be the attaining of sonic authenticity. However, it may also very well not be. It depends on a myriad of circumstances. It may seem perfectly plain that I shall get close to producing the intentional object of Bach's audience if I perform his cantatas and passions with the performing forces that were at his disposal. Yet not much reflection reveals that in important respects such an assumption is false. And this is but one simple example among countless others.

A great deal of effort has been put into the reproduction of what are taken to be the historical sounds of past musical performances, by those who think of themselves as pursuing the goal of the historically authentic performance by reproducing the physical sounds of the musical periods in which their repertoires lie. I do not wish to throw out this baby with its bath water. The achieving of sonic authenticity is a reasonable enterprise; and it produces an interesting result. But it does not, no matter how doggedly (or pedantically) pursued, constitute our sole or necessarily our best efforts toward historical authenticity in performance, just because sonic authenticity does not exhaust the concept of authenticity. Just as a particular mainstream performance *may* be the most historically authentic in light of our liberated notion of performing intentions, it also *may* be the most historically authentic in light of our liberated notion of authenticity of sound—the notion, that is, that includes sensible as well as sonic authenticity. Here, as elsewhere, there is not *one* "authenticity."

⊙

CHAPTER FOUR

Authenticity as Practice

Of the three candidates for the title of historically authentic performance, I think that the duplication of contemporary performance practice is the most problematical. This might sound like a strange thing to say. For the very study of historical performance is called, in most institutions of higher learning as well as in the literature, the study of "performance practice." It is called neither the study of composers' intentions nor the study of historical sound.

Well, from a certain vantage point, performance practice is not a problematical concept. That is the vantage point of ends-means; and it is from that vantage point, I would suggest, that the discipline of musicology —of which performance practice is a part—principally views it. Here is what I have in mind. There are, I suppose, two obvious reasons for musicologists to study historical performance practice: first, simply to satisfy their historical curiosity; but second, as a model for present-day musical performance practice applied to music of the past. And as a model for present-day practice, historical practice is seen by musicologists and musicologically minded performers not as an end in itself—the primary goal of their endeavors—but as a *means* to an *end*. What end? Clearly, the end of a historically authentic performance—which is to say, a performance that either realizes the composer's intentions or reproduces contemporary sound. In a word, historically authentic performance practice is not authentic performance per se but rather the means to authentic performance in one or another of the senses of historically authentic performance already canvassed. And understood thus, it is quite unproblematical.

Is this the conclusion in which we should rest? Or does it make sense to speak of historical performance practice as an end in itself—*another* form of historical authenticity, not merely a means to historically authentic sound or authorial intention? For it is in considering historical performance practice as, in itself, a separate form of historically authentic musical performance that its problematical nature becomes apparent.

.   .   .

We can best work our way into the problematical nature of historical performance practice by looking at a philosophical debate in the recent literature over whether or not it is inauthentic to perform music on instruments that are very different from the ones originally stipulated, even if the *sound* produced by them is exactly like the sound of the original ones. On this question, and in response to an essay by Stephen Davies, Jerrold Levinson has this to say:

> It seems to be that Davies's account misconstrues, or at least underplays, one factor that has an importance he does not explicitly recognize. This is the fact that performances are partly authentic in virtue of being performed *on the instruments for which they were intended* (or envisaged), for a reason wholly *other* than, and distinct from, their thus producing a *sound* that matches what an ideal contemporary performance would have delivered.[1]

So it seems, at first blush, as if Levinson is here making the strong claim that the way the music is played—in this particular instance, what instruments it is produced on—is not merely a means to the end of producing historically authentic *sound* but, beyond that, an end in itself—"that performances are partly authentic in virtue of being performed *on the instruments for which they were intended.* . . ." "What is left out of consideration"

[1] Levinson, "Performance and Performance Means," in *Music, Art, and Metaphysics*, p. 394. The essay by Davies referred to is "Authenticity in Musical Performance."

Authenticity as Practice

81

in Davies's account, he says, "is the fact that sounds are produced *in just that manner*; that is to say, *the way in which* the performance achieves its sound results is overlooked."[2] And although Levinson is just now talking only about instrumentation, the way he puts his case in the statement just quoted can well be taken as applying not merely to bowing and blowing but to performance *practice* across the board: "*just that manner . . . the way in which* the performance achieves its sound result."

But if, at the outset, Levinson seems to be treating performance practice as something beyond merely a means to the end of historically authentic sound, when he gets to his first examples, we find that is not the case. For these examples (and most of the others in Levinson's essay) have to do with the loss of *expressive* qualities when historically authentic instrumentation is abandoned. And expressive properties, as Levinson seems to be treating them in this essay, are *heard* properties of the music—not, to be sure, properties of the physical sounds alone. Rather, the point is: "Part of the expressive character of a piece of music *as heard* derives from our sense of how it is *being made* in performance and our correlation of that with its sonic aspect—its sound—narrowly speaking; and its expressive character *tout court* is partly a function of how it properly sounds taken in conjunction with how that sound is *meant* to be produced in performance."[3]

It thus turns out that when Levinson first contrasts the means of producing musical sound with the sound itself, he means by "sound" what I meant in the previous chapter by physical sound—the perturbations of the physical medium. But when he goes on to explain why, say, an electronic synthesizer, even though it produces the same "sounds" as a clarinet, cannot give an authentic performance of a piece for clarinet, his explanation is that it cannot reproduce the sounds "as heard," that is to say, what I called in the previous chapter "sensible authenticity"; and that because one's beliefs about how the sounds are produced—blowing on a reed rather than pushing buttons—has an effect on one's intentional object of musical perception. So even though it seems at first as if Levinson's argument is going to be that performance practice is not a servant to sound only but an authenticity in its own right, as the argument begins to

[2] Levinson, "Performance and Performance Means."
[3] Ibid., p. 395.

Authenticity as Practice

develop it becomes an argument simply that performance practice is a servant not merely to (in my terms) sonic authenticity but to sensible authenticity as well. Thus it *is* merely a servant to sound, when sound is broadly conceived (as it should be) to include sound as an intentional object.

Does Levinson ever get beyond the position that practice is the means to the end of sound broadly conceived? There are at least suggestions that he does. And I want to follow them up now.

·   ·   ·

In the final section of his essay, Levinson says:

> To conclude: Instrumentation in traditional music is not merely
> of instrumental value, so to speak, in achieving a certain sound,
> but is rather logically tied to a piece's expressiveness and aesthetic
> character in its own right. Recognizing this shows us that the notion
> of authenticity of performance cannot be analyzed exclusively in
> terms of a matching of sound per se, even the sound of an ideal
> contemporary performance.[4]

What are we to make of this conclusion? If we read Levinson closely here and take him literally at his word, then he does seem to be pushing beyond his original position, which seemed to have been merely that instrumentation is a means to the realization not just of physical sound but of the intentional object—especially its expressiveness—as well, even though he may mean no more by "the sound of an ideal contemporary performance" than the physical sounds that such a performance might produce. For if that were all he meant to imply here, then why say "is not of merely instrumental value . . . in achieving a certain sound," because that *is* all it would be if all it did beyond producing physically authentic sound was produce sound "as heard," that is to say, "intentional sound." Sound "as heard" is a "certain sound," and instrumentation, along with other performance practices, would be merely of instrumental value in attaining it.

This becomes a bit more apparent as Levinson amplifies his conclusion: "What I have said about the involvement of exact instrumentation in aesthetic content does have the implication that, to gauge that content fully

[4]Ibid., p. 408.

Authenticity   as   Practice

and accurately, or the expressiveness that is its major part, one must be familiar with instruments, their mechanics, their physical potentials, and perhaps most of all with how the manipulations of which they admit stand with respect to the broader repertoire of movements, gestures, and expressions of the embodied human being. . . ."[5] It seems *almost* as if Levinson is saying here that part of the expressiveness of a musical performance lies in the expressiveness of the instrumentalists' physical gestures as they play their instruments: *seen* rather than heard properties. It seems *almost* as if . . . But is that what Levinson really is saying? The last sentence of Levinson's essay is both enticingly suggestive and maddeningly inconclusive in coming to a definite and final answer: "Music is physical activity as well as spiritual product, and the latter cannot be properly grasped—or presented—without acknowledging the specific determining role of the former in it."[6] The enticing part is the beginning: "Music is physical activity as well as spiritual product." Compare: "Baseball is defense as well as offense." In saying this latter thing, I am saying that the whole that I am appreciating, when I go to a baseball game, is composed of two parts: defense and offense. I must appreciate *both* in order fully to appreciate baseball as a spectator sport. Is Levinson saying that music, as a "spectator sport," is composed of two things, activity (seen) and product (heard), such that a full musical experience is *both* visual and sonic; an experience of both activity and product? Is he saying that the expressive object, called "music," which we enjoy in performance, is a complex object, composed of both visual and sonic parts? That would be a very enticing thing to say; and I am going to pursue the possibility in this chapter.

But the rest of Levinson's concluding sentence seems to belie this enticing interpretation; for his last words seem to throw the whole weight of the thing on the *product* side of the equation. The final verdict is that "the latter," that is to say, the product, "cannot be properly grasped—or presented—without acknowledging the specific determining role of the former," that is to say, the activity, "in it." So we are back with the more conservative position that performance practice, and our knowledge of it as listeners, is not an end in itself but a means to a more authentic "product," musical sound, albeit that sound is construed not merely as physical sound but as intentional sound as well: sound "as heard."

[5] Ibid.
[6] Ibid.

Authenticity as Practice

· · ·

An ancillary point, which suggests that Levinson is not thinking of music as anything beyond a sonic art, is his rejection, at the beginning of his essay, of music's social context as playing any role at all in authentic performance practice. He registers agreement, in this regard, with Davies, when he says that "authenticity does not require reproduction of the social milieu in which a work was premiered. . . ."[7]

An initially puzzling, perhaps picky point about what Levinson is saying here is that he seems to be confining the interesting possibility of "social milieu" as a factor in performance practice authenticity to the "milieu in which a work was premiered." Taking "premiered" literally, either as "first performed" or as "first publicly performed," would have the overly restrictive result of making a performance of Mozart's "Haydn" Quartets inauthentic if they were not played in Mozart's flat in Vienna, or in a suitable replica of it, and a performance of the *Eroica* inauthentic if it were not performed in the same room in the Lobkowitz palace that has now become a musical shrine. But that would be absurd. We know that the social milieu in which Mozart's late quartets and Beethoven's *Eroica* were performed was a wider one than these two particular places would suggest.

But I don't think Levinson really meant to restrict the concept of social milieu in this way. Rather, I take it that Levinson's "social milieu in which a work was premiered" is shorthand for something like "social milieu in which a work was customarily performed during the composer's lifetime (or some other suitably circumscribed period)." And the question then is, Why should Levinson want to have denied the relevance of social milieu, so conceived, to performance practice authenticity, while including in it original instrumentation?

The answer to this question can best be got at, I think, by reverting to the original, and more expansive passage of Davies's with which, I take it, Levinson is registering agreement, in his rather truncated remark. Davies writes (and I quote at some length):

> The selectivity displayed in the search for authenticity in musical performance has been systematic in a way which suggests that the quest may be characterized as aiming at the production of a

[7]Ibid., p. 393.

Authenticity as Practice

85

particular *sound*, rather than at the production of, for example, the social ambience within which the music would or could be presented by the composer's contemporaries. This point is effectively illustrated as follows: orchestral music composed in the latter half of the eighteenth century might standardly have been performed in wood-panelled rooms. Nowadays such works would be performed in concert halls. Modern concert halls are designed with modifiable acoustics, the adjustments being made by the use of baffles, etc. In performing music of the period in question the acoustics of the concert hall would be set with a reverberation period such as one might find in a wood-panelled room containing a small audience. Although the music now is performed in a large concert hall in front of a large audience, the acoustic properties of the modern building are so arranged that they duplicate the acoustic properties of the sort of room in which the music would have been performed in the composer's day. Now, whilst one might prefer the intimacy of music performed in salons I take it that it will be accepted that the use of concert halls which reproduce the acoustic properties of wood-panelled rooms would be considered not *merely* as an adequate compromise between the demands of authenticity and, say, economic considerations, but, instead, would be accepted as a full-blooded attempt at authentic performance. That modern acoustic technology might serve the aim of authenticity in this way suggests strongly that musical authenticity aims at the creation of a particular sound and not at the production of a particular visual, social or other effect.[8]

Laid out in this more expansive way, I think we can now see directly what the argument—to some extent enthymematic—is, in both Davies and Levinson, for rejecting "social milieu" as a component of a historically authentic performance practice. Authenticity, on both accounts, is authenticity of sound, the difference being, as I would put it, that Davies seems to be construing sound more narrowly, as a physical phenomenon, and Levinson more broadly, as the intentional object of musical perception. There is an underlying assumption in all this, one is forced to conclude, and that is that music *is* just sound. (What else?) And so what else

[8]Davies, "Authenticity in Musical Performance," pp. 40–41.

Authenticity   as   Practice

can authentic musical practice be but a means to authentic sound? (One can't *hear* "practice"—one can only hear its result.) And so, as Davies puts it in the end, "musical authenticity aims at the creation of a particular sound and not at the production of a particular visual, social or other effect." Social milieu and visual effects cannot be part of musical authenticity as end because music is sound, and they cannot be heard. But nor can they be a part of the means to musical authenticity because—again, I think, an unspoken assumption—they cannot have any effect on musical sound. It is particularly because of this last assumption, I feel sure, that Levinson rejects social milieu out of hand as a goal of historically authentic performance practice. And the whole drift of the argument suggests as well that, contrary to the enticing remarks in Levinson's essay, previously alluded to, Levinson does not see the expressiveness of music as going beyond the audible.

As a quick aside, I find it puzzling, given Levinson's position on the role of instrumentation in imparting *heard* properties to music, that he should reject the social milieu, as he seems to do, as another source of the same phenomenon. For it seems no less (and perhaps more) plausible to think that the social setting in which one experiences a musical work should have an effect on how it sounds, *expressively*, than that one's knowledge of, say, how an eighteenth-century clarinet, as opposed to a modern French instrument, produces its sounds (one of Levinson's examples) would do. To instance a case in point, I would think that the more intimate social setting in which Haydn's string quartets were performed (and intended) during his career at Esterháza, as compared to the way they are performed today in the modern concert hall, might enhance or even impart an expressive quality of "domesticity"—a *heard* quality, mind you—to the works; and, similarly, a performance of Mozart's wind divertimentos during the kind of festive dinner parties for which *they* were intended (remember the *Harmoniemusik* in the penultimate scene of *Don Giovanni*), rather than as chamber music of the string quartet kind, might well enhance or impart to *them* the sparkling, elegant, suavely bantering quality, not to mention the undertext of sensuality and sexual innuendo, that must have characterized many such affairs.

As I say, this is in the nature of an aside at this point. But I will return to it in a later chapter, when we come to ask ourselves whether authenticity of performance practice, even as means rather than end, is a good thing to

Authenticity as Practice

achieve. For part of the answer to that question will turn on whether such claims as Levinson makes, about the relation of means of performance to expressiveness, are really true. I take them to be empirical claims (if they are not vacuous); and I take it that they can be evaluated as such, as can the claims I have just suggested might be made for the effects of social milieu on the expressive musical surface. For the nonce, though, this is the place to take stock of what we have so far discovered about the concept of historical authenticity as performance practice, before going on to explore it further.

· · ·

We have seen that, considered as a means to a sonic end, historically authentic performance practice is conceptually unproblematical. We do indeed need, as Levinson has done, to think of sound not merely as a physical entity but as an intentional object, to capture everything we want to say about performance practice as a sonic means; however, sonic means it remains in Levinson, some enticingly suggestive remarks to the contrary notwithstanding. It may well be a concept full of problems when we come to ask the further question of *why* a historically authentic performance practice might be a good thing to achieve. In particular, it will be necessary to ask whether a great many of the (to me) extravagant claims are true that Levinson and others have made about what the results of performance practice are in terms of sound "as heard." Yet as a concept, it seems straightforward enough.

Where historically authentic performance practice is thought of, however, not as a sonic means but as an end in itself to be aimed at by the performer, it immediately raises conceptual dust. And I think we are now in a position to see quite clearly why.

If I am correct in my interpretations of Davies and Levinson on this point, they both reject the pursuit of "social setting" and other such conditions of performance because they do not have any aesthetically significant effect whatever on *sound*, on both Levinson's and Davies's views. Furthermore, the underlying assumption driving the whole argument here must be that music just is, as aesthetically appreciated object, *sound* and nothing more.

From the premise that music is sound alone, and the line of argument it supports, I think the following tentative hypothesis can be drawn. It is that *if* performance practice—social milieu or any other part of it—is to

Authenticity as Practice

be thought of as an end in itself and not merely as a sonic means, then music as aesthetically appreciated object must be construed as being something beyond mere sound, even if sound is widely construed as intentional object of musical perception. For practice "as heard" is merely practice producing musical sound—a means to that end; and it can thus be an end in itself only if it is an unheard but otherwise perceived part of the total musical experience. We will then at least have to think of music as in part a visual object as well, appealing not just to the ear but to the eye also, if we are to think of practice as an end in itself and not merely sonic means. And now the problematical conceptual character of period performance practice is fully apparent. For the notion that music is, as aesthetic object of appreciation, not merely aural but also visual puzzles one mightily and tempts one to reject out of hand any attempt to make period performance practice anything beyond means to a sonic object.

In the remaining sections of this chapter I am going to explore the possibility that music is indeed something more than an aural object and that, therefore, certain aspects of performance practice are indeed to be pursued as musical ends in themselves. If this sounds like a scary prospect, perhaps even a mad one, I will remind the reader here, as I have done previously from time to time, that I am still exclusively involved with conceptual analysis. The question of *why* we might want to pursue "visual authenticity" in music must await our considerations in Part II; and these considerations will help, no doubt, to ameliorate this seemingly scary, mad prospect of a "visual music."

.   .   .

Let me begin my further explorations into historically authentic performance practice with a fairly clear and unproblematical example. I assume it would be agreed on all hands that a concert performance of an opera is not authentic, not a complete presentation of the work. And I further suppose that what is missing, all would agree, is a complex visual component—in a word, the "production." An opera is not merely music but a dramatic representation with singers that act (more or less) and wear costumes on a stage with scenery and props, lighting, and so forth. The point is trivial and requires no further elaboration.

But the concept of an opera, in concert version, is worth a little more consideration. Notice that the opposite of an opera in concert—that is to say, an "opera" in dramatic representation, scenery, costumes and the rest—*without the music*, would be a palpable absurdity. Who could bear a talked, acted dramatic presentation of even the best opera libretto? It would be a pointless exercise. Thus, as important as stage production, with all the frills, is to an authentic performance of an opera, it nevertheless pales in comparison with the importance of the music in the obvious respect that a performance of the opera sans mise en scène is a complete aesthetic experience of the work, if not an aesthetic experience of the complete work; whereas performance sans music is neither, but simply a freak.

Let me now move on to another example. In the early days of longplaying records I acquired a recording of Mozart's Coronation Mass (K. 317). On the record sleeve the program annotator dilated effusively on the annual Christmas Eve performance of the work in the Salzburg Cathedral. "You haven't really heard the Coronation Mass until you've heard it in the Salzburg Cathedral, with candlelight and all the trimmings," was the message, if not the exact words. Was that a credible message?

In certain respects such works as the Coronation Mass are very much like operas. Certainly Mozart wrote the mass to be "staged," although not, as a matter of fact, in the Salzburg Cathedral but for the annual coronation of the statue of the Virgin at the shrine of Maria Plain, near Salzburg. And there is, after all, plenty of theatricality in a religious ceremony of the kind for which most of Mozart's and Haydn's religious music was written. So one might perfectly well want to say that a performance of the Coronation Mass in Carnegie Hall is, in fact, a "concert performance" in the very same sense as if one were describing a performance of *Don Giovanni* under the same conditions. It is not completely authentic: something is missing, namely, the liturgical and ceremonial setting.

But suppose someone were to reply: "The cases are clearly different. The dramatic setting is *obviously* part of an opera. However, the liturgical or ceremonial setting of a mass—or vespers, litany, or anthem—is not part of such a work in any obvious way. Get thee gone, muddier of clear waters!"

Well, that is just the question—what *is* part of a musical work and what *isn't*. We cannot just beg the question because we are not used to the idea of the liturgical setting being part of the liturgical work but are used to the idea that the dramatic setting is part of an opera. I am trying to introduce here a new way of talking about some old facts; we need something more substantial to go on than that my way of talking is unfamiliar to make so serious a decision as that a feature is or is not part of a work.

So let's round up the usual suspects. We cannot, of course, reply that the music is only sound and that the liturgical setting cannot be heard, and therefore cannot be part of the musical work. For then we must say either that the dramatic setting is not a part of an opera because operas are musical works, and the dramatic setting not heard, or (as usually is done) that operas are mixed-media artworks, composed of both heard and seen elements. And if we say the latter, then I see no reason why we cannot (and should not) say that liturgical music is a mixed-media art form of which the liturgical setting and ceremony are a part. To insist, without further argument, that opera is a mixed-media art form and that classical or Renaissance church music, for example, are not, simply to avoid having to allow the liturgical setting and ceremony as parts of such works as Haydn's, Mozart's, and Palestrina's masses, is just to beg the question at issue.

Intention is, of course, another possible criterion to which one might appeal in winnowing out musical from nonmusical properties. No such appeal, however, will do any good here in trying to argue that the dramatic setting is, but the liturgical setting is not, part of the musical work. For clearly, just as Handel intended his operas to have dramatic settings, and fashioned the musical parameters accordingly, so too he intended his Coronation Anthems to have the liturgical cum ceremonial setting for which they were commissioned and for which his music was specially suited. ("Zadok the Priest" in Westminster Abbey is a far cry from the same work in the concert hall.)

To be sure, Mozart intended his Coronation Mass for a particular occasion and a particular place. But that does not in itself distinguish such works from operas. We must not forget that operas, like other "occasional" works, were also written with particular places *and* particular singers in mind. (And this is true of Wagner and Verdi as much as of earlier composers for the stage.) Mozart wrote the Coronation Mass for the shrine of Maria Plain, near Salzburg. *And* he wrote *Don Giovanni* for the opera house in Prague. But that implies neither that the only historically authentic way of performing the mass is in the shrine of Maria Plain near Salzburg nor, needless to say, that the only historically authentic way of performing *Don Giovanni* is in the Prague opera house. For, one assumes,

Mozart hoped, at least—if he did not expect—that these works would be performed elsewhere as well. So part of the historically authentic way of performing each is in *the kind of place* for which each was written, for *the kind of occasion*. So far, then, the analogy between opera and liturgical music has not broken down.

And we are prepared, too, to answer the possible objection that, of course, the analogy between opera and church music is not sound because whereas a liturgical work like Mozart's Coronation Mass is aesthetically complete without its liturgical and ceremonial accoutrements, an opera is *clearly* not aesthetically complete denuded of its dramatic setting. But this will not really wash. For we have already seen that operas in concert version *are* aesthetically complete: that is why the institution can exist. To be sure, an opera in concert form is not the complete opera. Similarly, though, I am arguing, the Coronation Mass is not the complete mass without its liturgical and ceremonial setting. And they are on all fours in that one can be aesthetically satisfied with a concert performance of the mass, as one can also be aesthetically satisfied by a concert performance of an opera.

At this point a concession surely must be made, although it is not destructive of the major point. In spite of the overarching importance of music to an opera or music drama, a larger hole, I am certain, is left in a concert performance of *Don Giovanni* or *Die Meistersinger* than in a concert performance of the Coronation Mass or a Bach cantata. That anyone must be willing to grant. We are dealing with degrees here; and it seems clearly to be the case that the degree to which the essential aesthetic of the Coronation Mass is diminished by a performance in Carnegie Hall rather than in a candlelit cathedral or the shrine of Maria Plain is smaller in magnitude than the degree to which the essential aesthetic of an opera or music drama is compromised by a concert performance. Or, to put it in a nutshell, the visual part of an opera is far greater than the visual part of a mass or cantata. But as this *is* a matter of degree, it is *also* a matter of *principle*; and the principle is, simply, that it makes rather good sense to think of musical works other than operas as musical works of mixed media. Indeed, I think what is beginning to emerge is that *all* musical works can be arranged, in principle if not in practice, in a continuum from opera and music drama (and ballet), which I take to be the ultimate mixed-media musical works, through such works as music, with or without text, for liturgical and other ceremonial occasions, down to works that, for all intents and purposes, have no visual component at all but *are* music purely for the ears: pure sonic art. We need further examples to pin this point down and elaborate it sufficiently.[9]

· · ·

Let us compare two rather different examples of absolute music, music for instruments alone, without text, title, or program: Mozart's Divertimento for Wind Sextet (K. 289) and the First Symphony of Johannes Brahms. I do not know exactly what the setting was for which Mozart composed this divertimento (or the other five for the same instruments), but we can hazard a reasonable enough guess for present purposes. Perhaps it was meant for a small dinner party like the one Don Giovanni gave for the Stone Guest, in which a similar ensemble was employed, or perhaps for an al fresco gathering in one of those wonderful Salzburg courtyards where I once heard Mozart's *Harmoniemusik* performed. In any case, the setting was not a public concert hall, with all that implies (and some of what it implies I shall get to in a moment) but a social gathering, of a somewhat grand and aristocratic kind, of which Mozart's suave, scintillating music was an aesthetic part. And because that setting is completely lost in a performance in Carnegie Hall by the Netherlands Wind Ensemble, the latter performance is historically inauthentic as regards performance practice in just the way that a concert performance of the Coronation Mass or *Don Giovanni* would be, although perhaps to a far lesser degree than both these others.

Brahams's First Symphony is another matter. Nothing about its performance in a modern concert hall is historically inauthentic with regard to that aspect of performance practice—that is to say, with regard to social setting—because it has no social setting other than the modern concert hall, which is, in a manner of speaking, the limiting case; and Brahms, of

[9] Actually, what a composer intends *not to be seen* may also be an essential "visual" part of a musical work. An interesting example of this occurs in the *Musikalische Exequien* of Heinrich Schütz, in the preface to which the composer specifically stipulates the placement of the choirs in such a way that the congregation would have heard *but not seen* the personified voice of the departed and his accompanying seraphim, thus underscoring their disembodied, ethereal nature not only by the sound of their musical utterance but by the invisibility of the source: "They would have heard the voices, incorporeal and migrant, emanating from different but indeterminate parts of the church." Johnston, "Rhetorical Personification of the Dead in Seventeenth-Century German Funeral Music," p. 205.

Authenticity as Practice

course, had just that setting in mind when he composed the work. We can see, then, that Mozart's K. 289 and Brahms's First Symphony fall on either side of a *great divide* in music performance practice—between an instrumental music that was composed with particular, diverse social settings in view, other than the modern concert hall (which has yet to be conceived of), and an instrumental music composed specifically for the modern concert hall, which had now become the standard showcase for the modern instrumental idiom. Haydn and Mozart, of course, straddled the line, with some of their large instrumental music written for one, some for the other, and some—Mozart's "Haffner" Symphony, for example—originally for the "old" practice and then reworked for the "new."

Musicologists tell us that the first public concerts (in the modern sense or something like it) took place in London, during Handel's hegemony there; and his later oratorios were, in fact, purely public entertainments, supported not by royal or even private patronage but by a paying middle-class audience. Nor is it insignificant that the modern concert hall and another modern artistic institution, the art museum, came into being during the same period. For the modern concert hall is, in many respects, a "sonic museum," and so I shall refer to it hereafter.

Let me now venture the suggestion that before the great divide—before, that is, the coming into being of the sonic museum—all music, including instrumental music, was a mixed-media art in the sense that it was all written for various and sundry domestic, social, public, and religious ceremonies that, as musical practice, formed part of its *appreciated aesthetic character*, fully envisioned by the composer. As practice, it was music's visual aesthetic part, like the dramatic setting of an opera. But almost all instrumental music composed after the great divide, and a good deal of vocal music as well—with the exception, of course, of ballet, opera, and music drama—was composed with the sonic museum specifically in mind, at least as the favored place of performance, and usually as the only one. (This is true, I believe, of even the great romantic chamber music literature, which must have far exceeded the musical capabilities of the domestic, amateur music maker.) And in the sonic museum, music is a purely aural art (with one possible emendation to that to be discussed in a moment). Indeed, as my name is meant to suggest, the concert hall, the "sonic museum," is a showcase for the express purpose of displaying

Authenticity as Practice

sonic artworks. From which it follows, of course, that the artworks created specifically with the sonic museum in mind—which is to say, most musical works, with the exception of opera, ballet, and music drama, composed after the great divide—were created as purely aural, purely sonic art works.[10]

Does this mean that instrumental music composed before the great divide should not be performed in the sonic museum? By no means. But it does mean that such instrumental music is, to a certain extent, being performed in a historically inauthentic performance practice, a practice that does not allow of visual musical properties that an earlier practice provided.

In this regard we can usefully compare the practice of the sonic museum with its visual analogue, the art museum. Here are two examples to ponder: an altar painting in the Museum of Fine Arts; and Handel's *Water Music* in the sonic museum.

Now, in the case of both the altar piece and the *Water Music* the art objects have been lifted from their original, intended settings and placed in the more antiseptic format of the museum, for the purpose of aesthetic "viewing." Furthermore, both suffer as a result of this aesthetic dislocation. The altar piece is deprived of the special, peculiarly shaped place for which it was designed, separated from the magnificent "theological" setting, and even viewed from a different visual perspective, having been contemplated, in situ, from below, by a kneeling penitent, but now, at eye level, by a standing observer.[11] (Indeed, if one wants to push things a bit further, the altar piece is deprived of its *sonic* setting as well, since the cathedral in which it was placed would frequently have been filled with music.)

Likewise, Handel's *Water Music*, presumably composed for a royal event on the Thames,[12] suffers palpable damage when moved into the more austere confines of the sonic museum. It is, after all, a somewhat amorphous collection of concerto grosso movements and dances, some twenty

---

[10] Cf. Higgins, *The Music of Our Lives*, p. 16: "Until recently, music in the West and elsewhere was almost always associated with community events that excited, entertained, or at least involved other senses besides the auditory."

[11] I am adopting here, for my own purposes, an example suggested by Arthur Danto in discussion.

[12] The exact historical circumstances of the original performance of the *Water Music* (c. 1717) are not known. I follow the familiar story.

Authenticity   as   Practice

or more, and lasts about as long as so tightly organized a work as Beethoven's Ninth Symphony, which was designed expressly for the sonic museum and is ideally suited to the kind of focused, concentrated listening that prevails there. Handel's suite, however, was designed for something else: an event, a "happening." Presumably performed on a royal barge, moving along a shimmering waterway, during a festive social gathering, it was really more like part of a pageant, the sonic element of an "orchestrated ballet," in which the "dancers" and the spectators were one and the same. It was not meant to, nor can it, sustain the kind of penetrating audition in every musical detail, throughout its entire length, for which the symphonies of Beethoven and Brahms were designed. Rather, it was part of a "multimedia event."

Even in the eighteenth century musicians must have already realized, one can safely surmise, that the *Water Music* was not perfectly suited to a "concert" performance; for the early published scores of the work already have the appearance of having been "arranged" (although I cannot prove this) into three, more self-contained suites, in which individual movements are vaguely organized into related keys. Nineteenth- and early twentieth-century arrangers laid even more violent hands on the work in trying to make it more suitable to the sonic museum. Nowadays, with the authenticity craze upon us, it is de rigeur, however, to hear the *Water Music*, in the sonic museum, in something like its original form, no concession made to mainstream symphonic performance practice. And in that form it clearly displays what it still has and what it has lost in the sonic museum. To be sure, it has lost all the visible "choreography" that made its considerable length yet lack of purely musical focus a virtue rather than a vice. But because Handel was a great composer and did indeed put so much musical artifice and inspiration into it, it survives, in spite of its "occasional" purpose, pretty well as an object of pure sonic concentration.

Other such musical examples, of course, come readily to mind: some fare well in the sonic museum, some not as well. The great tradition of English viol music, for example—the fantasias for the "chest of viols," by such composers as Byrd, Gibbons, and Purcell—were clearly written for domestic settings although certainly rather "grand" if measured by modern standards of domesticity. And one cannot help feeling that they must lose something vital of their intimacy in a public place—not merely, mind

Authenticity as Practice

you, their audible intimacy but something beyond that as well: the visual aspects of domestic music making and perhaps, more important still, the freedom of movement in such a setting that enables an auditor to alter his or her "point of view." Nevertheless, because there is so much to hear in these works—their composers being, after all, both sublime artists and master craftsmen—such works withstand transplantation to the sonic museum and can endure the exclusively aural attention that it is meant to focus as well as the greatest chamber works of Haydn, Mozart, Beethoven, and Brahms can, allowance having been made for the difficulty that the soft-voiced viols might have projecting in a large public space.

Similarly, the ricercare for instrumental ensemble, of Giovanni Gabrieli and other of his Venetian contemporaries, written expressly for the magnificent and "peculiar" space of San Marco, must lose some palpable musical qualities, expressive ones to a large degree, when deprived of this very special setting and, of course, the grand ceremonial pomp for which they served as the aural background. The antiphonal pieces particularly, obviously designed for the special architecture of San Marco, are hard to realize in the sonic museum with complete integrity. In a sense, this is the reverse of what happens in the case of the English fantasias. For whereas in the latter case it is moving from the small to the large setting that does the aesthetic damage, in the latter case it is moving from the large to the at least relatively small. (Few public performing spaces are a match for San Marco!) Nevertheless, there is so much of the pure musical parameters to hear in these pieces, particularly in those of Giovanni Gabrieli, that Gabrieli's ricercare have become the core literature of the modern brass ensemble, which treats them with something like the same performance attitude as the modern string player treats the quartets of Haydn, Mozart, and Beethoven. Here again, as in the case of the English fantasias, the sonic museum provides a favorable if not perfect environment.

In sharp contrast, however, to the fantasias of Byrd, Gibbons, and Purcell, or the ricercare of Gabrieli, are the numerous minuets and other social dances for orchestra written by Haydn, Mozart, and Beethoven for the Redoutensaal, and other such places in Vienna, which do not travel well; or, to take an example from the vocal literature, the graduals and other church music of Michael Haydn, which were much admired in the composer's lifetime (and of which I am particularly fond). There is not enough "real" music in such works: they do not withstand pure sonic

Authenticity as Practice

scrutiny for long. They were all part of a vast social or liturgical happening that must have been a stunning aesthetic experience, both to the ear and to the eye; and as part of such happenings, these works were, no doubt, a sparkling ornament. But no less than an opera, and perhaps more, they must be staged. In addition, the church music of Michael Haydn illustrates a point well taken about the revival of works by the *Kleinmeisters*, which is such a busy industry these days. Frequently such works, if they were composed before the great divide, will survive famously in situ, where they will not in the sonic museum, because, of course, their composers simply did not have enough pure music in them to give. Michael, after all, was not Joseph. Nevertheless, in spite of all of their obvious drawbacks, many of these works do possess enough musical interest to make a small sampler acceptable in the sonic museum, in concert performance.

The sonic museum is an institution, then, like the art museum, which serves two different kinds of artwork to the same basic end. It is no coincidence, I imagine, that both came into being at the same time as the very concept of an autonomous aesthetic experience, or aesthetic perception itself. For both seem, primarily, to be showcases for the aesthetic, places specially designed for aesthetic contemplation: in the one case the heard aesthetic; in the other, the seen. But each serves, in its own aesthetic domain, two kinds of artworks: those, before the great divide, that were made with settings other than the public museum in mind; and those after, with just that viewing environment as the intended one.

In serving our aesthetic needs, if I may so put it, the sonic museum can give us works to enjoy from before the great divide that we would have no access to otherwise. I don't want to wait for a royal water party on the Thames to hear the *Water Music*, and if I do, I am not likely to be on the guest list anyway. Nor can I hear a chest of viols in an English country estate. And it will be a long while before there will be an opportunity to hear Handel's Coronation Anthems in the grand setting and on the occasion for which they were designed: indeed, the interval one has to wait becomes longer and longer as life expectancy increases. But I can hear them all in that great democratic institution, the sonic museum, for the price of a ticket, with that sacrifice of authenticity that one always must suffer when one is hearing a mixed-media musical work—for that, in fact, is what I am claiming all music is before the great divide—in a concert version.

How great an effort should we make to restore, as an aesthetic end in itself, authentic performance as it was, in its many varieties, before the great divide? Would it be a good thing to do? Perhaps, to some extent, it would. But like any other of the authenticities we have already discussed, it would be subject to a kind of aesthetic "cost-benefit analysis"; and we must leave that inherently normative question for later on, with the preliminary observation that, however that analysis comes out, the sonic museum is not likely to be rejected as a musical institution, even for the performance of the music that preceded it. For its benefits, like those of its visual counterpart, the art museum, are too palpable to be easily overtaken by any movement to a more "environmental" performance practice, no matter how well intended or historically well justified.

The value question awaits us. But now is the right point in the argument to make good on an earlier promissory note. To that I now turn.

. . .

I said, it will be recalled, that we might have to amend slightly the blanket claim that music composed after the great divide, and expressly for the sonic museum, was a wholly sonic music, with no visual element at all. That amendment is now in order.

The sonic museum, I have been arguing, is expressly designed as a showcase for musical sound. But surely one brings eyes as well as ears to a performance there; one watches as well as listens, and, indeed, if one didn't, it might well be asked why one went to the sonic museum at all rather than listen to the performance on the radio or on a recording.

Of course there are many quite plausible and quite philosophically uninteresting answers to the question of why one was obliged or wanted to attend a live performance rather than tune in or turn on. The performance was not broadcast. You wanted to hear a piece that has never been recorded, or never recorded by those particular performers. You wanted to have an evening out. You wanted to see your friends. And so on.

But there is a deeper question lurking here that has at least occasionally been asked, and it is this: is there any *aesthetic* difference between a live performance of a musical work and a perfect sound reproduction of it? Indeed, this is no longer a *Gedankenexperiment* but very close to being a fait accompli, in the form of the compact disc. Has the modern high-fidelity sound system made the live concert obsolete?

If there is aesthetically more to the music composed after the great divide, and expressly for the sonic museum, than merely its audible part, and if that aesthetic something is the *visual act* of performing, then we have a way of saving the live performance of such music from obsolescence (at least until the perfect visual recording arrives). For what the sound system cannot capture is the visual aspect of performance, or its "social" aspect, in the form of audience involvement; and if that is even a small part of the aesthetic musical object, then the live performance will always be more aesthetically authentic, more aesthetically complete, than the sound reproduction can be.[13]

But *is* the visual aspect of a musical performance, in the sonic museum, an aesthetic part of the musical work? That is the crucial question; and it is a very difficult question to answer with any great conviction. Certainly the musician and music lover want very much to think that the live performance of, say, Brahms's Fourth Symphony is something aesthetically more than even the perfect recording of the work. Is this just a nostalgic longing after an outmoded past, or is there musical substance to the feeling of loss?

Well, as I say, I cannot answer this question either way with any great conviction. But there is this to consider in the way of at least a tentative argument: if you have found my previous argument at all plausible, to the effect that music before the great divide had an importantly aesthetic visual component, you will at least not be inclined to reject out of hand the suggestion that music composed after the great divide might have a visual component too. You may think it absurd to suggest that seeing performances in the sonic museum can be part of a symphony's aesthetic character; but you will not think it absurd because the aesthetic component is a *seen* component of an art that is commonly thought of as a purely *sonic* art. You are prepared now for that possibility, at least—that is, the possibility of a visual aesthetic component to the musical work of art.

But go a little bit further with me: observe that the *one* visual component of *all* music, before and after the great divide, that has endured is the sight of the performers playing and singing. Of all the dancers in the dance,

---

[13] Of course, a video sound reproduction will capture the whole shebang; but there will, nevertheless, have to be a live performance there for it to capture.

Authenticity as Practice

these have always been there. Can we know *these* dancers from the dance? In all the multimedia events of which music was a part, before the great divide—the coronation, the religious ceremony, the social dance, the water party, divertimentos al fresco, domestic music making, and so on—various people have "played their parts." Yet always the musicians as well. Are we to say that all these others were part of the choreography, and only the musicians, the very sine qua non, were not? Who is more intimately connected, in his or her motions, with the sound of the art than those who turn the notes into sounds? Are we to say that the celebrant of the mass is part of the visual aesthetic but the singer is not? That is a hard saying.

Here, then, is a better way to look at things. Music, before the great divide, was a richly ritualistic, participatory, "choreographed" art of which sound was an important but by no means the only aesthetic part.[14] With the advent of the sonic museum, whose major purpose is to display as effectively as possible the sound of music, the visual—ritualistic, social, choreographed—part has been cut to the bone, abstractly stylized, if you will, into one standard practice: men in tuxedos, women in evening gowns, playing or singing or moving their arms. But stylized and spare though it be, pale reflection of a water party on the Thames, or the Coronation Mass by candlelight in the Salzburg Cathedral, it remains that part of the music that is, and always has been, for the eyes. And in its reverberations of rituals past, it may have more aesthetic significance for us than at first might appear.[15]

Seen in this way, then, the real sonic museum—its ultimate expression—is not the concert hall but the perfect sound recording, where the visual has indeed been excised completely. For the concert hall still retains that vestige of the visual ceremony of music that is represented by the players and singers themselves, plying their various musical trades. And if my argument is correct, that visual aspect of performance practice is not merely of archeological interest to the nostalgic but part of the genuine, "authentic" musical work and musical experience.

· · ·

We might represent the aspects, both visual and aural, or any other you like, as a kind of cone. At the apex is the sound and visual appearance of

[14]I have discussed the ritualistic and participatory aspects of music, from a different viewpoint, in "Music and the Liberal Education," in Kivy, *The Fine Art of Repetition*.
[15]Ibid.

Authenticity as Practice

performance in the sonic museum: the limiting case. As the cone flares out, more and more aspects of performance practice are included. And this leads to a problem. How wide do we want the mouth of the cone to become? In other words, how widely do we want to construe the part of performance practice, before the great divide, that we think it sensible to restore, as an end in itself, in the name of historical authenticity? To put it in a nutshell, Bach's musicians wore wigs. Is *that* a part of an authentic performance practice?

The "wig problem," if I may so call it, is really this. In opening up authenticity in performance practice to the visual—in construing it not merely as sonic means but as end in itself—have I not become the easy victim of a *reductio ad absurdum*? If wigs, frock coats, and buckle shoes were part of the eighteenth-century musical scene, must I not insist that no authentic performance can be without them? Is this not a *reductio* of the notion that an aesthetic part of authentic performance practice can be a visual part? It would seem that, by claiming so, we have opened the floodgates to a rush of absurdities. Is there a reasoned way to keep the sense, and keep out the nonsense—a reasoned way to separate the aesthetic from the archeological?

The answer to this latter question is in the affirmative, I think, and really quite familiarly old-fashioned. If *interpretation* is a reasoned enterprise, then there is a reasoned way to separate the archeological part of visual performance practice from the aesthetic part, just as there is of separating any other unwanted way of performing music from what one thinks is an aesthetically correct way of doing the business. If you can give me a viable *interpretation* of Bach's Brandenburg Concertos that includes in it the necessity or desirability of performing them in wigs, then I will be ready to accept wigs as part of a historically authentic performance practice for them, just as, because you can give me a reasoned aesthetic interpretation of Mozart's Coronation Mass that makes performance in a candlelit Salzburg Cathedral, or other such place, more musically authentic than one in the sonic museum, I accept it as more musically authentic, even though I have accepted visual elements as musically relevant ones. I can give a plausible story about how the structure of the Coronation Mass and its shining musical surface have been aesthetically fashioned for ceremonial performance in a place of worship of a certain kind. I can give no such plausible story of how the Brandenburg Concertos were musically

Authenticity as Practice

102

fashioned for musicians wearing wigs. They could be wearing bowler hats or baseball caps for all that it matters aesthetically.

Now, perhaps you find this a disappointing answer. Here we are again, stuck with "interpretation"—that problematic, obstreperous concept that no one can really quite get a handle on, or get quite right. Well, we *are* stuck with it: that is the human condition. We have seen before, and we shall be seeing again, that no decision about authentic performance can be made, free of making interpretations about "how the music goes." And such interpretations are full of all those difficulties that crowd in upon us when we make "aesthetic" judgments, judgments of "taste," and the like. If you don't like these rules, don't play this game.

I cannot give a persuasive argument, a priori, to rule out wigs as part of an authentic performance practice for eighteenth-century music. All I can do is challenge any would-be wig supporter to give me an interpretation—tell me a reasonable story—according to which wearing wigs makes an aesthetic difference. And when I have such an interpretation, such a story in hand, I can evaluate it the way musical interpretations are customarily evaluated. My intuition is that no viable wig interpretation is in the offing. But that is just an intuition, and worth only what intuitions are in such matters.

But perhaps it will be objected that because, after all, whether or not wigs are aesthetically necessary *is* open to interpretation, and interpretation is notoriously hard to establish firmly one way or the other, I have still left myself open to a *reductio* in allowing visual features to intrude on the musical object; for one can never say with total assurance that *any* wig interpretation is absolutely off the wall, because one can never say that any interpretation at all is absolutely off the wall. But the problem with this objection is that, if allowed, it proves far too much, I would imagine, for even the objector to swallow. In fact, not only does it show that allowing visual features to be part of the musical work leaves one open to a *reductio ad absurdum*; it shows, in effect, that allowing *aural* features has a similar result.

It is equally absurd, one would think, to claim that the sound of horses' hoofs clattering by during a piano recital of works by Mozart is part of an authentic performance practice as to make that claim about the wearing of wigs; yet *both* were a part of the eighteenth-century musical scene, and *both* were to be expected by any composer of the period. And the only way

Authenticity as Practice

to rule out the former, as the latter, is to challenge the maker of such a claim to provide an interpretation of the music on which such noise comes out to be a part of the musical fabric and, if such an interpretation be tendered, to show, with as much persuasion as these matters allow, that the interpretation is implausible. More one cannot do. And if it be claimed that, because no interpretation, no matter how crazy, can be absolutely refuted, horses' noises cannot be confidently ruled out as part of Mozart's music for piano solo, one has reduced to the same "absurdity" the view that sound is an aesthetic part of the musical work as the wig argument is supposed to do for the view that the visual might be. This, I venture to say, is a *reductio* of the *reductio*.

It is important to bear in mind here that I do not wish to foreclose on the real possibility of actually finding a wholly plausible interpretation on which what might first appear to be an absurd candidate for a visual part of some musical work actually turns out to be quite sensible after all. Let me adduce a possible example of this from a familiar musical work: Haydn's "Farewell" Symphony (no. 45, in F♯ minor). Most music lovers know the story. Haydn's musicians were obliged to spend the summer months in Prince Nicolaus Esterhazy's Hungarian castle, Esterháza, without their wives and families, obviously a hardship for them. In 1772, the prince extended the season in Esterháza, which usually came to a close at the end of October, beyond the musicians' endurance. They appealed to Haydn for assistance. In the words of the composer's early biographer, Griesinger:

> Haydn had the inspiration of writing a symphony (which is
> known under the title of "Farewell" Symphony), in which one
> instrument after the other is silent. This symphony was performed
> as soon as possible in front of the Prince, and each of the musicians
> was instructed, as soon as his part was finished, to blow out his
> candle and to leave with his instrument under his arm. The Prince
> and the company understood the point of this pantomime at once,
> and the next day came the order to leave Esterhaz.[16]

No one is likely to object to the assertion that a really authentic performance of the last movement of the "Farewell" Symphony has to include some version of the little *scena* that Haydn had in mind when he com-

[16] Robbins Landon, *Haydn*, p. 79.

posed the work, even though, of course, it is a completely satisfying piece of purely instrumental music without it; for the last movement of the work is, after all, supposed to accompany a staged little "dramatic plot." And I have seen performances of it in which the musicians do, indeed, carry out the intended choreography, getting up from their seats in the appropriate time, flicking off their stand lights, and sauntering off stage, instruments in hand.

"Flicking off their stand lights?" you can hear the purist indignantly intoning. "Haydn did not score the Symphony no. 45 for electric stand lights! He scored it for *candles*! And it cannot be authentically performed without them."

On the face of it, this sounds suspiciously like a wig argument. What aesthetic difference could it possibly make whether Haydn's little pantomime is performed with candles or with modern electric lights. Actually, I want to make an interpretation of the symphony on which it does make a difference; and it is an interpretation that is based not only on plausible musical considerations but on a real musical experience of the difference as well.

Many years ago I saw a short film of the "Farewell" Symphony's last movement, played by musicians in eighteenth-century costumes, wigs and all, in a beautiful eighteenth-century concert room. They performed the accustomed ritual, down to the blowing out of the candles on their stands; and my memory of that film suggests to me that it does make a difference—a visual, musical difference—whether one switches off an electric light or blows out a candle. Here is why. The physical motion one goes through in rising from one's seat with an instrument under one's arm, bending over a candle, shielding it with the unoccupied hand, and gently blowing it out is necessarily a languid, graceful motion: if it isn't, one is quite likely, I imagine, to set one's wig on fire. On the other hand, getting up from one's seat and flicking off an electric light switch is accomplished in a rather quick, impulsive, jerky maneuver. And the aesthetic fact is that Haydn's music, a graceful Adagio into which the Presto finale segues, is written to accompany, obviously, a languid, graceful motion, not an impulsive jerky one. The choreography of candle blowing is right for the piece; the choreography of light switching completely wrong, because Haydn's rhythm, and the whole thematic, expressive character of the ending, are fashioned for the former, not the latter.

Authenticity as Practice

Is it absurd to say that candles are more authentic than electric lights—
not just more archeologically authentic but more *musically* authentic—in
a proper performance of the "Farewell" Symphony? Is it absurd to say
that they make an aesthetic difference? For the reason given in the preceding paragraph I do not think so. Of course, it is absurd to mess about
with candles on the music stands in Carnegie Hall. I am not saying that
the aesthetic payoff of candle blowing in the "Farewell" Symphony is
worth the trouble.[17] What I do mean to suggest is that the initial absurdity
of any claim about what might be authentic performance practice of the
visual kind—the "end-in-itself" kind—must, like any other claim about
how a piece of music should be played, undergo the "twofold test of interpretation": producing an interpretation, in the first place, that implies the
"absurdity"; and determining whether that interpretation is plausible. In
the absence of either, it would seem, we have a right to assume that what
appears absurd is just that, and can be dismissed until its proponent deliv-
ers the goods. This, I think, disposes of the "wig problem" once and for
all, and, with it, the claim that allowing visual elements into "pure" musical works will open the floodgates to archeological nonsense.

·   ·   ·

To summarize, I have examined in this chapter two different kinds of historically authentic performance practice: the "means-ends" kind and the
"end-in-itself" kind. Understood in the former way, performance practice
in itself raises no particular conceptual problems. It is quite simply the
means, whatever they might turn out to be, best suited to the production
of historically authentic sound or the realization of the composer's performing wishes and intentions. Disputes can certainly arise, as we shall
see in Part II, as to whether or not some sonic or intentional end is produced by some suggested "authentic" practice. But that casts no shadow
on the integrity of the concept of historically authentic practice itself so
understood.

Historically authentic performance practice viewed as an end in itself,
however, does raise conceptual issues; and that is because, viewed as end
in itself, it must needs be viewed as appealing to sense modalities other
than the ear; for to the extent that it does appeal to the ear, it is sonic

[17] I suppose a good compromise, with absolute authenticity in this regard, would be for
the musicians to turn off their electric lights in a more languid and graceful manner, in
rhythm with the music.

means, not end in itself. But that is exactly why the concept of performance practice as end in itself is conceptually problematic. For because music—with the exception of opera, music drama, and ballet—is customarily thought of as a sonic art, any suggestion that it can also aesthetically appeal to sense modalities other than the sense of hearing is bound to be contentious and problematic.

Confining myself to the visual aspects of performance practice that might possibly qualify as proper aesthetic parts of the musical work, because even a philosopher willing to take some risks in this regard is not likely to countenance musical tastes, smells, and "feels," I have argued that, at least before the advent of the modern concert hall, some very palpable aspects of what we might have seen in a musical performance can indeed plausibly be considered aesthetic, which is to say *musical*, content. I have said nothing, however, about the desirability or lack thereof of vigorously pursuing historically authentic visual performance practice as an end in itself. This question will be taken up later. But before such normative questions are broached, one further "authenticity" awaits our scrutiny.

Authenticity   as   Practice

⊙

CHAPTER FIVE

The Other Authenticity

We have examined in the preceding pages three candidates for the title of "historically authentic performance": authenticity as authorial intention, authenticity as contemporary sound, and authenticity as contemporary practice. But we noticed, also, in our preliminary examination of the concept of authenticity itself, that there seemed to be another sense besides the historical ones in which a performance might be said to be "authentic": the sense of authentically one's own, emanating from one's own person—authentic, in other words, as opposed to derivative or imitative. It will be my purpose in this chapter to examine with care this other, ostensibly nonhistorical sense of the authentic performance and to inquire as well into the possibility of either a connection or an inherent incompatibility between historical authenticity and this other kind, which I shall call, from now on, "personal authenticity."

What exactly am I saying about a musical performance, then, when I call it authentic in the sense of being "personally authentic"? And what sort of a thing would a performance have to be to be correctly so called?

. . .

When a certain well-known participant in a recent political scandal announced contritely that he had become a "born-again" Christian, many people would have said, I think, that his statement and expressive demeanor did not have the ring of authenticity. Either he was lying and emotively posing for obvious reasons of self-interest, or he was so self-deceived as to be rightly described as lying and posing to himself. In a word, his statement and expression seemed "insincere."

Here, then, is one very quick answer to the question both of what we might be ascribing to a musical performance by calling it personally authentic and of what kind of thing a performance would have to be to correctly bear such an appellation. We would be ascribing *sincerity* to it; and, of course, it would have to be the kind of thing that could or could not be sincere—either an *assertion* of some opinion or the *expression* of some emotion, or both, as the announcement of the exposed political gentleman was an *assertion* that he had converted and, at the same time, an *expression* of his contrition. But does it make sense to think of a musical performance as the expression of an emotion or an assertion at all? What emotion does a performance express? And what could it possibly assert?

Putting aside these questions for a moment, let us ask, first, whether we have any supporting reason for thinking that performances might be either assertions or emotive expressions besides the fact, already acknowledged, that we ascribe personal authenticity to them and that we could correctly do so if, but not necessarily only if, they were either assertions or expressions. Well, as we observed in the first chapter, performers are customarily referred to as "performing artists." And if performers are indeed *artists*, then it seems to follow directly that what they create *qua* artists—namely, performances—must be artworks. And because some artworks are thought by some people to be complex assertions, and by others to be complex emotive expressions, we do have further evidence that performances, being artworks, might also be assertions or emotive expressions.

Now it might, of course, be the case that the works of art we call musical performances are either expressions or assertions (or both) independently of their being works of art—that, in other words, the fact (if it is one) that they are expressions or assertions has nothing whatever to do with the fact (if it is one) that they are works of art. But if that does not strike one as immediately implausible, it certainly would begin to seem implausible as soon as one further concluded that the sincerity of the performance—its personal authenticity—would accrue to it not *qua* artwork but *qua* something else, because its sincerity or personal authenticity accrues to its assertive or expressive aspect, and by present hypothesis, its assertive or expressive aspect is not an aspect of it *qua* work of art, not an artistic aspect.

Because it seems implausible to me that performances being works of art has nothing to do with their being personally authentic, I am going to assume that the explanation we are now considering for how performances can be personally authentic is as follows. Performances are works of art. Works of art are either expressions of emotions or complex assertions of some kind, or both. To be personally authentic is to be sincere. Assertions and expressions are either sincere or insincere. So they are the kinds of things that can be personally authentic. Since performances are works of art, they are either expressions or assertions (or both) and, hence, the kinds of things of which it makes sense to predicate sincerity, which is to say, personal authenticity.

I shall treat the preceding explanation, however, for convenience as two explanations: the one depending upon the view that artworks are expressions, the other depending upon the view that they are assertions. I shall examine these views separately. If either view turns out to be plausible, the explanation of personal authenticity in performance as *sincerity* goes through. If both turn out to be false, it fails, and we shall have to try our luck elsewhere. Let's look at emotive expression first.

·   ·   ·

That art, *tout court*, can be defined as expression—the by now notorious as well as familiar "expression theory of art"—is not something necessarily or usefully discussed in these pages. There is no need to argue from the premise that all art is by definition expression to the conclusion that musical performance, being art, must be expression as well; nor need we even argue the weaker claim that performance is by definition expression. All we need claim, to make the point in question, is that performance is, among other things, expression and, therefore, that as expression , it can be sincere or insincere, personally authentic or inauthentic. That, then, is the claim we shall be examining.

There are a number of ways in which we might judge a musical perfor-

The Other Authenticity

mance good or unsatisfactory from the point of view of "expression." Sometimes we say that a performer has just played the notes, but without expression. And we sometimes say that the performer has failed to bring out the "expression"—that is, the expressive qualities—in the music. These ways of talking about performances certainly are well worth careful analysis. But that would not be to the present purpose; for neither of them seems to touch the question of sincerity. They are certainly both failures in performance; but neither seems a failure in sincerity. One can fail to play expressively or fail to bring out the expression "in" the music yet not be in emotional "bad faith." There seems to be no contradiction in saying that someone, in complete sincerity, played inexpressively: indeed, an inexpressive person would do so, if he or she were sincere in that respect. And a performer might, quite sincerely, miss completely the expressive features of a musical work or fail, because of ineptitude, to bring them out.

In order for the concept of emotive sincerity to do any work for us in explicating personal authenticity in performance there must be an emotion that the performer feels in performance but fails to express. And, furthermore, the failure must be due not to ineptitude but to purposeful dissimulation: deceit. For a failure to express can be a case of insincerity only if the person doing the deed gives the impression of expressing an emotion that he or she in fact does not have, or conceals an emotion that he or she might in fact have by showing no expression at all.

But once the matter is put this way it then becomes very difficult to see how the concept of sincerity or insincerity is going to help in explicating the concept of the personally authentic performance. For it is very difficult to see just what the emotion is that the performer might feel, and disguise, and that might have anything to do with his or her performance being a bad one. Yet the concept of personal authenticity is a value concept, which is to say, we are necessarily saying something good about a performance by calling it personally authentic, and something bad when calling it the opposite. And this value dimension must be preserved in any analysis of the concept of personal authenticity in performance.

What might we say the performer is feeling, and fails or succeeds at expressing, that would fill the bill, that would give us a handle on personal authenticity? Clearly, whatever we say it is must have some perceived relevance to the music, and to its correct or optimal performance, or the performer's failure to express it will have no reasonable connection with our evaluation of the performance. If a pianist is feeling sad, because her friend has died, and fails to express her sadness in playing a recital, we would hardly consider that relevant one way or the other to the question of whether she had played well or not. Nor would we be inclined to call the "failure" a failure—certainly not an example of "insincerity."

One obvious candidate for what the performer must feel and express might be the feeling or feelings that the music is expressive of—the emotions "in" the music. The further claim then would be, presumably, that a necessary condition for a proper or good performance of a musical work must be the performer's actually experiencing (during the performance) the emotions "expressed" in the music (however one might understand the way in which musical emotions are "expressed"). As a recent writer puts it, "the music will have the character he [the composer] wants only if the performer is in the proper frame of mind . . . ," which often means that "the composition will be properly performed only if the performer is in a kind of state of fury, animation, fervor, affection, sympathy, joy, distress, anxiety, hope, buoyancy, and so on . . . ," these all being "personal states *of mind* . . . always expressed or phrased as predicates or properties *of the music.*"[1] Sincerity, then, on such a view, would consist in the performer's feeling sad where the music is sad (and not some other emotion or no emotion at all), angry where the music is angry (and not some other emotion or no emotion at all), and so on, for whatever emotions the music might be expressive of; and insincerity would, of course, be the reverse—feeling some other emotion or no emotion at all where the music is sad, some other emotion or no emotion at all where the music is angry.

The first problem with such a view, although perhaps not fatal to it, is that whatever the congruity or incongruity might properly be said to be between the emotion in the music and the emotion in the performer, they are not literally sincerity and insincerity. If insincerity in emotive expression is feigning an emotion you do not have, or concealing an emotion altogether, then the performer has not necessarily done either by failing to feel an emotion in the music that he or she is playing. If I feel happy and express my happiness in playing a piece of sad music, then I have been perfectly sincere even though I have committed the sin (if it is one) of having my feelings out of phase with the feelings of the music.

[1] Aschenbrenner, *Analysis of Appraisive Characterizations*, p. 167.

The Other Authenticity

To this it might be replied that if the performer's feelings being out of phase with those in the music is not *literally* a case of expressive insincerity, it is enough like it to be called that at least in a metaphorical or attenuated sense, and that that is all one requires for present purposes. For the notion of sincerity is meant here as a gloss of the notion, in which we are principally interested, of personal authenticity in performance. And it does seem as if one might plausibly construe a performer's being out of phase, in his or her own feelings, with the feelings in the music as a kind of personal inauthenticity: feeling one thing while trying to project to an audience something else entirely.

But we are bound to wonder *why* it is a bad thing to feel sad while playing a happy passage, or happy while playing a sad one. To be insincere, in the literal sense of that word, is, except under mitigating circumstances, a moral defect, whereas there hardly seems to be a moral lapse involved in feeling happy and playing sad music. Why should morality come into the question at all, anyway? As I believe Humphrey Bogart once said, the only *duty* a performer has to his or her audience is to give a good performance.

Indeed, Bogart's remark merits a closer look, for it may be something beyond merely a *bon mot*. Assuming the performer's *only* "duty" is a good performance, then it would seem to follow that the performer's having his or her emotions in phase with the emotions in the music, if it is a good at all, must be an instrumental good—a state of affairs that is good because it is productive of a good performance. But then the question is quite naturally going to arise as to whether, as a matter of fact, such emotive involvement with the music is conducive to good performance and whether, furthermore, it is even a possible goal—whether, that is to say, one can really induce in oneself the emotive states ranging from anger, despondency, and melancholy through joy and exaltation that a work like, say, the *Hammerklavier* Sonata traces in its expressive progress. (How could one put oneself into those vastly diverse states voluntarily and on demand, in the course of fifty minutes on the concert stage? Can the *music* do that to one? Many, including myself, have come to deny music those powers; and those who have claimed them have never given us a plausible account of how the thing might be accomplished.)

As for the claim that feeling the emotions expressed in a piece of music might facilitate in any way the performance of it, I am reminded of an

The Other Authenticity

interview I once heard of the great Fritz Reiner, between two acts of
Tristan und Isolde, which he was conducting at the old Metropolitan Opera House. The interviewer was naive enough to ask Maestro Reiner
whether it wasn't a truly sublime experience to feel, *as he must*, the great
volcano of emotions that the opera spewed forth, in its tempestuous
course from the Prelude to the *Liebestodt*. Reiner's admirably pragmatic
reply—predictable enough to anyone who was fortunate enough to see
him ply his trade—was: "How could I *conduct* if I were experiencing those
emotions?" And if one were to reply that Leonard Bernstein was as emotional in his conducting as Reiner was calm and deliberate, I would suggest that we be very sure to distinguish between displaying one's enthusiasm for the music and for what one is doing, and being angry when the
music is angry, melancholy when the music is melancholy, and so on.
Even if it were possible literally to feel the emotions of which the *Hammerklavier* is expressive, one after the other, while performing it, such an
emotive feat would hardly seem conducive to the things one must do in
playing such a technically difficult work on the piano before a demanding
and discerning audience. Indeed, it would seem disastrous. But is it even
possible?

The idea that a performer could, in the words previously quoted,
arouse herself to "a kind of state of fury, animation, fervor, affection, sympathy, joy, distress, anxiety, hope, buoyancy" in the process of performing
a musical work runs counter to everything that recent philosophical
analysis has revealed to us about the structure of our emotions and how
they are really aroused, and is counter to plain common sense as well.
Emotions are aroused by the situations in which we find ourselves and by
the beliefs, true or false, that, in those circumstances, we come to have.
And these emotions are "intentional": they take objects. I am angry *at*
somebody because I have a belief that appropriately arouses that emotion. Such a process cannot answer, on instantaneous demand, to the human will. Whatever power we do have over our emotions must be exercised over fairly long periods of time and by indirection. I can no more
decide here and now to feel an emotion, and then feel it straightaway,
than I can decide to believe or to digest. But such is just what I would have
to do to fulfill the requirements of performance sincerity that the theory
under discussion implies. And that is just a plain, palpable impossibility,
bordering on the absurd.

The   Other   Authenticity

Now, there may well be other ways in which a performer might be correctly described as emotionally sincere or insincere. But it is not my purpose to try to canvass all the possibilities. I have looked at the one that most readily comes to mind and is most easily found in the literature, from the eighteenth century to the twentieth. This one anyway, it seems to me, comes to nothing. So I want now to leave the concept of emotive sincerity behind and go on to what might seem, on first reflection, to be an even less plausible alternative, namely, the sincerity of *assertion*. I say that this might seem an even less plausible alternative because, of course, it is much harder to imagine music as asserting anything than it is to imagine it as the expression of emotions. Nevertheless, a recent and very ingenious account of musical performance has made just that former claim: that music is a form of statement, and performance a kind of assertion. It is a possibility, then, not to be dismissed out of hand; and I turn to it now, in my search for a possible way to construe performances as sincere or insincere.

.   .   .

Thomas Carson Mark makes three major claims about musical performance, two rather surprising, in support of a third, unsurprising but extremely important, in which I acquiesce, that a performance—that is to say, the "thing" the performer produces in the act of performing—is a work of art. The first of these surprising and supporting claims is that the art of performing is very much like the speech act of "quoting," the second that the act of performing is, at the same time, very much like the speech act of "asserting" as well. In short, a musical performance (the product) is an artwork in the producing of which the performer both musically "quotes" something and musically "asserts" what he or she is quoting. But although Mark's view can be thus briefly stated, it cannot be fully appreciated or seem at all plausible until at least some of the details are laid before the reader.

Mark places three conditions on quotation: "For an utterance to be a quotation of S, it is necessary (1) that the words uttered be the precise words that constitute S. Furthermore, it is necessary (2) that the speaker intend that his words be the same as those which constitute S. . . . And . . . it must be the case (3) that it is the intention which effectively brings about the congruence of the utterance and S."[2]

[2] Mark, "The Philosophy of Piano Playing," p. 305.

The Other Authenticity

115

Moving quickly on to musical performance, Mark asserts: "The three conditions [on quotation] have exact analogues in performance. Obviously, in order to perform a Chopin nocturne, I must, first, produce a sequence of sounds identical with that prescribed by the score. . . . Secondly, I must intend that the notes I play be those of the nocturne. . . . Finally, my intention must effectively bring about the identity."[3]

But although musical performance may be a form of musical quotation (so understood), that cannot be the whole story. For, as can easily be shown, it is not a sufficient condition, because there is musical quotation that is not performance: "The professor of a course in chromatic harmony used to introduce his examples with the words 'When Brahms says *this* . . . ,' playing a few bars of (in this case) Brahms. He was quoting Brahms . . . but not performing, and his quotation was not a performance even when (as occasionally happened) he played the notes of an entire composition instead of just a few bars."[4]

What, then, beyond musical quotation, makes an act one of musical performance? On Mark's view, here is how the story goes.

When I quote, it is received doctrine to say that I *mention* what I quote, I do not *use* it. And this is, indeed, often the case. But, as Mark points out, I can also use a quotation to make an assertion; and when I do that I have quoted and asserted in one and the same utterance; or, to put it another way, the vocables are both the result of the speech act of quoting and the speech act of asserting. Thus, to use one of Mark's examples:

> Suppose that in some sort of contest I am getting the worst of it. My opponent asks me "Give up?" I reply "I have not yet begun to fight." I am obviously quoting. But, surely, I am also asserting something; that I am doing so is clear since my utterance would normally count as a *reply* to the question asked by my opponent, which it could not do if the situation included no assertion of mine. . . . Thus I assert, doing so by means of quoting.[5]

Performing, Mark wants to maintain, is a close analogue of using a quotation to assert, as in the preceding example: "Performance of a work of music is the simultaneous quotation and assertion of that work. Quo-

[3] Ibid., p. 306.
[4] Ibid., pp. 306–7.
[5] Ibid., p. 309.

The Other Authenticity

tation and assertion represent two different sorts of requirement, both necessary, and jointly sufficient for performance."[6]

But two further questions must be answered before we will have a reasonably complete account of what a performance is. First, what exactly is it to "assert," and, more particularly, what exactly is it to "assert" a musical work? Second, what role does interpretation play in all this? For performers are frequently referred to as "interpreters," and their performances as "interpretations" of the works performed.

As for what assertion is in the ordinary case of asserting in a natural language, "The principal requirement is an intentional one: the person must utter the words with the intention of their being *taken* as an assertion. . . . To take an utterance as an assertion is to take it as something which purports, at least, to state some fact or give an account of how things are."[7]

Now, this concept of assertion cannot, of course, literally apply to the musical cases, for it is very hard to see how a musical phrase could be literally true or false. Nevertheless, Mark thinks that there is enough of an analogy between what a speaker does when he asserts and what a pianist does when she performs to give sense to the notion of performance as a form of musical assertion. He writes in this regard that

> the performer intends that the sounds he produces will be taken as having cogency, as articulating how things musically are. Music is not true in the literal sense in which statements in language can be true, but I claim that as listeners we do distinguish between musical events which have a kind of authority and musical events which do not, and that our attitudes in the two cases are much like our attitudes toward sentences we take as purporting to be true as distinguished from sentences we do not take as purporting to be true. . . . The intention of a performer—the intention that makes his production of sounds a performance—is that his listeners will take the sounds produced to have this authority, this claim to attention which is analogous to the claim made on our belief by sentences that purport to be true. Performances, then, are very closely analogous to assertions.[8]

[6] Ibid., p. 313.
[7] Ibid., p. 310.
[8] Ibid., p. 312.

The Other Authenticity

But what now of interpretation? Well, put quite simply, in order to assert by quoting, I must have some idea of what the words mean that I am quoting, else I cannot, obviously, assert anything by quoting them. That is to say, I must *interpret* what I quote in order to know what I am asserting in quoting it. And analogously for musical performance: "Granted the similarity between assertion and performance, we can say that one cannot perform a work without attributing to it some 'meaning' (though the notion of 'meaning' is also not exactly the same as in language)."[9] To "assert" a musical work, then, and not merely to quote it, I must place a musical interpretation on it—opine what is musically happening in it; know how it goes. Hence the epithet "interpretation" as applied to a musical performance.

We now have a pretty good idea of why Mark wants to call musical performances both quotations and assertions. But we have yet to connect these two claims with the final and less contentious one, that they are also works of art. Making this connection will complete the account.

If we take a work of art to be an artifactual collection of aesthetically important properties, then it seems to follow that if a performance has aesthetically important properties of its own, apart from those of the work it quotes, it must be a work of art itself. But surely it must have its own aesthetically important properties. For: "If the only aesthetically important contribution comes from the composer then any minimally competent performance of a given work would be the aesthetic equivalent of any other, which is obviously false."[10] So it looks very much as if because musical performances do have aesthetically important features other than those in the works they are performances of, they are indeed works of art. And this conclusion, Mark points out, is quite congenial to his way of looking at performances: that is, as assertions or statements. For "works of art can be likened to statements: works of art can be thought of as entities which are accepted, in certain social or insitutional contexts, as making statements. . . ."[11]

We are now in a position to conclude that performances are works of art in virtue of being aesthetically important statements in themselves and not merely quotations of aesthetically important statements. "When

[9] Ibid., p. 317.
[10] Ibid., p. 319.
[11] Ibid., pp. 319–20.

The Other Authenticity

we have a performance of a work of music we have, thus, *two* assertions: there is the work of music itself, which is a statement or assertion by the composer, and there is the additional assertion which is the performance." Or, put another way: "The performance is not simply an interpretation (though it requires or involves one) or a presentation (though it requires that too since it includes producing an instance of the work): it is *another* work of art."[12]

* * *

Our goal, in laying out this elegant and sophisticated account of musical performance, it will be remembered, was to see if we could get, with it, a handle on what it might mean to call a performance personally authentic. That goal, at least insofar as it can be achieved through Mark's account, is now in our grasp. For we can now see that, on that account, it would make perfect sense to say that one of the defects in, for example, the playing of a Beethoven piano sonata might be "insincerity," in the form of playing the work without really believing it: in effect, quoting but not asserting—which, strictly speaking, would make the playing not a bad performance but a nonperformance, because assertion is a necessary condition for performance, and an insincere utterance to the effect that something is the case would not really be an "assertion" (properly so called) at all.

Indeed, Mark has really been sniffing around this point himself, where he says, "We use such words as 'convincing,' 'persuasive,' 'sincere,' 'assertive,' and their opposites [to describe musical performances]. Music teachers urge pupils to 'play it as if you believed it,' a comment which we can think of as elicited by a performance having an effect analogous to 'p but I don't believe that p.'"[13] Thus, whether one thinks of insincere playing as a bad performance or as a nonperformance, Mark's account gives us a framework in which to put sincerity and insincerity that makes a good deal of sense. And it then becomes easy to see, within this framework, what a personally authentic or inauthentic performance would be, as the concepts of sincerity and insincerity, in the form of sincere or insincere musical assertions, make the former distinction perfectly. On a Markian view of performance, the distinction between the personally authentic and the personally inauthentic is coextensive with the distinction

---

[12] Ibid., p. 320.
[13] Ibid., p. 313.

The   Other   Authenticity

between the sincere and insincere playing of a work, which is to say, a playing of a work that is both quotation and assertion and a playing of a work that is only quotation.

This is an elegant and rich solution of our problem. And I am in no position right now to refute it. But I do reject it, as not being the course that I would find congenial to follow—and I do so for two related reasons.

The first reason for my rejecting Mark's way is that, at least in its present form, it does not make clear enough to me just exactly what the concept of personal authenticity really is. Here is the trouble I am having. We wanted to know, at the outset, what it might mean for a performance to be personally authentic. The suggestion was made that it might mean "sincere," if a musical performance were a statement or assertion. Mark has argued that that is just what a performance is. But it is not *exactly* what it is; for assertions or statements are *literally* true or false, but musical performances cannot be. So when we say that a performance is an "assertion," we are using "assertion" here in an attenuated or metaphorical sense, and so must we be when we say a person who played a musical "assertion" but did not "believe" it was not being "sincere." "Assertion" and "believe" and "sincere" are all being used in attenuated, metaphorical senses, not literally. But then we are not very much, if at all, better off than when we started. For if "personally authentic" is being understood in terms of musical "assertion," musical "belief," and musical "sincerity," and all these are being used in nonliteral, attenuated, and not clearly defined senses, then so must "personally authentic" as well. One cannot understand the unclear in terms of the equally unclear and expect to make any progress in the way of clarity. We were using "personally authentic" loosely to start with and cannot improve on that by understanding the phrase in terms of other terms and phrases used in an equally loose way. It may, indeed, be a perfectly good first step to go from personal authenticity to metaphorical sincerity, by way of metaphorical assertion and metaphorical belief. But until more progress is made in firmly establishing the meaning, in the theory, of musical assertion, belief, and sincerity, there can be no second step.

Perhaps progress might be made in the further development of Mark's analysis that would help solve the personal authenticity problem. And that brings me to my second, deeper reason for not wanting to follow the direction in which Mark's theory points. I think it is based on a pro-

The Other Authenticity

120

foundly mistaken, though popular and long-standing, view of just what, *au fond*, music really is.

As we have seen, Mark proceeds from the observation that works of art are frequently likened to statements or assertions. Now, clearly, the works of art that would, quite naturally, be the paradigms of "statement art" would be literary works—which is to say, works consisting in sentences in natural languages. For, of course, it is only in language that we can assume, *uncontentiously*, that statements or assertions are made. To go to the visual arts, or to music, we must make an argument. Thus it is fair to say that one is not merely evincing an accepted platitude by declaring, "Art works are statements" but, rather, stating a *theory* of art that suggests a *literary* model for all the nonliterary arts. And that, it appears to me, is what Mark is essentially doing for music in his analysis of performance.

It is, indeed, a long-standing tradition, going back to the late eighteenth century, to represent pure instrumental music as a kind of musical "discourse," with, of course, literary discourse as the model. And that is the tradition in which Mark's analysis seems firmly planted. But I have come to believe that it is a profoundly misguided tradition. In plain words, the literary model is the wrong model for music, and words like "discourse" are quite inappropriate. Music is another kind of thing.

I have expressed my dissatisfaction with literary models of music at some length elsewhere and cannot do so again here.[14] But the reader is owed at least the basic, underlying reason for my dissatisfaction. And it is simply this: literary models of music as a kind of "discourse" or "assertion" or "statement" are completely incompatible with a palpably obvious and essential feature of musical form, to wit, the *literal musical repeat*. I am not even speaking here of the repetition of small musical patterns that constitutes the inner content of the larger musical forms, in the modern musical tradition, until the advent of serial composition in the early years of the present century. Indeed, such repetition is problem enough for literary models. But the fact that, for example, up to and including Brahms and Dvořák, the expositions of sonata movements are frequently to be repeated, as part of the full sonata form, is so recalcitrant to representing such movements as forms of musical "discourse," as to, for me, defeat the literary model of music at a single stroke, the sonata movement being, traditionally, the best, the paradigmatic case, indeed

[14] On this see Kivy, "The Fine Art of Repetition," in the volume of the same title.

The Other Authenticity

the instigation of the thing in the first place. And to go on to mention such other forms based on the principle of repetition, as minuet and trio, scherzo, binary dance forms, and the "da capo" movements of the baroque, is simply to rub salt in an already mortal wound.

To repeat the exposition of a large sonata movement—as is still happening, for example, in the first movement of Brahms's First Symphony— would be, in a literary context, like reading the first third of a speech and then reading it over again before going on. An art that not only suffers such repetition but does so regularly, and as an essential feature of its formal structure, cannot, at its heart, be a "literary" art. Its nature must lie elsewhere. Such, in any case, is my firm belief.

But if music cannot be understood on a literary model, then I do not see how it can in any way enlighten us to call it "statement" or "assertion," even in a metaphorical or attenuated sense: it just does not help; it leads nowhere. And with this realization comes the rejection of sincerity of belief as a possible explication for the personally authentic performance. If a musical performance is a work of art in its own right—and I thoroughly concur with Mark that it is—it cannot be the kind of work of art that is a "statement," or "assertion," or, therefore, the kind of work of art that might correctly be called "personally authentic" because it is a sincere "statement" or "assertion." A performance can be personally authentic *because* it is a work of art; but it cannot be because it is a "sincere" work of art. Its personal authenticity must lie elsewhere, in other concepts. Where, and in what concepts, must now be shown.

·   ·   ·

I have been laboring under the assumption that performances—that is to say, not the acts of performers but what those acts produce—are, quite uncontentiously, taken by everyone to be *works of art*. This is not perhaps altogether true. If ordinary language is our guide and standard, then I must say that I have seldom heard anyone call a performance a work of art. However, performers are pretty regularly called artists—performing artists. And if we take such talk seriously, I cannot see how we can avoid the conclusion that most people, at least implicitly, think of performances as artworks. What else would cause them to call the makers of performances "artists"?

We must, of course, ask ourselves just what kinds of artworks performances are, and what kinds of artists produce them. And so we shall. But

The Other Authenticity

given that performances *are* art works, there is, I think, a construction we can put on the notion of the "personally authentic" that will apply to all artworks *qua* artworks, irrespective of whether they are artworks that are statements or artworks that are not. For any artwork, whether it is a statement or some other kind of artifact, can be personally authentic in the sense of truly emanating from the artist, as a direct "extension" (so to say) of the artist's own personality, rather than a derivative imitation of some other artist's work. And it is our notion of the uniqueness of human personality that, it seems obvious enough, makes us want to say, further, that only through such personal authenticity can the artist achieve two of the most admired qualities of works of art: *style* and *originality*. If an artist "follows her star," is true to her own values and tastes and aesthetic intuitions, then, if she has the other necessary qualities and talents of a worthwhile artist, and if, of course, her values and tastes and intuitions are interesting and viable ones, her works may turn out to have an individual, unmistakable style all their own, and be original ones as well. But if she slavishly follows the works of others, whatever other admirable qualities her artworks might have, their style will be derivative, and they will be unoriginal works. Personal authenticity, though not a sufficient condition for artistic style or originality, is at least a necessary one. And that is why we admire it.

To put it quite simply, what I am going to suggest, then, is that when we say of a musical performance that it is "authentic" in the sense of being "personally authentic," we are praising it for bearing the special stamp of personality that marks it out from all others as Horowitz's or Serkin's, Bernstein's or Toscanini's, Casals's or Janigro's: we are marking it out as the unique product of a unique individual, something with an individual style of its own—"an original." Because performances are works of art, we can praise them for two qualities that they (but not only they) are particularly valued for having: the qualities of personal style and originality. Thus it appears to me that when we say a performance is personally authentic, that is shorthand for "having personal style," "being original," or both. We are praising the effect by naming the cause.

Now, here it might well be objected that I have hung my argument on far too slender a thread. To say that performances are artworks merely because performers are called "performing artists" is far from thoroughly convincing. The other day I heard a chef called an "artist" but was not by

The Other Authenticity

123

any means convinced by that that the dish he was preparing was a work
of art. "Artist," as we know, is frequently used as a compliment and not
much more; and to use it in this way is to imply neither that the recipient
of the compliment is literally an artist nor (by consequence) that his or
her productions are literally works of art. The last person I called "a
gentleman and a scholar" was neither: she was a travel agent. But if
calling performers "performing *artist*" is just an honorific—a "courtesy
meaning," as R. G. Collingwood called that sort of thing[15]—then it looks
as if the inference from such uses of "artist" to the conclusion that performances are artworks is quite fallacious.

To this it might be replied that the concept of personal authenticity certainly applies to artifacts other than artworks and, along with it, the concepts of style and originality. So losing the conclusion that performances
are artworks is not fatal to the enterprise. But, further, it might also be replied that the degree to which the epithet "performing artist" permeates
our discourse suggests something other than its being a mere honorific or
courtesy meaning. I may, in a gush of enthusiasm, call my plumber an
"artist"; it is not, however, my usual form of address. Whereas "performing artist" is not merely an occasional word of praise but a regularly applied, seemingly classificatory term, with bad as well as good instances:
the name of a profession.

But to the claim that performances are works of art a far more serious
and substantive objection has been raised by Paul Thom is his recent book
on performance. It is incumbent upon us to briefly canvass and answer
this objection before we can proceed:

> Performances themselves are not works of art. They are
> distinguished from works of art in that to perform is to engage in
> activity, and to that extent a performance is an event or process,
> whereas a work of art is a thing. Because it is an event or process,
> the parts of a performance are spread out over a stretch of time, at
> no substretch of which the whole is fully present. A thing's parts, by
> contrast, are simultaneous, and the whole thing is fully present at
> any substretch of the period of its existence.
>
> Events and processes do not endure, for to endure through a
> period of time is to be fully present at each of its subperiods.[16]

[15] Collingwood, *The Principles of Art*, pp. 8–9.
[16] Thom, *For an Audience*, p. 3.

The   Other   Authenticity

I must begin here by pointing out that Thom and I are obviously committed to widely divergent views concerning what aspect of musical performance is to be aesthetically relevant, and the object of discussion. He wishes to talk about the *act* of performance, and I am fixated on the *product* of that act, namely, the musical sound. And although, as can be gathered from Chapters 4 and 8, I envisage the possibility of visual aspects of the performance act being aesthetically relevant, I concentrate, quite unashamedly, on sound and offer, in Chapter 8, a defense of so doing. Nevertheless, on both Thom's view and mine, "performance" refers to an "event": for Thom an action, for me a sound event. Furthermore, since Thom's objection to considering performances as artworks is that they are *events*, his objection, if good, is good against my notion of performance as well as his own. So nothing more need be said on this regard. The question is, Is the objection good?

Thom's argument, as I understand it, is that:

1. artworks are things;

2. things endure through time;

3. performances are events;

4. events do not endure through time;

5. events are therefore not things;

6. performances, therefore, being events, are not things; and

7. performances, therefore, not being things, cannot be artworks.

It appears to me that Thom's argument is based on intuitions I simply do not share. Let us begin with "thing."

Pigs and pots and paper clips and paintings are paradigmatic "things." They are locatable in space and time. They endure (temporarily, of course).

Is a puff of smoke a "thing"? My own intuition is affirmative, and I think ordinary language bears me out. ("What's that thing up there? Is it a cloud?" "No, it's just a puff of smoke.") Does a puff of smoke "endure"? Well, not like a pig or a pot or a paper clip or a painting. I think it might be stretching things a bit to prove a point, to say that a puff of smoke "endures." But it is a "thing," at least the way my intuitions go.

The Other Authenticity

Well, forget about puffs of smoke. It is *events* that are the crux. Are they things? That they do not endure seems to me no reason to deny "thinghood" to them. I wouldn't deny it to the puff of smoke. My intuition is firmly in the direction of calling events "things," whether they endure or not. But my intuition is not, apparently, an unfounded one. For a quick glance at the *Shorter Oxford English Dictionary* reveals the following, by no means peripheral, range of meanings: "That which is done or to be done; a doing, act, deed, transaction; an event, occurrence, incident; a fact, circumstance, experience." I think that someone who wants to claim, in the face of this, that events cannot be things, has a tough fight on his hands. And so far as I can see, Thom puts up no fight at all. Thus, the argument that goes, Artworks are things; things endure; performances are events; events don't endure; therefore events are not things and so not artworks—comes to naught.

Here, I imagine, the defender of Thom's position is likely to let "thing" drop out of the argument altogether and simply take the more direct route, to wit: enduring is a necessary condition on being an artwork; performances are events; events do not endure; therefore performances cannot be artworks. But the problem for me with this argument is that I no more share Thom's intuition, if that is what it is, that artworks are of necessity *enduring*, like pigs and pots and paper clips and paintings, than I share his intuition, if that is what it is, that things are. The question is, Why should someone insist that artworks are enduring, in the face of obvious, prima facie *counterexamples* like improvisations, "happenings," and the like?

The reason, I suspect, is that since the advent of notations and scripts, some of what were once ephemeral arts have become enduring ones. The word "opus" itself, which, in modern times, composers have affixed to their favored works, the ones they have intended to endure, carries with it a sense of permanence. Perhaps, then, we should not call instances of ephemeral, nonenduring art *works* of art, and reserve the work-opus terminology for enduring art. Should we call them "art instances"? Or just "art"? I don't think it matters; we are now truly quibbling over words. The fact is that "work of art," in spite of whatever suggestions of permanence "work" might convey, is commonly used to refer to ephemeral as well as permanent instances of what ordinary people call "art." I myself think it would be counterproductive to cease to call such art "art*works*"

The Other Authenticity

and have no intention of doing so. Those who wish to withhold the term "work" from such instances are free to do so, with my blessing. Call them "instances" or "examples," or whatever; just continue to call them "art."

One further word before we go on. Performances are events. Do they, or some of them, *endure*? They do not need to do so, on my view, to be "art." But some of them—indeed, the ones most important to my argument—have one characteristic of permanence: they are repeatable; they are types with tokens. A great performing artist does not give a different "interpretation" every time she performs a work. Wanda Landowska, through the years, gave many performances of her version of the "Goldberg" Variations, tokens of the same type. A performer's interpretation may, of course, change, in which case one performance type may cease to be and another come to be. However, whereas a performance type continues to be given instances by the performer, my inclination is to say that it *endures*.

Again, Thom's intuition, on this regard, is quite different from my own. For, in discussion of Diderot's animadversions on acting, Thom says:

> A gesture that is repeatable might be thought to have the character of a work. Strictly speaking, this is nonsense. A gesture, whether repeatable or not, is no more a work than is any other event. It is true, however, that experiencing repeatable events is more like experiencing a work than is experiencing unrepeatable events. . . . A repeatable performance, like a work of art and unlike an unrepeatable performance, can be viewed and reviewed.[17]

Being repeatable, then, on Thom's view, does not make an event a "work" (of art). Indeed, it is "nonsense" to hold that it does; it is to fail to speak "strictly."

There is considerable arm waving here, and a paucity of argument. It is by no means obvious that the kind of repeatability some performances have—Horowitz's "Revolutionary" Etude, Toscanini's *La traviata*—does not bestow upon them endurance. And to high-handedly characterize such a claim as "nonsense" and loose talk is not going to convince anyone whose intuitions go in the opposite direction. One needn't be a metaphysician of a Platonic stripe to think that if a performance is repeatable, if there can be numerous tokens of that type, it can be said to persist

[17] Ibid., p. 151.

The Other Authenticity

through time in a full-blooded sense of "persist." Thus I feel strongly inclined to say that some performances—and those the most important for
my purposes—have instances and endure.

To sum up, then, my intuitions depart from Thom's in the following
particulars:

1.   things need not endure;

2.   events are things;

3.   some events endure;

4.   some artworks do not endure;

5.   some performances do endure;

6.   some performances are artworks; and

7.   some (but not all) performances are artworks that endure.

There is no good reason to be found in Thom's claims, then, for denying
that performances are works of art, and an important subset of these enduring works of art. We can go on, then, untroubled by these claims, with
our project of understanding performers as artists, performances as their
artworks.

                                    .   .   .

The conclusion that performances are works of art, even if proof against
the objections just examined, will hardly bring with it either confidence
or enlightenment unless it can be suitably fleshed out. What kind of artist
is the musical performer, anyway? And what kind of artwork does he or
she create? Unless we know these things we will not really know what
the cash value is of concepts like "style" and "originality" when applied
to musical performances.

In terms of what the performer had to put of him- or herself into the
performance, one of the most performer-oriented periods in the history
of Western art music was the high baroque. Two familiar aspects of baroque performance practice made this so: the so-called figured bass, and
the requirement that the soloist add ornaments to the melodic line, particularly in slow movements and repeated sections. We can learn a lot
about performance across the board by examining, very briefly, these two
techniques of baroque music making.

The   Other   Authenticity

Example 1. Tomaso Albinoni, Sonata in A minor for Violin and Figured Bass

As many of my musical readers will know, figured bass is a method of indicating, with numbers and other signs, the chords that are meant to be played by the keyboard, the almost omnipresent member of any baroque performing ensemble. The player is supposed to be able to do this "at sight," without rehearsal—that is to say, to "improvise" it. Example 1 shows the way a sonata for violin and figured bass looked to the performer (top and bottom staves), and how it might have been "realized" at a performance (middle staff).[18] (The realization is by J. S. Bach's pupil H. N. Gerber, with corrections by Bach himself.)

But although realizing a figured bass was, of course, a performance task of only keyboard players, the ornamenting of a melodic line in performance was the task of all soloists, whether instrumental or vocal. We can get an idea of what the art of ornamentation was like from the many written-out versions meant for instructional purposes. Example 2 shows a line for solo violin by Arcangelo Corelli, as ornamented by Francesco Geminiani. The lower staff is Corelli's line as written; the upper as it might have been performed.[19]

Now, both realizing a figured bass and ornamenting a melodic line are, clearly, *compositional* skills—in the former case, the art of composing in three or more real parts; in the latter, the art of thematic variation. In the exercise of these skills, the baroque performer, then, was a certain kind of artist, namely, a composer of music; and the results of exercising these skills were, it seems trivially to follow, certain kinds of artworks, namely, musical compositions. Let me amplify this thought a bit.

[18] Spitta, *Johann Sebastian Bach*, vol. 3, p. 388.
[19] Schmitz, *Die Kunst der Verzierung im 18. Jahrhundert*, p. 62.

The Other Authenticity

Example 2. Arcangelo Corelli, Sonata for Violin and Figured Bass, Op. 5, no. 9

Consider two performances of the Albinoni sonata, the opening measures of which are quoted here in Example 1. To make things interesting (and obvious), let's make them dream performances. In the first, the harpsichordist is Bach; in the second, Handel. And we shall say that each of the violinists is a distinguished practitioner of the art. Now, it ought to be quite plain that these will be very different performances of the work. Bach's accompaniment will be thick, complex, and (as we can see from his student's realization) in three real parts in the right hand. Handel's version we may expect to be leaner, more transparent, and not as contrapuntally strict. Each realization will bear, no doubt, the particular marks of the composer's individual style: each will be an original creation, and personally authentic. Furthermore, the violin parts, particularly in the slow movements, will be quite distinctively different, varying as the styles of the two players' *agréments*. In a word, these two performances of the same work will contain, in significant places, *very different notes*.

But this begins to look like a metaphysician's nightmare. How many *works* do we have here? One, or three? And if we have three, then we have as many works as there have been, and will be, performances of Albinoni's sonata, plus one (or at least as many, plus one, as the personally authentic performance types). And isn't even *two* one too many?

I am going to leave this for the metaphysicians to sort out. I don't think it need be a problem here and now, because musicians have been living with this kind of ambiguity for a few hundred years and have a terminology for dealing with it that will work perfectly well in the present situation. I do not mean by this to demean metaphysicians or to suggest that their problem on this regard is a trivial or uninteresting one. On the contrary, as a philosopher by trade I love metaphysicians as I do myself. All I am saying is that there is a musical apparatus already in place, and has

The Other Authenticity

130

been for a long time, for talking about these kinds of things. And we can use it without waiting for the metaphysicians to work out an acceptable ontology for all the cases.

Most concertgoers will be familiar with Mozart's Symphony no. 40 in G minor (K. 550); but perhaps few will know that it was originally written without clarinets: "Later Mozart replaced the two oboes by two clarinets, while two oboes were added with modified parts."[20] Two works, or one? The fastidious metaphysician may, for perfectly sound philosophical reasons, want to answer "two." But the number of Mozart's symphonies still stands at forty-one (or forty and a half, since no. 37 is by Michael Haydn, with only the slow introduction to the first movement by Mozart). What musicians say, simply, is that there are two *versions* of the same work, and leave it at that. But one thing they emphatically do *not* say (if one can be silent emphatically) is that there are two symphonies: two *works*.

Again, Beethoven "arranged" (that is a musician's word) his immensely popular Septet, Op. 20, for clarinet, cello, and piano. He gave it a separate opus number: Op. 38. One work, or two? In spite of the different opus numbers, no one in the music business is going to call the septet and the trio two separate works. Op. 38 is the trio version of the famous septet; or, if it is not the same thing but perhaps something marking a more radical departure, the trio is an "arrangement" of the septet.

Now, there would be, I suggest, as much perceptible, musical difference between Bach's and Handel's performances of the Albinoni sonata as between the two versions of K. 550, or between Op. 20 and Op. 38. Two works, or one? The answer seems to be that we have two versions—or arrangements, if you prefer—of the same work. The art of performing baroque music, then, when you are a soloist or continuo player, is in large measure the art of "arranging"—one of the peripheral skills of the composer but, obviously, a compositional skill. And the kinds of artworks that performances of baroque music are, where figured bass and ornamentation are involved, seem clearly to be arrangements: *versions* of the work.

All very well, it may well be said; but nothing very useful has been concluded so far by any of this about performance *tout court*, least of all what kind of art it might be. For baroque performance practice, as regards the

[20] Saint-Foix, *The Symphonies of Mozart*, p. 114.

The Other Authenticity

compositional input of the performer, is a very special case; and nothing general can be deduced from it: certainly not the conclusion that all performance is a form of composition, all performances (therefore) being musical works of art. In baroque performance, where figured bass is realized by the performer or where the performer ornaments a melodic line, notes are literally added to those the composer wrote; and notes that the composer wrote are literally changed, other notes being substituted for them. Nothing like this is permissible in the performance of classical, romantic, or most kinds of twentieth-century music, where the whole point is to play just the notes that are written, with no additions or omissions. To add or omit is not to perform but to vandalize.

Well, the lines cannot be so sharply drawn. Let me adduce another example to try to show this. In Example 3 are given some notes written by Bach, and beneath them those notes as played by Pablo Casals (and transcribed into notation with the help of a machine called the *Melograph*).[21]

Forget that this is a passage from Bach, so that we do not confuse the present case with that of baroque performance. It might just as well have been a passage from Beethoven or Brahms; for Casals would have taken the same "liberties" with them as well. The point is that Casals, like the baroque violinist who ornaments his part, has "added and subtracted notes." The Melograph shows that what Casals plays is not what is written, in the very same sense in which what Geminiani played was not what Corelli had written.[22] And our ear, after all, tells us as well: here is what Albinoni wrote, and what Bach played (Example 1); here is what Corelli wrote, and what Geminiani played (Example 2); here is what Bach wrote, and what Casals played (Example 3). We have here, I claim, three cases of the same sort of thing.

I think a similar argument can be run for various other parameters of the musical work that the performer "manipulates." But indeed we could, I think, have gotten our conclusion far more directly with the sim-

[21] Taken from Planer, "Sentimentality in the Performance of Absolute Music," p. 24.

[22] It is not easy to get a terminology that is unambiguous in this regard. In one sense both Geminiani and Casals have played the passages "as written": for the notation in each case, in the tradition in which it exists, mandates or permits just those things that Geminiani and Casals have done (although in the case of Casals this may be debated by the "purist"). But in another sense of "as written," which I think is just as transparently clear, both Geminiani (obviously) and Casals (less obviously) have "added and changed" notes. It is in this latter sense of "as written" and "adding and changing notes" that I am employing them in the present argument.

The Other Authenticity

Example 3. J. S. Bach, Suite in D minor for
Unaccompanied Violoncello (Saraband)

ple observation that various performances of the same work by different
performers don't sound the same. How could that be unless "the notes
were different"? To be sure, if the differences were, say, just in dynamics,
then the notes would be the same, even though the performances were
different. We know, however, that there are many differences other than
those of dynamics between a performance by Casals and one by Janigro,
a performance by Serkin and one by Horowitz, a performance by Toscanini and one by Bernstein: differences in note grouping, in phrasing, in
breathing, in articulation, in rest value, in note value. These will all be
registered on the Melograph as differences in "notes"; and so will they be
registered on our musical sensibilities.

What, then, does all this show? If we grant that things like realizing a
figured bass and ornamenting a melodic line—the jewels in the crown of
baroque performance practice—are, at least peripherally, compositional
skills, because within certain stylistic and "syntactical" limits "notes are
added and changed," then I think we must grant that all performance
practice, as we know it in the West, has been the same. In sum, then,
Western performance practice *tout court* is the exercise of a peripheral skill
of the composer's art, and its result is therefore the work of art that we call
a "musical composition."

Is there a name for this compositional skill? There is indeed: it is the art
of musical "arranging"; and it results in musical "arrangements." Just as
the clarinet version of K. 550 is an arrangement and not a new work, just
as Beethoven's Op. 38 is an arrangement of Op. 20 and not a new work,
so performances that exhibit personal authenticity are "arrangements" of
works, not new works themselves. And ordinary musical discourse reflects this conclusion. For just as we refer to the reworked K. 550 as the
clarinet "version" of the symphony, and Op. 38 as the trio "version" of

The Other Authenticity

Op. 20, so do we refer to Horowitz's "version" of a concerto, or Serkin's "version," Toscanini's "version" of a symphony, or Bernstein's "version," and so on. Performances are "versions" of works, and performers practice, in making them, the compositional skill of "arranging," when, that is to say, the performers are such as achieve personal authenticity in performance. For only when personal authenticity is achieved do performances take on the character of personal style and originality that mark them out as distinguishable "versions" of particular performance personalities.

At this point in the argument I think we must confront a serious objection waiting in the wings. It is the possible charge that I am employing a species of "slippery slope" argument that goes from composition to "arrangement" to a very special performance practice in which something akin to "arrangement" takes place and, finally, to something remotely like what is somewhat akin to "arrangement," thereby "proving" that all performance is "arrangement." But of course we are all quite rightly suspicious these days of slippery slope arguments. The slopes go both ways, so that the same argument proves the opposite also. And we know that slippery slope arguments lead to logical paradoxes: that all men are bald, as well as that all are hirsute; that everyone is rich and everyone poor; and, ancestor of them all, that a pebble is a heap, and that in fact there are no heaps.

I take this charge seriously, as I am no friend at all to slippery slope arguments. And the simple, direct answer to it is that I am not employing a slippery slope argument, nor am I trying to show that performers are composers, performing is composing, or performances are compositions. Composers are composers, performers are performers, and so on; and it is emphatically not my intention to break down these very reasonable distinctions. What my intention *is* I would like to now make clear. This will require retracing our steps.

The argument has gone something like this. We wanted to know what it might mean for a performance to be personally authentic. The suggestion was made that as performers are considered artists, performances, it would seem to follow, must be works of art. And if performances are works of art, there is a familiar sense in which they could be, *qua* works of art, the products of "personal authenticity." It is the sense that, having

The Other Authenticity

as their source as they sometimes might do, the strong, unique artistic personalities of outstanding performing *artists*, these performances would, on that account, have had imparted to them two of the most prized qualities that great works of art of all kinds are praised for having: style and originality.

The problem was, merely arguing from the fact that performers are customarily described as performing *artists* to the conclusion that performances must be works of art seemed to be hanging a pretty heavy conclusion on a pretty slender thread. And short of proving that performances are works of art, I suggested that we might make the thread somewhat less tenuous by trying to illuminate just what kinds of artworks performances might be. And by that I mean to lay emphasis on the word "kind" not so much in the strict sense of "species" as in the informal sense of "what they are like"; they are "the kind of thing," followed by a characterization.

Thus, the progression from arranging to baroque performance practice to performance practice across the board was not intended to show that performers are identical with composers, performing identical with the skill of arranging, and performances identical with arrangements. The performance is what it is and not another thing. What I *was* trying to do with this progression was draw an *analogy* between performers and arrangers, performing and arranging, performances and arrangements. I am not identifying them but analogizing them. I am suggesting that the artistic skill of performers, when they are exhibiting personal authenticity, is more like the compositional skill of arranging than like any other thing that I can think of; that performances, when they exhibit style and originality, are more like *versions* of musical works—the clarinet version of K. 550, the trio version of Op. 20—than like any other thing that I can think of. That was my purpose; that is my view. It is being very like musical arrangements in which performances have their character as works of art. And in that character, they gain the qualities of style and originality—when, that is, they emanate from performers of genius; when they are, in a word, personally authentic.

·   ·   ·

Having reached this conclusion—that performing is akin to the compositional skill of arranging, and performances (therefore) akin to musical arrangements or versions—we are in a position, I think, to meet an objec-

The   Other   Authenticity

135

tion that has been brought against the more general conclusion that performing is a kind of composing, *sans phrase*, and at the same time in a position to accommodate in our account a vital element that we have so far ignored. In an article on improvisation, Philip Alperson made the proposal some years ago that, as he put it, "the activity of performance seems necessarily to involve composition. A musical performance, whether public or in one's head, always involves formative decisions about how a piece shall sound. . . ."[23] Paul Vincent Spade has recently responded that this claim "is relatively, if not completely, non-controversial"[24] and suggested that the controversial part involves the role of *interpretation*:

> It may be objected, for example, that by grouping *all* decisions about "how the piece shall sound" under the rubric of "composition," Alperson has ignored the important, if not altogether clear, distinction we commonly make between composing and interpreting a work of music. . . . It is probably true that performing always does require decisions on the performer's part about "how the piece shall sound." But if that requirement can be satisfied by what we normally think of as *interpretive* decisions, and does not require "composition" in any stronger sense, then the interest of [the] claim . . . is considerably weakened.[25]

Of course it should come as no surprise to us that the concept of interpretation is a necessary ingredient in any account of musical performance. This was clear enough in Mark's account, examined previously, and clear enough, indeed, from ordinary musical discourse, where we find that performances are called not only "versions" of musical works but "interpretations" of them as well. And it seems to me to be a virtue of the account of performance that I am giving here that it can accommodate, at the same time, both locutions and the concepts they underwrite.

There are really two questions here. Is there a role for interpretation, as we feel there must be, if we see performing as a kind of composing? And can the aspects of performing that seem to require our thinking of it as a kind of composing not be accommodated just as well, and not so counterintuitively, by the concept of interpretation alone?

[23] Alperson, "On Musical Improvisation," p. 20.
[24] Spade, "Do Composers Have to Be Performers Too?" p. 366.
[25] Ibid., p. 369n.

The Other Authenticity

Let me begin with the second question. If we compare performing a piano sonata with what I take to be the paradigmatic instance of interpretation, namely, interpreting a literary work, we can, I think, plausibly characterize the latter as "telling us how things go" and the former as "showing us how things go." And in that both (to choose a neutral word) *"inform* us how things go," both can be thought of as "interpreting." But the relevant difference is, for our purposes, that in showing us, and not in telling us, what we are being informed about is brought into being before our very eyes (for which read "ears"). And it is because in this kind of interpreting there is not merely a telling but a bringing into being, an actualizing of the work, that the concept of interpreting alone cannot suffice. Something more is needed. In Mark's account the "something more" turned out to be quotation and assertion. In mine it is "composition" of a certain kind.

But the notion of composition, if unmodified, seems at odds with the concept of interpreting: the former excludes the latter. Interpretation informs us how things go. Composition, on the other hand, brings things into being that interpretation informs us about (or, if you are a Platonist in such matters, discovers and makes available to us what interpretation subsequently informs us about[26]). This brings us to the first question: can an account of performance as a kind of composition allow performance *also* to be, as we see it is, a kind of interpretation as well?

Well, it appears to me that construing performance not simply as a kind of composition, *sans phrase*, but akin to the specific compositional skill of arranging allows both for the kinds of "creative" artistic manipulations that make us want to call performers artists, and performances works of art, and for a prominent, indeed indispensable, role for interpretation. For the arranger, unlike the composer, cannot start from scratch. He or she starts with a preexistent work, of which a *version* must be contrived; and in order for his or her result to *be a version* of the work and not a new work in its own right it must be, whatever else it is, a possible, plausible way *that work goes*. Thus the arranger must have an idea of how the work goes in order to make a credible version of it. He or she must, in other words, have an interpretation, be an interpreter. And that gives us just the result we were seeking for performance. Because insofar as a performer is

[26] On composition as discovery, see Kivy, "Platonism in Music: A Kind of Defense" and "Platonism in Music: Another Kind of Defense," in *The Fine Art of Repetition*.

The Other Authenticity

1 3 7

akin to an arranger, he or she too must have an idea how the work "goes" that is being "arranged." He or she too requires an interpretation, and is an interpreter.

In seeing performers as akin to arrangers, then, we can accommodate both the notion that performers are "creative," their productions, at their best, original and uniquely styled, and the equally ubiquitous notion that they are interpreters, and their performances interpretations. And as originality and style flow out of personal authenticity, that latter concept too falls within our net, which was, of course, the original purpose of the exercise.

·   ·   ·

Our principal subject, however, is not, we should remind ourselves, personal authenticity in performance but, rather, the three forms of historical authenticity previously examined. Nevertheless, the high degree to which personal authenticity is valued in performance, as in other artistic endeavors, makes it absolutely imperative for us to ask whether the presence of personal authenticity in a performance is compatible with the presence of historical authenticity in any (or all) of its forms—whether, in fact or in principle, it is possible to pursue them both. And now that we have a clearer if not altogether satisfactory idea of what personal authenticity in performance might be, we are in a position to essay at least a preliminary answer (to be reviewed, later on, when we come to evaluate considerations).

Let us begin, for no particular reason, with "sound authenticity" (or "authenticity of sound"), which I will use as a term to cover both what I called "sonic authenticity" and what I called "sensible authenticity" (in Chapter 3). And let us ask whether a musical performance could be both sound-authentic and personally authentic. To make the question clearer, let us suppose that a single performer has, *per impossibile*, achieved a performance sound-authentic in every way, perfect in respect to authenticity of sound. Could this performance also be personally authentic? The answer, I would urge, is unequivocally *no*; for perfect sound-authenticity consists in the reduplication, the exact imitation of someone else's past performance, whether it is some specific person's performance or the "kind" of performance some contemporary or other would give; whereas our characterization of the personally authentic performance is one that emanates from the performer herself and is not derivative from or imitative of anyone else's (although here as elsewhere artistic "influence" is necessarily present). A performance might, indeed, be a sound-authentic performance that is so in virtue of being a perfect imitation of a personally authentic performance; but it would not on that account *be* a personally authentic performance.[27]

Indeed, looked at from the performer's point of view, the quest for the sound-authentic performance is completely at cross-purposes with the quest for a personally authentic one. For the former is a project in archeological reconstruction in which the personality of the agent must be submerged so as not to leave a mark of its own on the reconstructed object, because that would amount to an adulteration of the reconstruction; whereas the point of the personally authentic performance precisely is to leave the indelible mark of personal style and (one hopes) personal originality on the "object," that is, performance. I make no value judgments here as to which might be better; that is for later. All I say is that the single-minded quest for sound-authenticity in musical performance is incompatible with the quest for personal authenticity.

Two replies might be made here—both ineffectual, I think, and for the same basic reason. For one thing, it will be pointed out that my argument applies only to a performance in which sound-authenticity, *per impossibile*, is completely achieved. And since I have admitted in my very statement of the argument that such a performance is impossible, my argument is of no real practical interest at all. Any actual performance will be sound-authentic only in certain respects, because of inevitable gaps in our historical knowledge and our inherent inability to achieve our sonic goal in every instance, even when we know what that goal is. So where there is a gap in our knowledge, or where we cannot achieve sound-authenticity even though we know what it is, we are free, as performers,

---

[27] The philosophically sophisticated will probably have already framed the following problem example: a performer with neither the intention nor the knowledge to do so achieves a sound-authentic performance, by sheer accident, in the act of intentionally producing a personally authentic one. So here is a case in which personal authenticity and authenticity of sound coexist. There is no doubt that such a case is metaphysically and logically amusing. But it has no relevance for present purposes. For my analysis is of real musical practice; and what might happen in only the barest logical sense of "might" is of no interest here. Performance practice cannot rely on "accident" to legitimate it. And for the personally authentic performer to say that he too can achieve authenticity of sound, about as often as a monkey types *Macbeth*, is hardly to win an argument.

The Other Authenticity

to be personally authentic if we can. Authenticity of sound and personal authenticity *in practice*, though perhaps not in principle, are thus perfectly compatible.

Second, as is well known, no score and context of performance practice has ever fully determined the sound events of a performance. And where the score cum context do not determine the sound events, there is ample room for the performer to exercise his or her own personal taste and imagination and, perhaps, achieve personal authenticity, in those places.

I said that both these responses are similarly flawed. The flaw is that they both can allow only, so to speak, a *negative* role for personal authenticity. We settle for personal authenticity where we can't, for one reason or the other, get sound-authenticity. Personal authenticity is second best—the consolation prize. In a perfect performance world we would not need it (and could not have it). In the places where knowledge and ability, score and context fail us, style and originality may fill in the gaps. But their presence is the result of something sought-after failing to be there, not the result of their being sought after themselves, as goals intrinsically worth attaining.

This treating of personal authenticity as a negative quality is, however, completely out of phase with the way it in fact is treated in the musical community and has been, so far as I know, in a tradition of performance that goes back at least as far as the beginning of the modern era. Personal authenticity, under whatever different names it has been understood, is considered—along with personal style and originality—as one of the crowning achievements of the performer's art: something to be sought after and cherished for its own sake. And any approach to it that can maintain personal authenticity as only a quality of second choice, in the absence of what is really prized, has preserved merely the shadow of the thing, not its substance (or else is urging on us an entirely different attitude toward performance from what has heretofore prevailed). Personal authenticity is that which we actively seek, not that which we value only in lieu of something else that we have actively sought and failed to achieve.

The same argument can be run, pari passu, for historically authentic performance practice, in either of its two major roles: as means to the attainment of historically authentic sound or as an end worthy of attainment in itself. For in either case the goal is archeological restoration of a

The Other Authenticity

previously existing performance, which, we have seen, is completely at odds with the goal of personal authenticity and its requirement that a performance not be imitative or derivative of another person's performance but instead originate in the personality and initiative of the performer alone. There is no need, therefore, to consider authenticity of performance practice separately. What has been said about the relation of personal authenticity to authenticity of sound will suffice.

There remains, however, the question of compatibility between personal authenticity and the authenticity of composers' intentions and wishes. And here matters are quite different. A separate hearing is required.

· · ·

If it were always the composer's strong intention that all parameters of performance be totally controlled by him or her, then any performer who single-mindedly sought intentional authenticity would, ipso facto, be engaged in the archeological restoration of someone else's performance, namely, *the composer's,* just as much as it would be if the performer's goal were sound-authenticity or authenticity of performance practice. And this therefore would make intentional authenticity, both as a performer's end in view and as product produced, completely incompatible with personal authenticity.

There is, however, overwhelming evidence that, at least until the advent of certain musical movements of the twentieth century, composers not only did not wish or intend to control completely the parameters of musical performance but actually had a positive attitude toward personal authenticity in performance. That is to say, part of the network of wishes and intentions that has motivated the composition and performance of Western music (at least since the beginning of the modern era, if not before) are wishes and intentions that performers achieve, if they can, personal authenticity: individual style and originality. And if that is so, their seeking personal authenticity in performance is not merely compatible with seeking to realize the composer's wishes and intentions but a positive imperative of the latter enterprise. If it is one of the composer's wishes or intentions that his or her music be performed with personal authenticity, then in trying to realize this wish or intention of the composer, the performer must aim for personal authenticity; and if it is achieved, the performer has, in that particular regard, realized authorial intention.

The Other Authenticity

Now here, as elsewhere, there is no guarantee that a whole system of performance wishes and intentions will be consistent—which is to say, there is no guarantee that the achieving of personal authenticity will necessarily be compatible with *all* the other wishes and intentions of the composer with regard to the performance of a particular work. Thus, for example, if the composer has indicated a particular phrasing for a passage and the performer evolves an interpretation of the work in which a different phrasing is suggested, personal authenticity comes into conflict with a composer's performing intention or wish, even though the composer may have intended personal authenticity as well. And I do not think that a reasonable response to this kind of conflict is to enunciate some principle or other to the effect that a *specific* wish or intention of the composer— say, that a passage be phrased thus-and-so—always overrides the general wish or intent for personal authenticity in performance. Such a principle would essentially gut the concept of personal authenticity altogether. For what gives the concept its life, what bestows upon the performer the status of artist and on the performance the status of art, is the real, full-blooded possibility of the performer finding a better or at least *different* way of performing the music from the way the composer has specifically envisioned and explicitly instructed. This is what bestows upon the performance personal style and originality—what makes it the performer's "version" of the work and not just the composer's "version."

Thus here, as has so often happened in our consideration of *authenticities*, we find that achieving "authenticity" is always a trade-off: you get one, you lose one. And which one you want to get or lose is part of the normative problem of historical authenticity—that is to say, what it's good for. The normative problem we are now ready to face. The concepts are clarified to the extent I have been able. The authenticities are now before us, and how we evaluate them must at long last be explained.

The Other Authenticity

PART TWO

Why to Be Authentic

⊙

The Authority of Intention

F. H. Bradley, the English Hegelian, wrote a famous essay in moral theory that had as its title the perplexing question "Why Should I Be Moral?" "The question is natural," Bradley said, "and yet seems strange."[1] To many practicing musicians the question I mean to ask in this chapter, namely, "Why should the performer realize the composer's performing intentions?" may seem as perplexing and, indeed, self-defeating a question as the one that Bradley famously asked in 1876.

Without pressing *too* hard the similarity of my question to Bradley's—for the moral question is, after all, a very special one—it would be useful to press it at least a little. The reason Bradley's question seems strange, he thought, was this. "It appears to be one we ought to ask, and yet we feel when we ask it, that we are wholly removed from the moral point of view." The question seems natural, one we ought to ask: "To ask the question Why? is natural; for reason teaches us to do nothing blindly, nothing without end or aim. She teaches us that what is good must be good for something else, and what is good for nothing is not good at all." But, then, it seems strange, or inappropriate to ask it, of being moral, be-

[1] Bradley, *Ethical Studies*, p. 58.

cause morality seems a special case: "For morality (and she too is reason) teaches us that, if we look on her only as good for something else, we never in that case have seen her at all. She says that she is an end to be desired for her own sake, and not as a means to something beyond."[2]

It sometimes seems as if performers and musical scholars feel the same way about realizing the composer's performing intentions—and I am using "intention" now in the omnium gatherum sense that covers not only intentions but wishes, hypotheses, tentative suggestions, et alii—as Bradley suggested we feel about being moral: that is to say, to ask "Why?" somehow is to ask something logically inappropriate. One may ask why she should play a phrase slurred rather than detached. And the answer may be: because the slur is in the autograph. One may ask why she should follow the autograph in this matter. And the answer may be: because the autograph expresses the composer's intention. But one may *not* then go on to ask why she should follow, realize the composer's intention, any more than we can ask why someone should do the right thing. For realizing the composer's intentions just is the performer's vocation, the final end, the end worthy in itself, and not to some further end, as we might say, being moral just is the human vocation, the end worthy in itself of human action. And to ask the "Why?" question of either is to misunderstand the subject: in both instances, "if we look on her only as good for something else, we never in that case have seen her at all. She says that she is an end to be desired for her own sake, and not as a means to something beyond."[3]

Now, whatever can be said for being moral as an end in itself, it is not at all obvious that realizing the composer's intentions holds that status in the performer's vocation, however much performers and scholars may tend to treat it so in their practice. There is a prima facie strangeness in the question "Why should I be moral?" that the analogous question about realizing the composer's intentions lacks. Nevertheless, it might still be the case that there is something about the concept of performance itself, something perhaps implied by the concept, that makes the realizing of composers' intentions an end in itself and that performers and scholars are intuitively tuned into, even if it is not explicitly in their awareness. That possibility we must explore before we can feel confident in raising

[2] Ibid.
[3] Ibid.

The   Authority   of   Intention

the question at all of why or whether it is a good or necessary thing to realize the composer's performing intentions.

Here is the best argument I can think of to show that realizing the composer's intentions is analytic to the concept of performing and performance. A performance (product) of a work simply *is* the work, or (if you
are a Platonist in these matters) an instance of the work. And the performance (act) is the human action of making the *work* aurally available to
the listener.

Now if I ask a violinist why she played the following notes:

rather than these others:

she will quite rightly reply that the former are what the composer, J. S.
Bach, intended: they constitute the first measure of the Giga from his Partita for Unaccompanied Violin in D minor (BWV 1004), and the others do
not. It is her vocation, *qua* performer, to make aurally available to us that
piece; and that piece just *is* a complicated system of the composer's expressed intentions as to how his piece goes. Part of that complicated set of
intentions is the intention that the opening notes of the Giga should go
thus,

and not:

The Authority of Intention

And to play them in the second way would be, ipso facto, not to be a performer of that piece. It is analytic to the notion of being a performer that these and other such intentions of the composer are to be realized in the performance. So it makes no sense to ask either why or whether such intentions should be realized. From the point of view of being a performer, realizing such intentions is not a means to something else but an end in itself.

But now suppose we ask the violinist, Why do you play the notes this way,

rather than this:

She replies that the former articulation is that given in the *Neue Bach Ausgabe*, and that edition of the work, in her judgment, best reflects the performing intentions of the composer. And if we ask, further, *why* she thinks it proper or incumbent upon her to realize this intention, she makes a similar reply to the one she made when she told us previously why—to not put too fine a point on it—she felt obliged to play the right notes of the Giga. The piece is a complicated set of intentions, expressed by J. S. Bach, of how the notes should go. They are different notes—the passage has a different sound—if articulated one way rather than the

The Authority of Intention

148

other. That sound is part of the work; and it is analytic to the notion of performing that it result in a presentation of *the work*. The particular articulation Bach intended, as all other performing intentions, is part of the whole complicated system of intentions that constitutes the work. It is therefore analytic to the concept of performing that the composer's performing intentions should be realized: realizing performing intentions is part of the end, not part of a means to an end, in performing. And thus it makes no more sense to ask why or whether we should, *qua* performers, realize the composer's performing intentions than it would to ask why, or whether, *qua* performers, we should play the right notes; indeed, *it is part of playing the right notes.*

I said this is the best argument I can think of for the claim that realizing (or trying to realize) the composer's performing intentions is analytic to the notion of performance, either as act or as product; and so it is. It is neat and complete. It connects performing intentions to the other intentions that, as a system, make up the musical work in a way that seems, on the face of it, to satisfy intuition.

Would that things were so unproblematical. But readers of Chapter 2, "Authenticity as Intention," will know straightaway that there is one very obvious objection to this neat analysis. For I have been using "intention" here in its broad sense, to cover not only intentions properly so called (as in "the general intends the seventh regiment to advance") but all sorts of "weaker" performing attitudes as well: wishes, hypotheses, tentative suggestions, and so on. And if it may seem intuitively obvious to some that performing *intentions*, properly so called, are partly constitutive of the musical work, it would by no means be obvious to *anyone* that performing wishes, hypotheses, or tentative suggestions should be thought to be so. So there is going to be a large number of performing intentions, usually referred to in the literature as composer's "intentions," that no one thinks are constitutive of the work; and, therefore, the realizing of these "intentions" is by no means shown to be analytic to the notion of performer or performance by the preceding argument. By consequence, if the realizing of *these* intentions is an end in itself and not a means to some further end, a different argument is wanted to show it; and I have no idea what such an argument would look like.

But, really, a second look at "intentions," properly so called, will reveal that our argument is in jeopardy even with regard to them. For, to begin

The   Authority   of   Intention

with, our intuitions are by no means clear or undivided as to whether or not performing intentions, properly so called, *are* themselves constitutive of the musical work. If we *were* clear and undivided, I suppose there would be no purpose in the phrase "performing intentions" at all, because what the phrase seems to imply is that these are intentions as to how *the work* is to be made aurally available to the listener; and so we must have *two* things here: *the work* already constituted, apart from the composer's performing intentions, and the performing intentions themselves, which are directed to *the work*.

I am far from suggesting that this little sojourn into "ordinary language analysis" proves that composers' performing intentions, properly so called, are not, any of them, partly constitutive of musical works. But it does demonstrate, I think, that without a satisfactory philosophical account of just what the musical work is, a case cannot convincingly be made for composers' performing intentions either being or *not* being constitutive of musical works. Intuition simply won't settle the matter. And, as experience shows, the work status of performing intentions is not invariant with philosophical analysis of the work itself; witness the fact that on a Goodmanian analysis of score and work, tempo intentions expressed verbally "in" the score are neither part of the score nor (by consequence) part of the work,[4] whereas intuition and alternative analyses might suggest otherwise.

Nor will it help matters any by maintaining that composers' performing intentions, properly so called—that is, as opposed to wishes, hypotheses, tentative suggestions, and so forth—are just those performing attitudes that are work-constitutive. For that would simply beg the question by stipulative definition. If the position that performing intentions, in the narrow sense of "intention," are part of *the work*, whereas performing wishes, hypotheses, and tentative suggestions are not, is to have real content and not just be a disguised meaning rule, there must be a way of determining whether something is a performing intention (in the narrow sense) independent of whether it is part of *the work*. Without such a method of determination, the claim becomes merely a "conventionalist sulk." So all comes down again to having, first, an adequate analysis of the musical work.

I have no such analysis of the nature of the musical work to offer or en-

[4]See Goodman, *Languages of Art*, pp. 184ff.

The Authority of Intention

dorse that would either enfranchise or disenfranchise performing intentions, properly so called, as part of the musical work. In lieu of such an analysis, since it must constitute the heart of the best argument I can think of for the view that realizing the composer's performing intentions is, for performance, an end in itself, I shall conclude, at least for the purposes of this book, the opposite view. I shall assume, that is to say, that if realizing the composer's performing intentions, wishes, tentative suggestions, and so forth is a good at all, it must be (if a pun may be excused) an *instrumental good*. Realizing the composer's performing intentions must be evaluated, in other words, in terms of its payoff.

• • •

There are two fairly obvious ways to evaluate the consequences of realizing the composer's performing intentions: *aesthetically* and *ethically*. That is to say, we can evaluate the consequences of realizing the composer's performing intentions in terms of the aesthetic goodness and badness of the resultant performance (product), or we can evaluate these consequences in terms of moral goodness or badness, and the performance (act) producing them in terms of moral rightness and wrongness (following the convention of applying "right" and "wrong" to actions, and "good" and "bad" to their consequences).

I have written at some length elsewhere on the possibility of an ethical defense and concluded that there is, indeed, more of a case than one might initially have thought for the view that we have at least a prima facie although defeasible moral obligation to realize the composer's performing intentions.[5] I have no wish either to repeat those arguments or to make any use of the ethical defense here, since I now think that, for the most part, any prima facie moral obligation we may have to honor the performance wishes and intentions of dead composers, in the way of respecting, so to say, their musical last will and testament is far weaker in any given instance than our moral obligation to realize what we deem to be the best performance possible, the latter obligation owing not merely to the composer but to his or her posterity. In other words, any prima facie obligation I might have to play in a way mandated by the composer would, it seems to me, be overridden by the blanket obligation to place that composer's work in the best light possible and the determination that

---

[5] See Kivy, "Live Performances and Dead Composers: On the Ethics of Musical Interpretation," in *The Fine Art of Repetition*.

The Authority of Intention

this would *not* be accomplished by playing the work as originally de-
manded (or suggested) by the composer. So I will be considering in this
chapter only the defense of realizing composers' performing intentions
based on the aesthetic payoff of doing so.

Nevertheless, there is one dimension of the ethical defense that was not
apparent to me in my original treatment of the subject and that does de-
serve some attention here, before I get to my main business. For it has created some confusion in the debate over the relevance and importance of
composers' performing intentions that I think should be cleared up before we go on to the aesthetic defense.

It has become increasingly common to refer to composers' scores as
"texts," obviously under the influence of textual scholarship, criticism,
and interpretation in the literary arts. And it is, of course, a commonplace
that a historically authentic performance of a musical work must be
premised upon a historically authentic "text." The modern industry of
"Urtext" and scholarly editions is, of course, the practical expression of
this commonplace.

But the concept of an authentic musical text, I believe, is responsible for
bringing into the argument another, and potentially obfuscating concept—that of the musical "message." For a "text" in its usual form, either
literary or expository, is a *verbal* document; and verbal documents are
commonly the bearers of "meaning" (in the literal sense of that term).
And so the benign habit of referring to a musical score as a "text" leads to
the more dangerous habit of referring to what it possesses, and must be
passed on by the performer as its "message" or "meaning." As one writer,
more circumspect than most, puts it, within the safety of scare quotes, "a
concern with authenticity takes its point ultimately from the authority of
authorship, from a concern to present accurately (to an audience) what
the composer 'had to say.' "[6] Or, less circumspectly and more out front, as
another author puts it: "Our interest in creating the authentic sounds of
music can be justified only by our belief that they lead us closer to its authentic meanings."[7]

[6] Davies, "Transcription, Authenticity, and Performance," p. 223.
[7] Tomlinson, "The Historian, the Performer, and Authentic Meaning in Music," in Kenyon, *Authenticity and Early Music*, p. 115. I should perhaps add here that another quite
legitimate sense in which a composer may literally *mean* may tend to creep into the discussion and cloud the issue. Peter le Huray writes, for example, "If, then, composers
mean what they write, it is our duty as performers to try to find out as much as possible

The Authority of Intention

Let me suggest that the plea for scrupulous adherence to the composer's performing intentions tends to escalate in passion to the level of
moral fervor under the influence of the notion, shorn of its scare quotes,
that when we transgress in respect to the composer's performing intentions, we misrepresent what the composer had "to say," what the "authentic meanings" of his or her text were. We are unfaithful to the musical "message." The moral opprobrium that some may feel attaches to the
transgression of the composer's performing intentions thereby becomes
clear. It derives from their way of expressing the result, namely, as misrepresenting the "content" of the composer's "text." Where the text is verbal,
and its meaning "meaning" in the literal sense of that term, any misinter-
pretation of the text's meaning, either purposeful or due to *inexcusable*
lack of competence, is rightly viewed as a moral lapse; it violates the "ethics of inquiry."

It is thus a quite justified sense of moral outrage at purposefully, with
malice aforethought, misrepresenting an author's opinions, as expressed
in his or her text, that transfers in a quite unjustified way, I think, to the
case of ignoring for one reason or another a composer's expressed intentions as to how his or her work is to be performed. The transfer is unjustified precisely because musical "text," musical "message" or "content"
or "meaning"—what the composer had "to say"—all are or, where they
aren't, *should be* in scare quotes, to indicate attenuated senses. And there
is no reason at all to think that the moral obligation we owe to the author
to correctly represent her meanings and messages, what she had to say in
her text, implies a similar moral obligation to the composer to correctly
"represent" his "meanings" and "messages," what he had "to say" in his

---

about that meaning. It is as much a question of ethics as aesthetics" (le Huray, *Authenticity in Performance*, p. 3). Now, I take it that le Huray is talking here about *score* meaning, not *musical* meaning, although, unfortunately, he says in the very next sentence:
"This is not for a moment to suggest, however, that musical 'meaning' has a fixed and
absolute value—that there can be only *one* way of playing a particular piece." He
should, of course, have said "score meaning" rather than "musical 'meaning'"; for his
thought here is that scores "say things." Indeed, we can verbally paraphrase what they
say. And if we are telling people what a composer's *score* says, whether we are performers, scholars, or anyone else, we of course have the same moral obligation to tell the
truth as if we were telling people what the text of *Das Kapital* or *The Republic* says. But in
the act of *performing*, as I understand that act, it is not the act of telling people what the
score says; and, therefore, in *that act* the ethical obligation to tell truthfully what the
score says simply does not apply. We go to concerts to hear performances. We go to musicology seminars to find out what scores say.

The Authority of Intention

"text," where all the morally operative terms are figurative. Whatever musical imprudence we may commit by not starting trills on the upper note where the composer intended it, we are not garbling his message or misrepresenting his case and are subject to none of the moral opprobrium that may accrue to such interpretational malfeasance.

In claiming that it makes little sense to speak of music's literally possessing a message or content, or saying anything, I have reference of course only to absolute music: music without text, title, or program; music alone. But music with words and, perhaps, a mise en scène, is quite another matter. And without trying to unravel the logical niceties of "mixed-media" arts—that is to say, *which* is doing *what*—I think it can safely be said, without fear of contradiction, that operas, oratorios, cantatas, masses, songs, motets, and things of that kind are *musical works* that may possess content, convey messages, say something in the quite literal senses of all those terms. Furthermore, performing such works in any way that serves knowingly to obscure or alter content, message, what is said, is tainted with the same moral opprobrium that would attach to purposely misrepresenting the meaning of Plato or Marx. And if cold-bloodedly ignoring the composer's performing intentions should be the instrument of that obfuscation or meaning change, it too would be a morally guilty act.

But such considerations have little relevance for us here. For this is a book about performance of the "pure musical parameters." And few *real* examples, I think, can be adduced where differences in performing them will lead not merely to (perhaps) emphasizing or deemphasizing message or content but actually to *falsifying* it. To illustrate with the most obvious kind of case: what can happen on the podium, in the pit, or in the voice coach's studio that can really alter, misrepresent, or obscure the "philosophical" message of Wagner's *Die Meistersinger*? Where that can happen, needless to say, is at the hands of the director; witness the famous 1956 production of the work in which the nationalistic significance of Wagner's Nuremberg atmosphere, anathema to audiences immediately following the Second World War, was stripped away with purposeful intent in what a recent author has called "Wieland Wagner's *Meistersingers without Nuremberg*."[8]

Whatever laudable (or perhaps not so laudable?) intentions that Wie-

[8] Spencer, "Wagner's Nuremberg," p. 41.

The Authority of Intention

land Wagner might have had in obscuring *Die Meistersinger*'s palpable
message of German cultural ascendancy, it is as clear a case as one can
find of the way performance can misrepresent the idea content of a musical work. And such misrepresentation of an author's ideas, here or anywhere else, is a moral lapse, subject to justified moral condemnation of
the appropriate kind (although perhaps outweighed by other moral considerations pulling in the opposite direction). But the "performer," in
such cases, pretty clearly falls well outside of the category of "musical performer" and so well beyond the purview of this book.

Those who think I may be underestimating the power of the musical
performer to obfuscate or even contradict the message or content of
texted musical works will, of course, place more importance on the moral
defense of realizing the composer's performing intentions than I am here
suggesting is reasonable. Nevertheless, I hardly think that anyone will
want to place enough importance on it to deflect in any way the notion
that if realizing the performing intentions of the composer is to have a defense capable of enfranchising it as the principal, overarching goal of musical performance, it must be a defense based on an aesthetic payoff. And
to that possible defense I now turn my attention for the remainder of this
chapter.

·   ·   ·

Why should the performer realize the composer's performing intentions?
There can be only one interesting answer to this question: because it will
ipso facto realize the best performance of the work. But is that answer
true? That is what we must find out. And before we can, we must first
have a general idea—and a general idea is all we can have—of what the
best, or a good, performance would be. That is what immediately concerns us.

For the purpose of somewhat simplifying the argument, I shall confine
my remarks in what follows to the performance of absolute music: music
without text, title, or program. Much of what I say will also apply, pari
passu, to program music and texted music as well. But certain complications involved with the performance of texted and program music will
not be covered. I do not, however, believe that such complications sub-
stantially affect the general drift of my argument, and so I feel no qualms
about leaving them alone.

With the preceding qualification in mind, then, we can go on to ask what, in general, would constitute a good, or an optimal, performance of a work. To begin with, let us remind ourselves just what I take a performance (product) of a musical work to be. It is akin, I suggested in Chapter 5, to an arrangement of the work: that is to say, a version of it. But if that is the case, then in general a good performance (product) of a work will possess those characteristics to the fullest extent possible that make something a good musical work—a good musical work of art. Thus, in the most general terms, performance P_1 of work W will be a better performance of W than performance P_2 if it is more unified, presents more variety within that unity, is more expressive, has more effectively brought-off climaxes, resolves tensions in a more satisfying manner, is more lively, vibrant—anything in the way of what makes one work better than another and makes W as good as it may be. For P_1 and P_2 *are*, in the sense carefully made out in Chapter 5, different musical works: something like but not exactly like the sense, say, in which Beethoven's arrangement of his String and Wind Septet (Op. 20) for clarinet, cello, and piano (Op. 38) is a different work from the standard arrangement of Op. 20 for woodwind quintet.

But I have laid matters out in excessively general terms. And now some important qualifications must be made in the nature of a little fine-tuning. First, the criteria of work excellence that I have adduced, and any others that might be, must be relativized to particular genres, forms, composers, periods. Thus unity may be a good-making feature of a late eighteenth-century symphonic movement but not of a seventeenth-century dance suite, expressiveness a virtue of a Schumann piano piece but not of one of Stravinsky's so-called neoclassical pieces, climaxes and resolutions a good-making feature of a Bach aria but not of some compositions by Ravel and Debussy, and so on. And the same, of course, would hold true of performances of these works. But I need go into this complex subject no further; for I am not in the business, here, of analyzing the concept and paraphernalia of musical value. All I wish to maintain is that however we go about, in our everyday encounters with musical works, evaluating them and ranking them is just the way we go about evaluating and ranking performances.

Second, the following objection might here be interjected. If we are to say that P_1 is superior to P_2 by virtue of its having more of the features that make a musical work a good one, why should we not say—which clearly

The Authority of Intention

we would not—that P_1 is superior to P_2 in bringing out the sadness in bars 33–35 of W by virtue of the performer adding some diminished chords that the composer had not thought to put there? Bars 33–35 are expressive of sadness: the sadness there is part of W. And P_1 has succeeded, by the addition of the diminished chords, in intensifying that sadness to a degree P_2 cannot match. So why should we not say that, with regard to the expression in bars 33–35, P_1 is a better performance than P_2?

The answer must be that those diminished chords in P_1 are not part of W. Thus neither the act of which the playing of those notes is a part, nor the aural product of that act, which contains those notes, is a "performance" (properly so called) of W. Because I do not pretend to have a philosophical analysis of the musical work, I cannot give any adequate logical grounds for saying that. But I am taking it for granted that although there are going to be plenty of borderline cases, all my readers will possess a set similar to mine of well-founded intuitions about what would be beyond the bounds of performance and into the area of altering or arranging a musical work; and adding some diminished chords to intensify expression is clearly, I think all would agree, in the latter area. That being the case, P_1, at least with respect to those diminished chords, is not a performance of W at all and hence, a fortiori, not a *better* performance of W than P_2. Thus our intuition that we would not call P_1 a better performance of W than P_2 by virtue of the additional expressiveness that the diminished chords impart is saved.

Furthermore, this rather crude and obvious case in which an act and its product fail to be performances can be extended to more subtle and more likely cases, which can be dealt with in the same manner. In fact, the crude case itself can be looked at in a more subtle way by making a slight emendation. Let us suppose that the addition of these diminished chords not only intensifies the sadness in mm. 33–35 of P_1 beyond the intensity achieved by P_2 but (as is almost certain to be the case) does so beyond the intensity of sadness in W as well. The rejection of P_1 as a true performance of W is now overdetermined. We can reject it not only because it possesses chords that are not in W but because it possesses a level of emotional intensity that is not in W either. Of course, exactly *what* level of emotional intensity a given work possesses at a certain place is going to be a far more controversial matter, more difficult to settle, and based on considerably "softer" evidence than whether or not it contains diminished chords at

The Authority of Intention

that place, which is a "hard" textual question. But in principle, anyway, I think we must assume that within admittedly vague boundaries there is a certain intensity of sadness at mm. 33–35 of W and that a playing of those measures with an intensity higher (or lower) than that would be not a bad performance of those measures but rather no performance at all.

Of course, the usual and accepted way of bringing out or intensifying the emotive expression of a musical passage in performance is not by re-writing it but by playing it "in a certain way"—by, in other words, *manner* of performance. But even where intensity of expression is achieved by, so to say, "legitimate" means, by manner of performance and not by rewriting, I would want to insist that if the intensity achieved is beyond that of the work, the playing is to be judged not as a bad performance of W but as a nonperformance. And this applies to any other of the features that make a work—hence on my view, a performance of a work—a good one. P_1 is better than P_2 to the extent that it has more unity, or more variety, or more complexity, or more simplicity, or whatever feature is relevant to the evaluation of W. But only within the limits of W itself. For if it possesses more unity than W, or less, or whatever, then it is not a *performance* of W (in that respect) at all.

Here a caveat must be entered. It may seem as if I am endorsing Good-man's notion that a single wrong note, or some other small regional mistake in score compliance can render a playing a nonperformance of the work. But that is not the case. What I want to say is that if, for example, P_1 intensifies the expression at mm. 33–35 of W beyond the intensity possessed by W, then it is not a performance of W *in respect of those measures and that feature*. But it still *is* a performance of W *sans phrase*. If, of course, *enough* of such departures occur in P_1, then we might want to say not merely that it is not a performance of W in this respect or that but that it is not a performance of W at all, *tout court*. Nevertheless, it is logically important, for present purposes, to keep distinct ways of playing a part of a work that are bad performances *of that part* and ways of playing it that are, for one reason or another, not performances *of that part* at all. And one can maintain that distinction without endorsing the Goodmanian precept of notorious reputation, that one misdemeanor in regard to score compliance makes a playing not a performance (of that work).

What I am suggesting, then, with all the above qualifications read into it, is that when we evaluate a performance (product), we evaluate it in terms of just those good-making features that we would adduce in evaluating the work performed. But of course there will be, in many musical works if not all, features other than good-making ones, namely, those that are negative (i.e., bad-making) and those that may be neutral. Their presence requires us to have a more complicated description of performance evaluation: a good performance generally will be one that maximizes to the greatest extent possible all the good-making features of the work performed, minimizes to the greatest extent possible all the bad-making features, and includes to the greatest extent possible the neutral ones. If a good-making feature is maximized, however, beyond the degree to which the work possesses it, then in that respect it is not a performance of the work; and if, similarly, a bad-making feature is minimized below the degree to which the work possesses it, then in that respect it is not a performance of the work. And, finally, if the performer omits a neutral feature, then in that respect it is not a performance of the work. (It of course may be—indeed, I think, probably is the case—that no performance can maximize *all* positive features of the work while minimizing *all* negative ones. Such a set of properties may simply be, in practice, inconsistent. Which is only to say, really, what everyone already knows intuitively: that there is no *one* perfect or optimal performance but a wide variety of different performances, both attractive and unattractive for various reasons. The world of performance, in other words, on my view as on everyone else's, is a pluralistic one.)

And now a final objection must be entertained before we can get on to the question of intentions. I am saying that we evaluate a performance (product) the same way we evaluate the work performed, since the performance just is a version, an "arrangement" of the work. But this, it may be objected, goes against received opinion and common sense; for there are, clearly (so the objection goes), good-making and bad-making features of performances that are not features at all of works. For example: a performance of a movement can be too fast or too slow; but the movement cannot be either, *at least in the same sense*. Let me explain that last qualification.

It does make some kind of sense to say, for example, "The second movement of this symphony is too fast: a true adagio was needed here for contrast, and the andante is just not appropriate." But it does not make quite the same kind of sense as when we say, of an andante, "The performance

The   Authority   of   Intention

was too fast: it was really an allegro moderato." And it is in *that* sense that we can say "too fast" or "too slow" of a performance but not of the work performed.

I want to make two responses to this potential objection. First, I am not claiming that all good-making or bad-making features of work can be predicated of performance, and vice versa. There may well be some features exclusive to each. What I am claiming is that, *by and large, for the most part*, we can understand the evaluation of a performance in terms of its presenting, to the highest degree possible, those features of the work performed that tend to make it a good work and presenting, to the lowest degree possible, those that may tend to make it a bad one: in other words, it is the task of the performer, in the words of the song, to accentuate the positive (within the parameters of the work) and eliminate the negative (consistent with work fidelity).

Second, it would be useful to observe that at least some of the features applicable only to performances but not to works nevertheless can be fitted into my scheme because their real payoff is in features that can be predicated both of performance and of work. Thus, to stick with our previous example, if I say, "She played the andante too fast: it was made really into an allegro moderato," I cannot let my criticism rest with that. I must add some reason, having to do with the nature of the work, why it was too fast, why allegro moderato didn't work. And that answer, eventually, would have to be in terms of some feature shared by work and performance—for example, *contrast* between the andante and its preceding or following movement. Thus, the evaluative moment of "too fast," a feature of the performance but not of the work, is cashed out in terms of *contrast*, a feature of the work and, in a good performance, of the performance as well. And the same could also be said of other evaluative terms that refer exclusively (in a given context) to the performance. It may not be true in all such cases, but it will be true in a significant number of them, I think, that the value term, be it positive or negative, appropriate only to the performance, will when defended turn out to have its justificatory foundation in a shared feature of work and performance. For our purposes, however, I think there is no need to adduce further examples.

To summarize briefly, then, a performance of a work is to be evaluated, comparatively to another, in the same way that the arrangements of, say, Beethoven's Septet—the one for piano trio and the one for woodwind quintet—are to be evaluated vis-à-vis one another: as works of art, works of music, *but* works of art and music that are *both*, at the same time, *the* work of art of which they are the versions. Which is the best arrangement of Op. 20, the one for piano trio or the one for woodwind quintet? Answer: the one that is the best work of art, the best musical work; the one that is the best "Op. 20." Which is the best performance of Beethoven's *Hammerklavier*, this one by Serkin or that one by Schnabel? Answer: the one that is the best work of art, the best musical work; the one that is the best "Op. 106."

Now, there are those who will, for various reasons, find this analysis unsatisfactory, and maybe even outrageous, in its conflation of performance evaluation with work evaluation; for received opinion is certainly against that. And in all fairness to them I must admit that what I have given here is a mere sketch, which faces far more difficulties and requires far more spelling out than can be undertaken here. So I lay it down as a hypothesis and a promissory note. But I offer in conclusion, before I go on to the intention question, the following reassurance: even if my account of performance, and its evaluation, proves unsatisfactory, the rest of what I have to say will, I feel certain, be consistent with any other account that succeeds. So, with that assurance made, and with my own cards on the table, I can now get on with the business.

I argued in the previous section that a performance, being a work of art in its own right—in effect, an "arrangement" of a work—is to be evaluated for the most part by adducing the same good-making and bad-making features one would adduce in evaluating the work of which it is the performance. Further, I argued that, given two performances of W, P_1 and P_2, P_1 would be the better performance by virtue of maximizing, to the greatest permissible extent the good-making features of W and minimizing to the greatest permissible extent the bad-making ones. The question before us is, What reason might we have for believing that the better performance, the one most successfully maximizing the good-making features and minimizing the bad-making ones, is the performance that realizes to the greatest extent possible the composer's performing intentions, wishes, hypotheses, tentative suggestions, and so on? Why, in short, should we believe the composer's plan for performance of his work must necessarily be the best one?

The Authority of Intention

161

To state the matter very briefly, before going into it in detail, the notion that realizing the composer's intentions (in the broad sense of the term) produces the optimal performance seems predicated on two axioms, sometimes explicitly stated and defended but more frequently unspoken, unexplained, and implicit: what I shall call here the axiom that *the composer knows best* (CKB), and the related axiom of *the delicate balance* (DB).

CKB is, of course, fairly obvious on the face of it. It simply is the belief that because the composer is the maker, the creator of the work, he or she, common sense would dictate, is the most intimately acquainted with it in all its detail and, therefore, is the one in the most favored position to know how it might be best made aurally available to an audience.

DB is perhaps more elusive; but what it amounts to, in brief, is the belief that every work of art—at least, every great or good or important work of art—is an arrangement of parts in such a delicate balance and adjustment of interrelationships that even the slightest change anywhere will upset the equilibrium and worsen the whole. This is, of course, a palpably romantic notion. But in essence it is, after all, one of the oldest philosophical precepts that we possess about the arts, having had a very mature and highly influential statement in Aristotle's *Poetics*, where, it will be recalled, the Philosopher compared the well-wrought tragic plot, in its unity, to the closely knit parts of a living organism and averred that "its parts (the incidents) ought to be so constructed that, when some part is transposed or removed, the whole is disrupted and disturbed."[9]

The relation between CKB and DB is this. The delicate balance, it is believed, is so finely tuned that even the slightest deviation from the composer's performing intentions (broadly speaking) will upset it. It may seem, so the faithful would have it, that a local "improvement" might be possible, using, say, a modern flute to improve ensemble, or fingering a passage in a way undeveloped in the composer's lifetime, to execute a scale more smoothly; but such local changes are bound, overall, even if they have a favorable local payoff, to upset in the long term the "delicate balance" and so are never to be entered upon. The composer knows best. Only the composer has the intimate connection with the work that can enable one to contrive and fully comprehend the delicate balance; and to go against the composer's performing intentions, even if it seems an im-

[9] Aristotle, *Poetics*, p. 12 (51a).

The Authority of Intention

provement, cannot, in the event, be one. "Stay close to nurse for fear of something worse."

In what follows we must ask ourselves if either of these axioms, CKB or DB, is true. More precisely, I shall argue that there is no convincing argument or evidence in favor of either of them. I shall not, however, try to demonstrate their falsity absolutely; for, as will become apparent, that would be an impossible task. But, I take it, if there is no convincing argument or evidence for either one of them, there is no reason to adopt either one of them in our musical practice. And let me add, before getting on with it, that my criterion for "convincing argument or evidence" is neither Cartesian certainty nor even the absence of reasonable doubt as it is conceived of in a court of law but merely the evidence and arguments that convince us in our everyday lives and guide us in our ordinary affairs. It is even that latter kind and degree of evidence and argument that, so far as I can see, fails to be forthcoming for either of the axioms that underlie faith in the composer as the *fons et origo* of performance practice. And if the evidence is not there, even in this weak, practical sense, for either CKB or DB, I see no reason to predicate musical practice upon them. For those with religious fervor or the will to believe, of course, such an argument falls on deaf ears.

·   ·   ·

Common sense might suggest that CKB is a nonstarter. Composing is one kind of skill, performing another. Why should anyone think that talent or expertise in the one should imply either in the other?

Here are some analogies. Miss Tinker is very good at inventing labor-saving devices. Mr. Faber knows how to manufacture them; Miss Tinker does not. So Miss Tinker takes her inventions to Mr. Faber, who figures out how to mass-produce them, to their mutual benefit.

Miss Schuster makes extremely good shoes but hasn't the foggiest notion how to market them. Mr. Handelman is a super salesman with no talent at all for making anything (except money). So Miss Schuster makes the shoes, Mr. Handelman sells them, and both are in the chips.

Well, isn't the relation between the composer and the performer something like that—something like the relation between the inventor and the manufacturer, or between the maker and the seller? One knows how to bring the things into existence, the other how to present them to a con-

The Authority of Intention

163

sumer. It is to the mutual benefit of both to make use of the expertise of the other, doing only the job for which he or she is best suited by nature and expertise.

Hume might say that we have here two "species of common sense" that "oppose" each other.[10] On the one hand, there is a "species of common sense" to the effect that *obviously* the composer knows best, given his or her intimate relation to the work, as God-like creator of it. That nobody could know better than he or she how to present the work in performance is just "common sense." Yet now we have a completely opposite "species of common sense," based on perfectly transparent models of the relation between "making" and "marketing," that seems to imply just the reverse. For what can be more obvious, more commonsensical, than that creating things is one kind of expertise and presenting them for public consumption or appreciation another—and that it is highly unlikely (though not impossible) for the same person to exhibit both kinds of expertise at the world-class level?

Well, the solution of this antinomy is really not very interesting philosophically, but it is nevertheless essential to our enterprise. Obviously—at least so it seems to me—the truth about the relation between composition and performance lies somewhere *between* the "two species of common sense." And the best way to show this, perhaps, is to chip away at the maker-marketer model until a more accurate model of the composer-performer relation emerges.

One thing we know that must cause us to modify the maker-marketer model as applied to composition and performance is that in the Western musical tradition the composer, until very recently, has usually been a distinguished, not infrequently a fabled and lionized, virtuoso as well, usually on keyboard instruments. And another well-known fact that must prevent us from taking the maker-marketer model *too* literally is the role *improvisation* has played, until very recently, in the composer-performer's bag of tricks. For when a Frescobaldi or Bach, Mozart or Beethoven, Chopin or Liszt was praised as a performer, it was not merely as a performer of his own music or of that of others but especially as a composer "on the spot."

We know, furthermore, both from anecdote and from fairly trivial inference, that a lot of the composer-performer's musical compositions

[10] Cf. Hume, "Of the Standard of Taste," in *Essays*, pp. 234–35.

The Authority of Intention

must contain material that had its origin in improvisational performance, thus, of course, further collapsing the composer-performer distinction. And we can straightforwardly infer, too, one would think, from all this— from the thoroughgoing way in which composition and performance are intertwined with each other in the tradition—that the composer's opinions about how his or her work is to be performed are not to be taken lightly. It is not an outsider's advice but the advice (usually) of an expert; nor is there an alienation of "product" from "means of marketing." For the work or parts thereof may very well have been born in performance, that is to say, in improvisation, and so to separate composer from performer as one does shoemaker from shoe salesman might be tantamount to separating the smile from the smiler.

But—and it is a big "but"—there is no justification for chopping away at the maker-marketer model until there is nothing left of it at all. For the person of the performing artist in his or her own right, the practicing musician known solely for instrumental virtuosity, is also a part of the tradition with which we are concerned. And there is a long history in that tradition of cooperation, of beneficial interaction between composer and performer, which suggests that the arena of performance, far from being a military discipline under the ringmaster's whip, is more in the spirit of commedia dell'arte, where we make it up as we go along.

There is, in other words, in the tradition that the "historical" performer wishes faithfully to reproduce, a very mixed message. Part of that message certainly is, in anecdote and established practice, "Do it my way or else." But another part of the message, again in anecdote and established practice, and equally compelling, is "Let us reason together." And this mixed message leads us to a rather paradoxical-looking impasse.

CKB essentially has it that the composer is infallible when it comes to the best way of performing his or her work: the performing intentions of the composer are, according to CKB, indefeasible. But the message of the tradition is mixed. And this implies that part of most composers' system of performing intentions is the intention to learn by the experience of performers and sometimes to take the performer's explicit or implicit advice. Is *this* intention infallible? If so, then the composer's specific performing intentions cannot be, because it is the composer's *indefeasible* policy that his specific performing intentions are *defeasible*. If we want to insist that with regard to performance *tout court* the composer knows best, then we

The Authority of Intention

165

shall have to accept that he does not necessarily know best in every specific case how his individual works are to be played, for he knows best that his own individual ideas about how his works are specifically to be played are not always the best ideas, and the performer's may be.

Thus CKB, given what the mixed message of the performance tradition tells us, seems to be a self-defeating doctrine. If the composer knows best about how his specific works are to be performed, then to say that he also knows best that sometimes the performer knows better—which is, as well, part of CKB broadly conceived—must be false; so CKB must be false overall. But if one wants to have just the part of CKB true that says that the composer always knows best about how the individual work should be played, and is always mistaken in thinking, when he does sometimes, that someone else has found a better way, we must have some method of establishing what I shall call modified CKB, independent of "common sense." For common sense, as we have seen, goes both ways; and, in any case, the "common sense" that pushes us toward our original CKB is pushing us toward a self-defeating, paradoxical doctrine.

Why, indeed, should we even think that *any* of the composer's performing intentions are infallible, if we accept that at least one of them, his intention sometimes to acquiesce in the performer's way over his own, is *always* to be counted mistaken? Once you allow one performing intention of the composer to be open to at least reasonable doubt and possible denial, you have let the fox into the henhouse, and everything is vulnerable.

What might we appeal to in establishing modified CKB? A possible answer seems to be that modified CKB stands or falls with DB. It is because the composer's performing intentions are part of that delicate balance for which any change is a change for the worse. And, it may then be argued, we can well understand why there is no absurdity—as some might think there is—in asserting that a composer can quite possibly be mistaken about the infallibility of his performing intentions. For he may be quite unaware of the delicate balance that he has achieved by a combination of instinct, genius, and craft, even though that may have been what he was aiming at all along; and he may thus be quite unmindful of how what he accepts from the performer as a "better" way of performing some passage than the way he has indicated is detrimental to that balance and, hence, to the work in question.

In order to push this inquiry into DB further, however, we had better get straight about what it amounts to. For there seem to be two possibilities.

There is a sense of DB in which it could be true that one masterpiece has it and another does not. It is the sense in which the "delicate balance" is taken to be a good-making property that some particular works have and some do not but that is certainly not a necessary condition for being a great musical work. Thus, for example, Mozart's *Eine Kleine Nachtmusik* has a perfection about it that makes us feel as if it were in perfect equilibrium: change one detail and that perfection is lost. Whereas Schubert's great B♭ Piano Sonata gives us no such sense of balanced perfection but rather one of craggy vastness, of overwhelming magnificence, flawed yet so powerful as to make the flaws insignificant in contrast to the overall effect.

What I am stating here is something like the early eighteenth-century formulation of the distinction between the beautiful and the sublime, in which Virgil represented the neoclassical ideal of balanced perfection whereas Homer was held up as the example of overpowering but flawed grandeur. And when the distinction came to be extended, as inevitably it was, to music, it was such masters as the "chaste and perfect Corelli" that stood for Virgilian beauty and, of course, in England, Handel as the powerful, flawed Homeric.[11]

Now, this first sense of the DB that I am explicating here can itself be understood two ways: either what we might call "objectively," or "impressionistically." In its objective sense, DB has it that *Eine Kleine Nachtmusik*, say, gives an impression of a delicate balance, a perfect equilibrium that *in fact* could be destroyed if the slightest alteration were made in the work: that is to say, any change whatever would *in fact* destroy that impression of balance and equilibrium the work conveys. Whereas, in its impressionistic version, DB says that *Eine Kleine Nachtmusik* gives the *impression* of delicate balance, of perfect equilibrium, in which any change would upset the apple cart, but that that is all it is: an *impression*, an aesthetic effect, the fact of the matter being that Mozart could have given the same impression of balance and equilibrium by changing the work in various ways, just as long as the changes were consistent with that impression—an impression that Schubert's B♭ Sonata, for all its greatness, does not give at all.

[11] On Handel and the sublime, see Kivy, "Mainwaring's *Handel*," passim.

The Authority of Intention

It appears to me, although it would be difficult to prove, that only in its impressionistic reading is this version of DB true. It is undoubtedly true that certain works—particularly, of course, those of "classical" periods or by composers of a "classical" taste—give the impression of the delicate balance. But I tend to doubt that that implies the real impossibility of alternative ways of achieving that same impression by, in the case of, say, *Eine Kleine Nachtmusik*, adding a movement or replacing a movement with another. As a matter of fact, I believe *Eine Kleine Nachtmusik* did have at least one extra movement in an earlier version, and Mozart's "Paris" Symphony had its slow movement exchanged for another on the advice of people who knew Parisian taste and convinced Mozart that the original slow movement would not please in Paris. I see no compelling reason to think these works would fail to maintain their impression of balance in their alternate versions. And, of course, we know many examples of such tinkering in all musical periods.

But whether I am right about this is completely immaterial in present circumstances. For in neither the impressionistic nor the objective reading will this version of DB do the job of vouchsafing CKB. First of all, it would require an additional argument, even if this version of DB were true in the objective sense, to show that the delicate balance would be lost if such a work as possessed it were performed not in accordance with the composer's performing intentions. And I doubt if such an argument could be run successfully. As a matter of fact, I came to know *Eine Kleine Nachtmusik* a long time ago, on 78-rpm recordings, and in singularly "inauthentic" performances under the batons of the likes of Weingartner and Toscanini; and yet I was aware of the work's delicate balance even in these versions. Apparently, then, where the delicate balance is present, it survives various kinds of performance, even the "inauthentic" kind that are not faithful in all respects to the composer's performing intentions. This I know from *experience*; and I have no idea what *argument* would counter that.

Second, though, even if this version of DB were a successful argument for CKB where the delicate balance obtains, it would fail to have any effect where the delicate balance is absent, as, for example, in the case of Schubert's B♭ Sonata. That is to say, it *would* be an argument for performing *Eine Kleine Nahtmusik* according to the composer's performing intentions, if true, that failing to do so would destroy the feeling of balance and equilibrium possessed by the work. But since by hypothesis Schubert's B♭ Sonata does not possess that feeling of balance and equilibrium, it cannot be an argument for recognizing the performing intentions of the composer in performance that failing to do so tends to destroy the feeling of delicate balance and equilibrium—it is simply not there to destroy.

Third, and this is quite important, even where a work does possess that delicate balance and equilibrium, and even if failure to conform to the composer's performing intentions always destroys it, it *still* does not follow that conforming to the composer's performing intentions will be better than not doing so, for the following reason: the delicate balance, on this version of DB, is only one among many good-making features of the works to which it belongs. And it is therefore perfectly possible that a performance in which it is lost might so highlight other of a work's good-making features as to make the total aesthetic payoff of the performance a higher one than the payoff of the performance that adheres to the composer's performing intentions and preserves the delicate balance. In short, even where we assume everything favorable that we can for the present version of DB, it fails to legitimate CKB. Another version of DB is required; and to such a version I shall now turn my attention.

. . .

The third objection to DB as initially construed calls our attention to what we really need, and what it fails to give: a version of DB that will, as a support for CKB, always yield the result of the optimal performance being the one in conformity to the composer's performing intentions. So let us, with this as our end in view, construe DB as maintaining the following. Every work is a system of the composer's work and performance intentions, so delicately balanced and organically interconnected that a single change *anywhere*, even if it seems like a local improvement, will lessen the overall effect of the work. That is to say, even if a change in one place increases the aesthetic payoff *there*, it will lessen the aesthetic payoff overall. A musical work, on this reading of DB, is rather like an image of the Leibnizian best of all possible worlds. For just as God has maximized good and minimized evil in the world he chose to create, consistent with logical possibility, so the composer, as the god of his work, has created a perfectly balanced little world of sound, consistent with certain externally and internally imposed parameters, such that aesthetic good is maximized, aesthetic evil minimized. It might *seem* as if this is not the best of all possible

The Authority of Intention

worlds—that it would have been a better one without the Lisbon earthquake—but if we were able, like God, to take in the whole picture, we
would see that a world without the Lisbon earthquake, no matter how
God adjusted its parts, would be a worse one than the one that contains
it: the world as it is. Likewise, it may seem as if a departure from the composer's instructions for performance in one place might make an improvement, and, indeed, in that place it will; but the work overall must
suffer and have less overall aesthetic value than it would have had if that
instruction were followed to the letter.

Now, this reading of DB does indeed seem to support CKB fully: indeed, it is really just a way of stating the latter. But the problem with it,
straightaway, is that one wonders *why* anyone in his right mind should
believe it. *As stated* it is wildly implausible. Why should it be true of *all*
musical works that each of them, as it stands, *is* such that no performance
change from the composer's intentions can do aught but lower its aesthetic payoff?

Consider three baroque trio sonatas: one by J. S. Bach, one by Georg
Philipp Telemann, and one by Frederick the Great. There is some initial
plausibility in the contention that Bach's work is, if any work is, a structure of such excellence and sophistication of execution that none but the
master himself dare tamper with it. If CKB and DB (under the present
reading) apply to any composers and works, it is to the composers and
works we revere as at the highest level of musical attainment. It is of the
works of those composers that we are likely to say: "We cannot make it
better. If Bach intended it to be played thus-and-so, then even if it may
seem that playing it differently here or there will be better, we can be sure
that that is not true. We may not see the harm, but Bach from his God-like
perspective could."

Well, my esteem for Bach is of such a high order that it amounts to reverence. And for that reason I find it at least a real option that such composers, at the absolute pinnacle of musical genius, should have contrived
works of such sensitive balance and equilibrium that any change whatever, even in manner of performance, from what they themselves had in
mind must lessen the aesthetic value of the works. But, to begin with
something of a *reductio*, I hardly feel for the musical talent of Frederick the
Great the kind of reverence that would lead me to think his trio sonata a
work that cannot be improved or his performing intentions either infalli-

ble or even of more authority than those of the ordinary performers of today on the baroque circuit. And although I certainly have a good deal
more respect for a Georg Philipp Telemann or a Heinrich Graun, worthy
practitioners of the art, I hardly hold them in the reverence I hold a Bach
or a Haydn. So why should I think that they have achieved that God-like
adjustment in their works that makes *their* trio sonatas, like the handi-
work of God, untouchable? DB and CKB seem to have at least a fighting
chance of being correct with regard to masters and masterpieces. But they
scarcely seem even plausible with regard to the *Kleinmeisters* that the "authentic performance" movement has so enthusiastically championed. Indeed, they just seem flat-out false with regard to the likes of Frederick the
Great, or even the likes of Telemann or Graun.

Thus, DB (as currently construed) and, by consequence, CKB, if they
are valid at all, can be valid only for composers at what we take to be the
highest level of attainment. Let us now inquire whether they are valid
even for them.

. . .

I compared the delicate balance that is supposed to hold in the works of
the masters to the Leibnizian concept of the best of all possible worlds.
And so I shall from now on refer sometimes to the present version of the
DB as the Leibnizian version. According to Leibniz, the sum of goodness
in the world is the greatest logically possible; and any local change seemingly for the better would, in the long run and from the broadest perspective—that is to say, the perspective of God—in fact be perceived to be a
change for the worse. The Leibnizian version of DB says as much for the
masterpieces of music, in particular, seeming "improvements" over the
composer's performing intentions. For such seeming local improvements,
the Leibnizian DB holds, will always in the long run and from the composer's God-like perspective result in a lower overall aesthetic payoff than
would have accrued to faithfully adhering to the composer's performing
intentions throughout.

I hope I may be forgiven for indulging in this well-known textbook the-
ology; for I think it actually illuminates the musical performance problem
in an unsuspected way. So let me continue. Leibniz's claim, that this is the
best of all possible worlds, is notoriously both unverifiable and irrefutable:
completely immune to empirical failure. The "long run" is never run, and
the God-like perspective remains always unattainable. And thus we are

The Authority of Intention

forever faced with the "possibility" that in the long run that we will never experience, from a perspective we can never attain, this is a better world, in spite of the Lisbon earthquake and other such horrors, for reasons we can never comprehend, than any of the possible worlds without them.

But now one may get the sneaking suspicion that if Leibniz's famous world hypothesis is unverifiable in practice if not in principle, perhaps the Leibnizian version of DB is as well. And, indeed, it can certainly be stated in such a way as to make it just as immune from empirical falsification as the Leibnizian solution to the problem of evil. For if I should claim that a performance of a Bach trio sonata departing from the master's perform- ing intentions in certain respects sounds better to me than as performed with those intentions in place, you may reply: "Well, my man, your ear is not as fastidious as Bach's (needless to say). But if you listen to Bach's way *long enough*, you will come inevitably to like it better." How long is *long enough*? "Why, just as long as it takes to like Bach's way better than the 'inauthentic' one." Of course, I may die having never achieved enlight- enment; but that will not falsify DB. I just didn't live *long enough*.

Now if this really is the status of DB, a kind of Leibnizian world of the musical work, *possibly true*, which is merely to say, *logically possible* but *completely immune to empirical refutation*, we must ask some hard questions about it, even as applied to our most revered composers. For even Bach, after all, is not God. And one hard question we should ask, straightaway, is *why* in God's name we should believe something that is barely "possi- ble" and only at the cost of, in a completely ad hoc manner, always keep- ing the evidence of our musical sense from refuting it?

If we ask the same question about Leibniz's solution to the problem of evil—Why should anyone believe the barely possible but (to the common sensibility) wildly implausible suggestion that this is the best world pos- sible?—the answer is very clear. The believer in this hypothesis is *already* committed to belief in God, belief in His omnipotence, omniscience, and moral perfection; and this prior commitment is nonnegotiable. That being the case, belief in the Leibnizian world hypothesis is a rational pol- icy: better to believe the barely possible but wildly implausible than to en- tertain a logically inconsistent set of beliefs.

But the philosopher of music—at least *this* one—is in no such position vis-à-vis the Leibnizian version of DB as the Christian believer is vis-à-vis the Leibnizian world hypothesis. I have no prior beliefs so strongly held

The Authority of Intention

that only belief in the Leibnizian DB can save me from logical contradiction. And in the absence of such beliefs, there is no reason for me to believe the Leibnizian DB—a doctrine that, although logically possible, bears all the obvious earmarks of a vacuous one, fully armed against all empirical refutation. For surely no one would suggest as a rational policy believing something *just* because it is *possible*.

I think we are now in a position to make some summary conclusions. First, although the Leibnizian version of DB is barely possible, under the stipulation that if we listen long *enough* (with "enough" left completely open-ended) it will be verified, at least for every work at the highest musical level, there seems no real reason to believe it. The Leibnizian version of DB, as we have already seen, is a palpable nonstarter with regard to works below the level of masterwork. But nor is there any reason, as we have now seen, to believe that Leibnizian DB holds even for these. This is not, however, to deny that some masterworks are such that any departure from the composer's performing intentions will produce a lower aesthetic payoff than strict adherence to them. That, however, must be decided empirically, on a case-by-case basis.

Second, if the Leibnizian version of DB falls then so also does CKB, which it was meant to support. For if it is false that all musical works, even all musical masterworks, are such that any departure from the composer's performing intentions will result in a lower aesthetic payoff than would accrue to strict adherence, it must also be false that the composer always knows best as to how his or her work is optimally to be performed in every respect; and *that* is what CKB amounts to. But again, as with the case of DB, this is not to deny that sometimes, for some works, it is the case that the composer's performing intentions constitute the best way of performing the work—that is to say, the way with the highest aesthetic payoff. And again, as with DB, the question of where CKB applies and where it does not must be decided empirically, case by case.

But how does such an empirical, case-by-case procedure work? Until we know that we will not really know what the authority of the composer's performing intentions really amounts to. As might be expected, what it means to verify or disconfirm empirically for a given work, either DB or CKB, is not an uncomplicated matter. It will occupy us in the concluding sections of this chapter.

. . .

The Authority of Intention

When the "historical performance" movement, in its recent form, was in its infancy, in the 1950s (which is when I first encountered it), one used to hear pleas for restoring the great baroque choral literature, the Mass in B minor, and the familiar (and less familiar) oratorios of Handel to a manner of performance more in accord with the composers' intentions. Those were simpler days; and the things being proselytized for were so basic that it is hard to believe there was once a time when they were not in place: smaller performing forces, the original orchestration (but on modern instruments), including a harpsichord continuo, starting trills on the upper note, adding an appoggiatura here or there at the cadence of a recitative. These seem to us practices hardly in need of defense or argument. Yet they *were* defended and argued for then, for there were plenty of distinguished performers who by no means agreed that any of these were good ideas. And it will be salutary, I think, to recall some of these arguments and defenses. The point of doing so will become apparent.

We were told, in those early days, that one needed the continuo to fill in the missing harmonies, one needed the harpsichord rather than the piano or added wind parts so that just the right balance might be achieved: the piano or winds "obtruded"; the harpsichord's genius was just to "be there," not too obtrusive. We were told that trills, in this period, were not just "ornaments" but expressive gestures and that starting them slowly, on the dissonant upper note, made them expressive rather than ornamental. We were told that the bloated Victorian choral society, two thousand strong, muddied the contrapuntal waters of Bach and Handel and that an ensemble of more modest proportions, as the composer intended, would make these muddied waters transparent, the counterpoint intelligible. And so on.

We heard these new ways—which were old ways—of performing *Messiah* and the B-minor Mass and *gradually* came to like them better than the ways we were used to. Many of us did not like them at first (I still have a great fondness for the "old" *Messiah*); and that is why I underscore that it took time for our taste in these matters to change. This is a complication that must be taken into account by any appeal to "experience" in judging whether one way of performing a work is "better" than another. So I shall be returning to it later on.

There are, then, three things that have emerged from this little reminiscence of earlier times in the movement to revive the composer's inten-

The Authority of Intention

tions in the performance of the baroque choral literature (and they are meant to apply, pari passu, of course, to any musical style or tradition whatever). First, we have a right to expect a "story" about how adherence to the performing intentions of the composer will make the performance of the work better—in what respects better. And this will require having an interpretation of the whole work, in which to place this "story."

Second, whether or not this story is true, whether or not adhering to the composer's performing intentions does improve the performance in the stated respects, is an empirical matter, a matter of the listener's musical taste. It cannot be decided a priori, from the heights of theory, but only in the workshop of musical practice.

Third, musical taste is not a constant but a variable. It does not sit as an unwavering judge of a changing musical practice but is itself changed by the changing practice that it judges. This means that appeal to the judgment of musical taste cannot but be an appeal over time, and *how much* time is a debatable question. Furthermore, taste is not merely a descriptive concept; it is a value-laden, normative one, at least in its standard contexts. And thus the appeal to its judgment involves not merely an appeal to taste as it is but to taste *as we might want it to become*, under the influence of a changing practice.

Each of these three points must now be examined separately, before we can reach a reasonable conclusion about how appeal to the composer's performing intentions can really have merit.

· · ·

Under the influence of the "historical performance" movement, appeal to the composer's performing intentions has taken on such an aura of supernatural invulnerability as to seem to require, now, no further defense. This is natural enough in the process in which a movement becomes an established religion. But I am reminded, in this regard, of John Stuart Mill's defense of freedom of expression, in *On Liberty*, in which he argued that even those propositions taken for established truth must continually be open to dissent; for where such propositions cease to be dissented from, at least in argument, they literally cease be understood. And that, it appears to me, is what has now happened to the appeal to composers' performing intentions. In allowing them to become unquestioned dogma, we have forgotten why we wanted to retrieve them in the first place; and in forgetting that, we have allowed slavish adherence to them

The Authority of Intention

(or what we take them to be) at times to defeat the very purpose that such adherence was called upon to serve.

It is thus not enough to say "Perform it this way: it is the composer's way." What we will want to know is in what respect the work will sound better played this way rather than some other way. We will be entitled to an account, based on some overall view, some interpretation, of how this work goes, of how it is put together, that tells us why performing it the composer's way, rather than some other plausible way, will improve this particular work.

In addition, we should expect that the story we are told is a believable one, with a real payoff for the listener, not a possible payoff for an imaginary one. Let me try to spell this out. What follows is a brief for playing works of the past on "original instruments," by a recent and very astute philosophical commentator.

The deliberate exploitation in composition of features of the instruments to be used is at least a possibility when the composer can assume that instruments of a particular type *will* be used. To a certain extent the availability of this assumption is assumed when the composer specifies the instruments of her work. But a composer who is not composing for distant posterity knows a good deal more about the instruments which will be used to perform her works than just that the violin parts will be played on violins, the bassoon parts on bassoons, and so on. She knows that the parts will be performed (in the performances that are most salient for her) on the violins, bassoons, and so on of her here-and-now, and she is apt to know very well what those instruments are like. She will, then, be able to rely on features more specific than the generic characteristics of violins-through-history or bassoons-through-history or pianos-through-history. It is at least possible that Bach or Mozart or Beethoven or Chopin made various decisions in composing with the intention of exploiting features of the instruments they knew which are not features of later versions of the same instruments (later violins, bassoons, pianos, etc.). And again, even if such conscious intentions played no role in their composing, it seems likely that many composers respond consciously or unconsciously to their awareness of the features of the instruments with which

The Authority of Intention

they are familiar in ways which might (persisting with a somewhat extended sense of "idiomatic") be gathered within the general category of writing idiomatically for those instruments. To the extent that this is so (and it will differ from composer to composer and from work to work), works and instruments will be suited to each other in ways that reflect the musical judgment of the composer. Such a matching of work and instrument can be expected to produce aesthetic values that can be realized only in performances on period instruments.[12]

Let me call attention to two obvious features of this spirited defense of adhering to the composer's intentions with regard to period instruments—which is to say, by the way, not intentions to have the music played on period instruments rather than on modern ones (which choice, of course, was not open to composers of the past) but intentions, *simpliciter*, that the work be played on *these very instruments*, familiar to and thoroughly understood by the composer in question. The two features are, first, that no specific way is ever mentioned in which a work would be better played on a period instrument than on its modern counterpart; and, second, that the whole argument is couched in terms of a "possible" rather than an actual outcome: "It is at least *possible* that Bach or Mozart or Beethoven or Chopin made various decisions in composing with the intention of exploiting features of the instruments they knew which are not features of later versions of the same instruments."

Now, it would perhaps seem unfair to expect the above-quoted author, Aron Edidin, who is writing in a philosophical vein and not as a musician, to cite chapter and verse on the specific merits of, say, the eighteenth-century basset horn over the twentieth-century one in performance of the great concertante aria for that instrument in *La Clemenza di Tito*. And to a degree, I suppose that *would* be an unfair expectation. But even allowing for the fact that we are dealing here with a philosophical argument and not practical advice on performance practice, we are not mistaken, I think, in the distinct feeling that Edidin's argument is suspended in air.

It is of course "possible"—logically possible, anyway—that all the

[12] Aron Edidin, "Look What They've Done to My Song," in French, Uehling, and Wettstein, *Midwest Studies in Philosophy*, vol. 16, p. 407.

The Authority of Intention

works of the great masters are so finely adjusted to the strengths and weaknesses of the instruments of their times that the substitution of a modern one, even though technically improved over its older counterpart in some respects, will upset the "delicate balance" and result, overall, in the long run, in a lower aesthetic payoff. Alternatively, however, we also know that composers make demands upon instruments—particularly instruments with which they are not on intimate terms—that are "unidiomatic" and even beyond the real capabilities of those instruments, demands that are part of the motivating force that drives instrument makers to make technical improvements to their products. Edidin's view represents only the "conservative" compositional attitude toward instruments, not the "revolutionary" one; and if the revolutionary one were not extant as well it seems doubtful that we would today have woodwinds with keys, trumpets with pistons, or the rest.

In any event, we have been brought, I hope, to that point in the argument where we will not so easily be satisfied with mere "metaphysical possibilities." It is "possible" that the Lisbon earthquake is a blessing in disguise; but it requires some pretty strong and serious presuppositions to make that possibility significant to anyone. And the "possibility" that every change from period to modern instrument, for all the advantages it might bestow, will be outweighed by unforeseen and unspecified disadvantages is one of the new "dogmas" that Peter le Huray may be crying down when he quite correctly warns: "There is however a danger that new 'authentic' dogmas of style and interpretation will come to replace the anachronistic dogmas of a late Romantic tradition, the shortcomings of which are now increasingly realized by informed professionals and an informed musical public."[13]

I hope I have made it clear, by this time, that there appears to be no a priori argument to support the precept, in danger of becoming dogma, that adherence to the composer's performing intentions, of which the "period instrument" movement can be seen as a special case, must always have a greater aesthetic payoff than any other policy. And the "possibility" argument, of which Edidin's is a good but by no means isolated example, is the last refuge, before one simply acquiesces in the fact that the composer's performing intentions, wishes, suggestions, and tentative hypotheses are, like anyone else's, subject only to the tribunal of experience,

[13] Le Huray, *Authenticity in Performance*, p. xv.

The Authority of Intention

178

of musical taste, and must be verified or disconfirmed case by case, in the hurly-burly of musical practice. And the first step in that verification or disconfirmation process is a plausible story about what one policy or another will result in: what it will do for the work to which it is applied. The true believer may be in a position where he or she is forced to accept the mere "possibility" that every cloud has a silver lining, without describing what particular silver lining accrues to what particular cloud. But the musician and the musician's audience are in no such position with regard to any performance policy, including the composer's, on pain of its being an article of faith: a new "authentic" dogma, as le Huray happily puts it.

So we shall now be impatient of any argument for adhering to the composer's performing intentions that does not cite chapter and verse. We shall insist on a plausible, verifiable story: how will the "period" basset horn make the performance of Mozart better? How will a modern instrument make it worse? On which side of the ledger does each choice fall?

This brings us to the point where "verification" now becomes an issue. How are we to confirm or disconfirm a performance strategy? The criterion is clear in principle, if not in practice. That local or overall performing policy that makes aesthetically the best version of the work is the best policy. And how are we to determine what the best version is? Again, the answer is in principle clear, though in practice not. The best version is the version that gives "the listener" the most aesthetic satisfaction: in less pretentious terms, the one that sounds best. But now we begin to have problems. Who is this "listener"? How do we evaluate this listener's satisfaction or dissatisfaction? Here things get murky. It is our next task to try to clear them up.

· · ·

Let's tackle "the listener" (henceforth "audience") first. Won't it make a very big difference how we evaluate performance strategies, in terms of audience response, who constitutes the audience? In practice, of course, it will. An audience of professional musicians will, no doubt, be able to hear things that an audience of laypersons will not. (And would it be too "democratic" of me to add that an audience of laypersons will be able to hear things that an audience of experts might not be able to hear *anymore*?) But as it turns out, in principle, what I have to say about evaluating audience response will be applicable, with proper, nonessential adjustments, to any audience, no matter how defined.

The Authority of Intention

It would be well, nonetheless, to have some image before our minds when the term "audience" or "listener" occurs in what follows. And I can do no better, I think, than to adopt for this purpose what le Huray called, in a passage quoted earlier, "an informed musical public," which I imagine to be, say, the concertgoing public of a large metropolitan city, or a Midwestern "college town." That is what my "audience" is; and I shall not try to characterize it in any greater detail, for it conveys, as it stands, all that is necessary for my argument.

Now, we want to characterize the relationship between performer and audience to the end of spelling out how a performance strategy—in particular, the composer's—is evaluated: confirmed or disconfirmed. We shall start off with the ideal case, as a scientist might do, and then see how it can serve as an approximation of the actual state of affairs in which we find ourselves. So let's imagine one performer, a pianist, say, and an audience of one, with whom the performer can converse for the purpose of eliciting responses to his or her rendition.

The performer, we must assume, has some pretty strong feelings and convictions about how particular pieces are to be played, the result of years of study and innumerable influences. Suppose, for the sake of argument, that she has come to think she is being most faithful to Beethoven's intentions for his Sonata in A♭, Op. 110, by playing it on a replica of Beethoven's last piano (Conrad Graf, Vienna, c. 1825), with a markedly incisive and choppy articulation in the fugue rather than a smoother, more legato style of performance. Her audience of one, we shall assume, has only heard the work on a modern Steinway or Bechstein, with a far more legato fugue.

"Did you like the way I played the Beethoven?" our performer asks hopefully. "No," is the abrupt reply.

I suppose we might say that we have just experienced, in this minimal conversation, a *minimal* refutation of the performer's conviction that following the composer's performing intentions in the ways specified vis-à-vis Op. 110 is a good strategy. It doesn't much matter whether we call it that or whether we do not want to call it a refutation at all. For certainly we would hardly think it *conclusive*, nor doubtless would the performer.

The next step, I imagine, is that the performer will want to know why, in what respect, the listener found the performance displeasing. Recall that we are dealing with an "informed" listener. That by no means implies a listener with any technical knowledge or vocabulary. But nor does lack of technical knowledge or vocabulary imply that a listener cannot understand and describe the music he or she is familiar with.[14] And to remain consistent with this latter point, I will put in the listener's mouth no technical musical vocabulary at all, only plain English.

As I say, the performer will want to know what it was in her performance that displeased the listener. But I think that must be put more strongly. The performer, I think, has a right to demand from the listener more than a "like" or "don't like" if the listener's response is to be taken seriously. We are not, after all, dealing here with ice cream cones but with a level and complexity of satisfaction that cannot be cashed out in the coin of direct titillation of the senses *simpliciter*.

So now for our "informed" listener's reply. Here is what I imagine he says: "There were two things I didn't like about your performance. First of all, the high notes sounded tinny, anemic, and dull. It sounded as if you were absolutely pounding the keys and still getting not enough sound. And, second, in the part where the melody comes in, one time after another, sometimes high, sometimes low, it all sounded kind of jerky and jumpy, not as smooth and tranquil as I like it."

This is a fair accounting but elicits a fairly predictable and justified response from the performer: "It takes time to get used to this new way of performing Beethoven; but if you give it the time, you will get more satisfaction than you ever got out of the old way. Furthermore, you must listen to the right things, and listen to them in the right ways. What you call the tinny, anemic, and dull sound of the high notes is characteristic of pianos in Beethoven's day. But like all great artists, Beethoven makes a virtue of this fault. This music is supposed to be expressive of power surpassing all human limitations; and that expressive character is intensified by the pounding of those keys in the high register of the right hand, which is necessary to get them to 'speak.' That extra expression is lost on a modern Steinway, with its more powerful and richer treble, which easily and effortlessly accommodates the phrases; whereas Beethoven brought the right hand to the very limits of his own instrument. As for the place where you find my playing too jerky and jumpy, lacking in smoothness, that is because I want to bring out the structure of this movement, which is a fugue, by marking out as clearly as possible the entrances of the subject,

[14] I have written at some length on this question in *Music Alone*, pp. 101–9.

The Authority of Intention

as they occur at various places, speeds, and registers. A certain smoothness has to be sacrificed for this; but it pays off in a fuller comprehension
of the fugal structure, which is, on my interpretation of the work, the
most important thing." And so on.

Now perhaps the listener, with the performer's admonitions ringing in
his ears, will indeed get the aesthetic payoff that the performer promises.
Or perhaps he won't and will come up, instead, with a further reply. He
may declare himself glad to sacrifice some *expression* in the high register
for a more beautiful sound. He may, indeed, find the "story" about how
pounding the keys adds to the expression, to that feeling of boundary
bashing, an unbelievable one, objecting that he doubts Beethoven could
have had any such outlandish intention and really would have liked better treble notes on his piano, requiring less pounding of the keys. This
kind of objection on the listener's part illustrates my stipulated requirement that the "story" told about how doing things as the composer intended will produce an optimal performance must be a plausible one.
And in response to the claim that it isn't, the performer will be compelled
to find arguments and evidence to the contrary.

Again, the listener may reply that he would be glad to give up some
clarity of structure in the fugue for a more legato texture. Pushing it further, he may suggest that to *interpret* this movement as a "fugue" in the
traditional sense and therefore to make structure rather than "expression"
its principal aesthetic feature is to place a mistaken interpretation on it.
And this illustrates another of my stipulations concerning composers'
performing intentions, namely, that arguments that purport to show how
following the composer's intentions produces a higher aesthetic payoff
must be based on an overall view, an "interpretation" of what the musical
nature of the work in question is: what makes it "go." In the case in hand,
it is no argument for a better performance that a less legato style brings
out the structure more clearly, if the listener's interpretation of the fugue
downplays structure in the interest of expression. So the performer must,
in response, dislodge the listener's interpretation and convince him of her
own, if she is to make progress in this regard.

How long should this give-and-take go on? At some point, one assumes, the listener has a right to object, if the promised payoff doesn't
come, that it is an irrational policy to postpone satisfaction indefinitely.

The Authority of Intention

"Better a performance I like *now* rather than a performance I *may* like in the great by-and-by." To postpone satisfaction permanently in deference to the composer's performing intentions, or to conclude finally that those can't *really* be the composer's performing intentions because they fail to give optimal satisfaction, is to remove the composer's performing intentions entirely from the realm of the empirical.

Nevertheless, to expect the performer to acquiesce too readily in the listener's dissatisfaction is, I think, seriously to underestimate the kind of commitment to his or her own judgment in the matter that any superior performer must have. But to focus this give-and-take between performer and audience I think we must now bring our ideal case into the real musical marketplace.

Obviously the performer and the listener do not have the kind of one-on-one relationship exemplified by the ideal case, any more than do elected officials and their constituency in a representative democracy. The audience, the performer, the critic, the impresario, the publisher, and the recording company are all intertwined in a complex social dance in which it would be very hard for any single listener to feel that he or she had any perceptible influence on how the performer presents her wares. Nonetheless, as remote and as complicated as the connection may be, what audiences like does have an effect on how performers perform, and how performers perform does have an effect on what audiences like. Within this complex social structure, then, what taste the performer decides to promulgate by her interpretations is not merely a personal choice but a social policy as well—and likewise for what the listener accepts or rejects.

It is because of the fact that the audience and performer are locked in this complex social embrace that the "verification" of a performance strategy is not the direct, transparent registering of preference or aversion one expects to find in, say, a marketing research project to determine whether or not the American household prefers crunchies to munchies. The manufacturer is indifferent to the results but merely wants to accommodate public taste in the matter for the purpose of turning a profit; he has no ideological commitment. But how one performs Beethoven and how one wants one's audience to appreciate and understand Beethoven is a value-laden commitment. The performer is not merely a purveyor of

The Authority of Intention

musical pleasure who wishes to operate at a profit, although she is that too. She is committed to an ideal or an ideology that she wants her audience to share.

One can perhaps more easily understand this in the context, familiar to moral philosophers, of the utilitarian calculus. A committed utilitarian wishes, by his acts, to maximize happiness and minimize unhappiness. But he will also know that happiness (as old-fashioned utilitarians used to put it) has a qualitative as well as a quantitative dimension. And there may come a point at which he will have to decide not only which action produces more happiness but what *kind* of things he would like the things to be that make people happy. So that on normative grounds he might prefer a world in which poetry rather than pushpin is what makes people happy, even though there is nothing to choose between them as regards *quantity*, or even though the quantity of happiness in the pushpin world is actually greater.

In like manner, a performer may very well feel toward the performing intentions of Beethoven an attitude of something like "reverence," if you like, such that the fact that her audiences do not like the music performed that way as well as some other would not dissuade her from doing it Beethoven's way, on the grounds that she envisions, and hopes eventually by her unswerving attitude to bring about, a world in which audiences are so "sophisticated," so musically "enlightened," that they *will* enjoy Beethoven his way, which is, in her eyes, the better way *qualitatively*, poetry rather than pushpin. This is what I meant to bring out by saying that evaluating a performance policy is not merely "marketing research" but "ideology" as well. And that certainly complicates matters. Nevertheless, if "ideology" comes to so overpower "market research" that the composer's performing intentions cease to be negotiable and become simply an article of religious faith, then the policy has ceased to be a rational one. However complicated by ideology and normative considerations the performer-listener relation may be, it is, in the last analysis, one of consumer to provider, in which any performance strategy, including the composer's, ultimately stands or falls at the pleasure and is measured by the pleasure of the audience. In the long run, no manner of performance will prevail against it, at least not in a "free market."

·   ·   ·

The Authority of Intention

It appears to me that I have taken a very long time, and followed a tor-
tuous route, only to arrive at an utter banality, no less banal for its truth,
that the performing intentions of the composer, like any other set of pro-
posals for performing a musical work, might turn out to be a good way of
doing the business, or might not; and if not, should, like any other plan
that doesn't work out, be discarded in favor of one that does. Who could
quarrel with that? And why should it take so long to reach such a
platitude?

But if from one vantage point the defeasibility of the composer's plan
for performance seems a trivial truth, from another it seems a palpable
falsehood. And now having followed me through my argument to its
truth, the dissenter may well see a way of turning my own argument
against me. I should like to conclude this chapter by considering this maneuver and coming to some accommodation with it.

"You have gained a cheap victory," I imagine the dissenter beginning.
"You have, indeed, quite convinced me that the *mere possibility* of the
composer's performing intentions always being optimal is an inadequate
defense of them. But you have also taught me to beware of *mere possibility*
wherever it rears its head. And so far as I can see, all you really can say, in
the last analysis, about the defeasibility of the composer's performing intentions is that there is always the possibility, the *mere possibility*, of their
not constituting the best strategy. But *mere possibility*, you have made
abundantly clear, is an empty conclusion. And let's face it, *for all practical
purposes*, the composer's performing intentions, where available, are
going to be the performer's best bet. Of course it is possible, *merely possible*,
that someone else might have a better plan. Then, again, it is possible,
merely possible, that the next crank letter to the physics department really
will refute the theory of relativity. The physicist, quite rightly, ignores this
mere possibility. So too should the performer."

Well, there is a grain of truth in this response. Let's see if we can extract
it.

The grain of truth certainly is *not* that the defeat of the composer's performing intentions is just *merely possible*. But that may be a hyperbolic way
of saying what the truth *is*: namely, that the composer's performing intentions do hold some special, prima facie authority over all others. That is to
say, they are not necessarily where we stop; but they are perhaps neces-

The Authority of Intention

sarily where we must begin. A performer who played a work her way without first determining and evaluating the composer's way, if available, would, we think, be guilty of some kind of musical hubris.

Thus it would appear that the composer's performing intentions may have something like the weight, in "performing ethics," of what moralists have referred to as a prima facie duty or obligation. Like the admonition "Pay our debts," "Do it the composer's way" is what, in the absence of defeating conditions, we are obligated to do. But just as paying your debt is precisely the wrong thing to do when (to use Socrates' famous example) it means returning a borrowed sword to a man subsequently gone mad, so doing it the composer's way is inadvisable (not in any obvious sense morally wrong) if it turns out not to yield the best aesthetic results. However, pointing out that conforming to the composer's performing intentions "has the feel" (so to say) of a prima facie obligation, or is treated that way, does not fully solve our problem. For it may be that this feel, this appearance, is without a foundation. So we are compelled to ask, further, what the source of this prima facie obligation, if it is one, can be. (I use "obligation" here in an attenuated sense.)

The ease with which, in talking about the intentions of composers, one slips into metaphors of religious fervor and ideology may suggest there is nothing more to be said than that it is the leap of faith. But I suspect there is more to it than that; that the authority of the composer's performing intentions as a prima facie "obligation" has its source in virtue of being a part of a "system"—what we might call the "culture of authorship."

For reasons some of which I think I know, but many of which I am sure I do not, it means a great deal to us "who did what" and, specifically in the present context, "who wrote what." Anonymity is Public Enemy Number One, and scholarship will not rest until a suspect is turned up, no matter how tenuous the evidential thread.

It need not be thus; and it hasn't always been. We know that there have been times and places at which authorship was of no particular importance and had no particular proprietary rights or aspirations; where Anonymous 2 added at pleasure to Anonymous 1, only to be treated in kind by Anonymous 3. It is *we* who care whether Anonymous 1 was Tom, Dick, or Harry, and what constitutes the original "text." And it is within this system of wants and goals that the composer's performing intentions

The   Authority   of   Intention

function: a peripheral (or perhaps more than peripheral) result of the culture of author and text.

We have heard some proclamations in recent years (mostly in French) about the death of the author and of the author's text (in favor of the reader's). Perhaps that might be a good thing if it happened, perhaps not; that is not the point. Rather, this is just another case of exaggerated demise, particularly so in the world of music and musicology, where the cult of author and text is alive, well, and flourishing as never before, thank you very much. It is within this cult or culture that, I believe, the composer's performing intentions gain their prima facie authority. It is an authority, as we have seen, open to empirical defeat, on an individual, case-by-case basis. But its primacy of place, as the starting point for all performance decisions, can be defeated only by an overthrow of the culture of the author itself. For in the culture of anonymity, the composer's authority holds no more sway than anyone else's, over his text, which *is* no longer *his*, or over its destiny, which, a fortiori, is his no longer.

So in the culture of the author and the text—our culture—the composer's performing intentions have their prima facie authority from the system in which they are embedded; but, individually, they relinquish that authority to human practice in the marketplace of music. That, at last, is as close as I can come to understanding the magnetic charm of the composer's performing intentions and, in spite of that, their ultimate mortality.

The Authority of Intention

⊙

The Authority of Sound

To inaugurate discussion of the possible rationale—in the normative sense—for realizing historically authentic sound in musical performance we must reintroduce an important distinction, and some of its implications, already made out in Chapter 3. The distinction is between what I called "sonic authenticity" and "sensible authenticity."

By sonic authenticity, it will be recalled, I intended the reproduction of physical sounds, perturbations of the air just like those that were, or would have been, produced at a contemporary performance of the kind deemed worthy of emulation. In this sense of sonic authenticity, I am "hearing" an authentic performance if these "historically authentic" perturbations of the air are entering my ear and mechanically interacting with the physical organ in the way they would have done vis-à-vis the physical organ of the contemporary listener who is paying "musical" attention to the sounds. And it is a matter of no small significance, from the practical musician's point of view, that it matters not, on this way of construing historical authenticity of sound, what *means* of production are employed to make the noise. If the physical perturbations of air are of the

188

right kind, then the performance is "historically authentic" whether they are caused by a rebec or a gadget, a clarinet or a contraption.

It is perfectly apparent, however, that there is another sense of "hear" in which all these conditions might be in place, but we would not want to say that a twentieth-century listener was "hearing" the same "sounds" as her baroque counterpart. For, to take a simple and obvious example adduced earlier, Johann Sebastian Bach's congregation, in hearing the opening chorus of the *St. Matthew Passion*, would be hearing very loud musical sounds, whereas in "hearing" a sonically authentic twentieth-century performance, the modern listener would be hearing rather subdued musical sounds, to her almost of a chamber-music quality: two hearers, same physical perturbations, different sounds, different hearings. Both the baroque listener and her twentieth-century relative have heard a sonically authentic performance; only the baroque listener, however, has heard, in respect to dynamics, a sensibly authentic one. For although the twentieth-century and eighteenth-century listener have both "heard" the same physical sounds, they have not heard the same "phenomenological" ones. Or, to put it in more contemporary terms, the intentional objects of their hearings have been different ones.

All this will of course be totally familiar to the reader of Chapter 3, and in greater detail than it is necessary to go into here. For a reminder of this vital distinction is all we require to point out that the possible rationale for realizing historically authentic sound in musical performance is really two questions, not one: is there a rationale for realizing sonic authenticity? And is there a rationale for realizing sensible authenticity? For even if they were the same in practice, which they are manifestly not, they are manifestly not the same in principle. Two questions, then, not one; and I turn first to the question of sonic authenticity.

•   •   •

The question of why the performer should wish to achieve sonic authenticity can be easily answered in two ways that would dispose of it immediately in a consequentialist manner by simply reducing it to another question. Thus, one possible answer to the question of why sonic authenticity is desirable would be: "Because it realizes the composer's intentions. The composer intended just those sounds that you are describing as 'sonic authenticity.'" If that answer satisfies you, then it remains but for me to refer you back to the previous chapter for an answer to the question of why realizing the composer's performing intentions might be a desirable thing to do.

Alternatively, it might be answered, to the question of why the realization of sonic authenticity is a desirable goal, "The goal, really, is to achieve sensible authenticity; and the best way, or at least part of the best way, of achieving it is by means of sonic authenticity. Sonic authenticity is a means; sensible authenticity the end." If that answer satisfies you, then it remains but for me to refer you ahead to the bulk of this chapter, where the possible rationale for sensible authenticity will be the subject.

In point of fact I do think that if the achieving of sonic authenticity is to have any rationale at all, part of that rationale must lie in its propensity to produce sensible authenticity; and whether a case can be made out for this instrumental value of sonic authenticity is a question that will be broached in our consideration of sensible authenticity to come. But it is apparent that much of the writing on nuts-and-bolts historical performance practice, as well as a good deal of the musicologists' theoretical pronouncements, operate under the assumption that sonic authenticity is somehow a desirable end unto itself. In any case, that assumption, among the faithful, is never questioned. So it behooves us to examine it now, and question it if we must.

Of course no one, no matter how devoted to sonic authenticity, believes that it is an "end in itself," in the senses in which Aristotle thought happiness is, or in which Bradley thought being moral is. It is an end, one must assume, pursued for one of two, possibly interrelated, reasons: to achieve the best performance or to restore the "unadulterated object," which might itself be an end or, perhaps, a means to the best performance. Let us look at the "restoration" argument first.

·   ·   ·

Because sonic authenticity amounts to the reconstruction, if you will, of a "material object"—that is to say, certain perturbations of the physical medium of air—it becomes tempting to think of it as of a piece with the physical restoration of oil paintings, and the like. For just as an old oil painting will bear the encrustation of three hundred years of dirt and grime, so too, in a manner of speaking, the sonic "object," through modernization of instruments and departure from historical performance practice, will have become encrusted with generations of sonic detritus.

The Authority of Sound

Just as, then, the goal of the restorer's art is to give us, as near as possible, the physical object as it issued from Rembrandt's studio, so, analogously, the goal of the historically authentic performance is to give us, as near as possible, the physical object as it issued from Bach's "studio"—which is to say, his own or his contemporaries' instruments and performances. Finally, closing the analogy, just as it seems self-evident, without need of further argument, that the restored Rembrandt is a more desirable object than the dirty one, so too the sonically authentic object, cleansed of its pollution, is self-evidently more desirable than any of the "dirty" versions that subsequent performance has produced.

As enticing as this analogy seems, however, it is conceptually flawed in a serious way. For the two arts we are analogizing are logically and ontologically quite distinct. And although no one expects an analogy to be exact, the present one fails in such a conceptually deep way that no argument founded on it can stand. The problem is, simply, that painting is what Nelson Goodman calls an autographic art, whereas Western classical music, since the invention of modern notational systems, is an allographic one.[1] Which is to say that, among other things, there is an "original," a physical object locatable in space and time, in the art of painting, where there is not in the art of music. (Where is the *Eroica* located?) And there are performances of the work, there is a work-performance relation in music, where there is not in painting, although there is an original-fake and an original-reproduction relation. (What could it mean for there to be performances of the *Mona Lisa*?)

For present purposes this logical and ontological gap between painting and music means that the concept of "restoration," although it may be perfectly applicable to both art forms, will have a different "logic" and different "ontological" implications for each. If we understand "restoration" as the attempt to restore, to its pristine condition, *the artwork*, which indeed is how it seems to be understood among physical restorers of oil paintings, then it does seem as if such restoration requires no further argument for its desirability. It seems clear, and there's an end on't, that it would be better to have a clean *Mona Lisa*, and a *Venus de Milo* with arms.

But if it is clear that a restored original is, unqualifiedly and without argument, better than a dirty or broken one, that self-evidence certainly cannot transfer to sonic authenticity, because what is being restored, in

[1]Goodman, *Languages of Art*, pp. 113–15.

The Authority of Sound

the latter case, is not an original, not *the* work of art, but a *performance*. And it is simply not obvious *at all* that a "restored" performance is better than some other kind. The fact that we must put the word "restored" in scare quotes, in this context, is already warning enough that the implications of restoration in the autographic arts cannot pass freely to *performances*, even if they may to the *works* that the performances instantiate. To restore an original means to make a unique object as it was at a certain time. But performances are many, not one, and diverse, not uniform; so such a concept of restoration simply does not apply to them. Further, since it is from the notion of restoring an original, unique object that the self-evidence of restoration as a desirable goal derives its force, that force fails with regard to the restoration of performance—which is to say, sonic authenticity.

This is even clearer if one turns the argument on its head and looks at the *opposite* of restoration, which, I suppose, is defacement. If a vandal knocks Michelangelo's *David* off of its pedestal, he ends up in jail. But when Horowitz "defaced" Mozart by playing him like Chopin and on a modern Steinway, he ended up on a pedestal.

To sum up, then, there is a self-evidence attached to the desirability of restoring paintings, statues, and the other works of the autographic arts to their original, pristine condition. The enterprise seems to *require* no argument for its legitimation (although such an argument there well might be). This is not the case, however, when the concept of restoration is carried over to musical performance, viewed as physical perturbations of air. For it is not obvious, where sonic authenticity is concerned, that anything has been "lost" or (therefore) in need of restoring; and the mere fact that paintings and sound vibrations are both of them "physical" is now seen as quite irrelevant. Certainly nothing of *the work* has been lost, when sonic authenticity is lacking, because no performance *is* the work (although each is a version of it). And no intuition draws us, so far as I can see, to the restoration of sonic authenticity as a *transparently* desirable goal.

The same intuition that draws us to the cleaning of a Rembrandt, as a goal in no need of rational support, does indeed draw us to the restoration of musical *works*—for example, discovering the original manuscript, in Mozart's hand, of the lost *Sinfonia concertante* for winds, which we have

The Authority of Sound

now only in a corrupt version, or, failing that, reconstructing the *Urtext* by analysis and conjecture. But restoring a performance, in the sense of achieving sonic authenticity, is not doing any such thing as that, unless you have an argument for showing that sonic authenticity is part of the work. And such arguments would suffer the same fate and face the same difficulties as those already considered in the previous chapter, aiming to make composers' performing intentions constitutive of works. In short, the *authentic* work can be presented in a sonically *inauthentic* performance, unless you have an argument about the nature of works to preclude it. That being the case, "restoring" performance to sonic authenticity has none of the prima facie clout of restoring the Rembrandt to pristine condition.

And, in fact, prima facie clout may be all that it is. Indeed, restoring paintings and other physical artifacts turns out to be, as we are about to see, as deeply problematical as "restoring" performances and, therefore, no support for "restoring" performances, even if the "logic" and "metaphysics" of the two were the same (which, I have just argued, they are not).

•   •   •

The reader may have noticed that I have peppered my prose, in the preceding section, with such qualifiers as "*seems* self-evident," "*if* it is clear," "*seems* to require no argument," and so forth, with regard to the restoration of paintings to their "original" physical states. These qualifications were entered quite self-consciously. For, as David Carrier amply demonstrated not so long ago, the physical restoration of paintings is neither an obvious desideratum nor even as transparent a concept as it might at first appear: "The aim of restorers is (deceptively) simple to state: show as best as possible what the artist intended us to see. We desire to see what the artist made, without later additions or subtractions from the artwork. Changes in paintings include both natural aging and damage."[2]

The reason the simplicity of the restorer's aim is deceptive is that as soon as one begins to spell out that aim, it becomes far from clear what the aim really is, what the nature of the "object" to be restored, what it is to be restored *to*, and *why*. To begin with, if we want to restore what we

[2]Carrier, "Art and Its Preservation," p. 291. Cf. Wilsmore, "Unmasking Skepticism about Restoration," pp. 304–6.

The Authority of Sound

have to what the artist made, we find it not at all clear that we are necessarily doing that by "repairing" what changes have occurred merely in
the natural aging process. Thus:

> Titian's *Bacchus and Ariadne* may be thought of either as a work now
> over 450 years old or as a painting which, because made in 1523,
> today requires cleaning. What Titian made was a pigmented surface,
> and such things change with time. To restore the work is to change
> what he made. Alternatively, what Titian made was a painting in
> which Bacchus has a bright red cloak: Titian wanted us to appreciate
> the appearance of that image, so if with age its color has changed,
> we can best preserve what he made by cleaning that object.[3]

So if one wants to make an accounting of the vagaries of physical restoration, a beginning might consist in flagging the ambiguity inherent in restoring, putting to rights *the thing the artist made that has changed over time*;
for if we are putting to rights *the thing that the artist made*, which has
changed over time, then, by all means, we want to repair the ravages of
time and circumstances; but if we are putting to rights *the thing changed
over time*, which is what the artist made, then there is nothing to do, for
that thing we already have.

Well, which *is* the aim of restoration? In posing this question, another
vagary immediately emerges. "Some art historians hold that color
changes produced by aging varnish were desired by the artist."[4] If so, then
the artist didn't intend her painting to have the same physical properties
in the future that it had when she created it. And so what appeared to be
the simple process of restoring the authentic object, easily identified in
principle, if not in practice, as the original, unique physical object, now
becomes the problematical process we have come to know all too well, in
this book, of determining the artist's intentions. Carrier takes a skeptical
view of intentional arguments, as being nothing more than disguised
expressions of likes and dislikes: "The art historian desires that the work
be cleaned or not, and underlines that opinion by adding; and I am sure
that this is what the artist intended."[5] As is clear from what has gone before, I take intentions and intentional arguments far more seriously than

[3] Carrier, "Art and Its Preservation," p. 291.
[4] Ibid.
[5] Ibid., p. 292.

The Authority of Sound

does Carrier here. But however that may be, it is also clear that as soon as artists' intentions perturb the concept of physical restoration, another reason emerges for believing it far from the simple, unproblematical thing it may at first appear to be.

Of equal interest, for present purposes, is the appearance in the equation of "historicism." For it then becomes clear that the notion of physical authenticity in regard to painting is bifurcated in exactly the same manner as the authenticity of sound in regard to musical performance.

Let us say we opt, never mind the reason, for *not* leaving the painting alone but restoring it to its "original" condition; and let us say, further, that it is the colors we are principally interested in restoring. Even here we will not have a simple, transparent aim:

> Suppose we adopt the historicist suggestion; seeing paintings by postimpressionists influences our view of Titians. What follows is that even perfect preservation of a Titian's colors would not preserve their original effect; that system of color relations will look different in 1985 than in 1523 because we bring to it different expectations. Preservation of the work's artistic value could be attempted only by meddling with the original.[6]

Thus restoring colors in paintings to their original, authentic state has the same ambiguity as the analogous project, in performance practice, of restoring the original, authentic sounds. Are we restoring the physical object or the perceptual object, the light waves and sound waves, or the intentional objects they produce?

One could go on a good while enumerating and dilating upon the vagaries embedded in the project of physical restoration in the visual arts. The subject is by no means exhausted by what I have said so far; but neither exhausting it nor examining Carrier's positive suggestions in the direction of answering the skeptical doubts with regard to that project that he has raised is to the present purpose. The point I wish to make has already been amply demonstrated: it simply is that the authority of sonic authenticity cannot be established by appeal to the more self-evident case of the physical restoration of paintings, even if their "logic" and "metaphysics" were compatible (which, I have already argued, they are *not*), because the case of physical restoration of physical artifacts simply is *not*

[6]Ibid., p. 294.

The Authority of Sound

more self-evident. We do not escape the problems of sonic authenticity by moving to the more "obvious" case of authentic physical artifacts like restored paintings, statues, or buildings. We just regenerate them in another medium.

· · ·

If the plausibility of sonic authenticity does not lie in the concept of work restoration, the next place to look, one would surmise, is simply to the concept of the optimal performance. Indeed, it might well be asked, why *else* would one want to have a sonically authentic performance, or any other for that matter, except that it sounded best? So our next task, it appears, is to determine what arguments might be adduced for the claim that sonic authenticity is musically desirable, above all other performance goals.

Well, one thing we can say, obvious enough, is that the physical sounds of a sonically authentic performance were just the sounds in the ears of every composer in history. That is to say, what entered Bach's or Josquin's ears, when *they* listened to music, were just those sounds, just those perturbations of the physical medium that we are trying to produce when we aim at sonic authenticity in the performance of their works. And, by consequence, the sounds that were in their heads were just the mental representations that had their casual origin in those very same physical perturbations. But it was those mental representations, those "sounds in the head," that were the materials they were manipulating, at their writing desks and in their heads, into their musical compositions. So if there is going to be an argument for the musical desirability of sonic authenticity, it must begin with those "sounds in the head" and go on from there.

But a problem arises straightaway. For "sounds in the head" are not physical stimuli or perturbations of the air, obviously; they are intentional objects of musical attention, mental representations. So if there is to be an argument, starting with these intentional objects, for the desirability of sonic authenticity, then it seems obvious enough that sonic authenticity is going to end up, assuming the argument goes through, possessing merely instrumental value, desirability as a means to the end of sensible authenticity. Whatever the details of the argument, its general point is going to have to be that because musical compositions are made with the sound materials "in the composer's head," it is those sound materials that must be retrieved in performance. Such a view of performance, however, answers not to the description "sonic authenticity" but rather to the description "sensible authenticity," and sonic authenticity, if it is to be a goal of performance at all, must serve the end of sensible authenticity and itself be a means only.

Thus the defense of sonic authenticity devolves on establishing two things: first, that sonic authenticity is a reliable means to sensible authenticity; and second, that sensible authenticity is a desirable end in itself. Of course, it by no means follows that if sonic authenticity is *not* a reliable means to sensible authenticity, then sensible authenticity is itself indefensible as the (or a) goal of musical performance. The desirability of sensible authenticity is a separate and important issue. I shall indeed be devoting the major part of this chapter to it. And I think that it should be first in order of exposition. For it will be easier, I think, to evaluate sonic authenticity as a means, after we have discussed the end at length, renewing our acquaintance with its substance as we investigate its value.

·   ·   ·

To remind ourselves just what really is involved in sensible authenticity, let us recall that there are various ways in which we would want to say that two listeners—say, an eighteenth-century one and a modern one—are hearing the same sounds, conceived as physical stimuli, but yet different sounds, conceived as intentional objects of musical appreciation. So let us imagine baroque Johann, listening to a performance of the *St. Matthew Passion* in the Thomaskirche, and thoroughly modern John, listening to a sonically authentic performance of it in Wigmore Hall.

Johann listens to the opening chorus and hears a monumental, overwhelming musical sound. John hears a rather subdued, almost chamber music–like musical fabric. Johann hears a brand-new contemporary work, with various daring harmonies and innovations that he finds difficult. (He wistfully longs for good old familiar Kuhnau.) John, on the other hand, hears a somewhat "archaic" but nevertheless comfortable work. But at one place Johann and John do both hear a rather daring, startling harmonic progression. However, John also hears that gesture as rather romantic, somewhat Schubertian, as a matter of fact; and, of course, Johann hears no such thing, although he may hear the particular musical quality that John so describes in a distinctive way related to John's: *empfindlich*, or something like that.

Furthermore, while we are on the subject of functional harmony, there

The Authority of Sound

is a certain level at which we assume, if Johann and John are sophisticated listeners, they will be hearing the music to a certain degree "grammatically" and will both be hearing the same "grammar." But here again there may be very marked differences. Because, although Johann may be hearing this "grammar" within the framework of a Rameau-like analysis, John might be understanding it under a Schenkerian description completely unavailable (obviously) to Johann.

Moving ahead a couple of generations, Johann's grandson Johann III, fortunate enough to have been present at the world premiere of Beethoven's First Symphony, will have heard a startling, harmonically innovative slow introduction to the first movement, and throughout a rather heavy, perhaps overly heavy orchestration, especially in the use of the winds.[7] Whereas John will hear, at a modern, sonically authentic performance of the work, Beethoven's *First* Symphony, not *yet* the *Eroica*, Beethoven in spots, but certainly a mild, balanced, "classical" work with a balanced "classical" orchestration, and so on. Furthermore, John, when he hears sonically authentic performances of the *St. Matthew Passion* and Beethoven's First Symphony will hear, of course, examples of the "historical performance" movement: an attempt to "restore" a lost performance practice. Whereas Johann and Johann III will be hearing performances in their own, "mainstream" performance tradition; they are not having a "historical" experience at all but a contemporary musical one, with no taint of twentieth-century "historicism."[8]

Now, of course, one can multiply indefinitely the individual differences, in individual works of various periods, between the intentional objects of a contemporary listener's experience and the intentional objects of a present-day listener's. Such a project would certainly be an interesting and rewarding one, as a venture into historical criticism and the history of musical taste. But what I wish to do, rather, is explore a more general question, which, it appears to me, underlies such a project and is more directly relevant to present concerns. The question, quite simply, is this: is it desirable to hear music the way it was heard by its contemporaries? Or, to put it in modern, intentionalistic terms: is it desirable that

[7] I seem to remember that excessive use of the winds was a contemporary charge brought against Op. 21.
[8] On this see Kivy, "On the Concept of the 'Historically Authentic Performance,'" in *The Fine Art of Repetition.*

The   Authority   of   Sound

our intentional objects of musical appreciation be similar to those of contemporary listeners, at least so far as is possible? That is the question I
wish to pursue. And I begin on something of a tangent.

Let me introduce at this point two theses about musical appreciation. I
shall call them the romantic thesis and the historicist thesis. At least the
first, I think, will be quite familiar, and probably the second as well.

According to the romantic thesis, "They laughed at Beethoven." And,
indeed, "they"—at least some of them—did, as can be surmised by a
glance at Nicolas Slonimsky's *Lexicon of Musical Invective*, from which I
quote some choice expletives.

> Beethoven's Second Symphony is a crass monster, a hideously
> writhing wounded dragon, that refuses to expire, and though
> bleeding, in the Finale, furiously beats about with its tail erect.
> (*Zeitung für die Elegente Welt*, Vienna, May 1804)

> Recently there was given the overture to Beethoven's opera *Fidelio*,
> and all impartial musicians and music lovers were in perfect
> agreement that never was anything so incoherent, shrill, chaotic
> and ear-splitting produced in music. The most piercing dissonances
> clash in a really atrocious harmony, and a few puny ideas only
> increase the disagreeable and deafening effect. (August von
> Kotzebue, *Der Freimütige*, Vienna, 11 September 1806)

> We find Beethoven's Ninth Symphony to be precisely one hour and
> five minutes long; a fearful period indeed, which puts the muscles
> and lungs of the band, and the patience of the audience to a severe
> trial. . . . The last movement, a chorus, is heterogeneous. What
> relation it bears to the symphony we could not make out; and here,
> as well as in other parts, the want of intelligible design is too
> apparent. (*Harmonicon*, London, April 1825)

> The merits of Beethoven's Seventh Symphony we have before
> discussed, and we repeat that . . . it is a composition in which the
> author had indulged in a great deal of disagreeable eccentricity.
> Often as we now have heard it, we cannot yet discover any design in

The Authority of Sound

it, neither can we trace any connection in its parts. Altogether it seems to have been intended as a kind of enigma—we had almost said a hoax. (*Harmonicon*, London, July 1825)[9]

The sum total of the romantic thesis is not, needless, to say, merely that they laughed at Beethoven (or Bach or Brahms) but that, after a while, they stopped laughing and started clapping. It is a corollary of the cult of artistic genius that was passed on from Kant, by way of Schopenhauer to the romantic *Weltanschauung*, which is why I have called it the romantic thesis. And it teaches that the products of artistic genius are always, in the nature of the case, misunderstood, undervalued, and never fully enjoyed, or perhaps enjoyed at all. Slonimsky's *Lexicon* is, of course, an exaggerated as well as humorous illustration of the romantic thesis, and the quotations that I have selected concerning contemporary reception of Beethoven's music display all three phenomena: lack of comprehension, lack of esteem, and absence of enjoyment.

I shall return, in a moment, to further consideration of the romantic thesis. But before I do I want to place beside it its opposite number, so to speak—the historicist thesis. For it is by playing one off against the other that the full significance of sensible authenticity, and the possible rationale for its quest, will emerge.

They say that the Age of Enlightenment was "unhistorical" and that historicism is a nineteenth-century discovery. However that may be, it nevertheless amuses me to introduce the historicist thesis with a quotation from David Hume's ever-intriguing essay "Of the Standard of Taste."

> We may observe, that every work of art, in order to produce its due
> effect on the mind, must be surveyed in a certain point of view,
> and cannot be fully relished by persons whose situation, real or
> imaginary, is not conformable to that which is required by the
> performance. An orator addresses himself to a particular audience,
> and must have a regard to their particular genius, interests,
> opinions, passions, and prejudices; otherwise he hopes in vain to
> govern their resolutions, and influence their affections. . . . A critic
> of a different age or nation, who should peruse this discourse, must
> have all these circumstances in his eye, and must place himself in
> the same situation as the audience, in order to form a true judgment

[9] Slonimsky, *Lexicon of Musical Invective*, pp. 42–44.

The   Authority   of   Sound

of the oration. . . . A person influenced by prejudice complies not with this condition. . . . If the work be addressed to persons of a different age or nation, he makes no allowance for their peculiar views and prejudices; but, full of the manners of his own age and country, rashly condemns what seemed admirable in the eyes of those for whom alone the discourse was calculated.[10]

The historicist thesis, as I am calling it, seems then to be the reverse image of the romantic thesis. For while the romantic thesis would have it that an artist's contemporaries will fail to appreciate him whereas posterity will succeed, the historicist thesis (and such I take Hume to be adumbrating) would have it that posterity, if left to its own devices, uncorrected by historical self-examination, is likely to "rashly condemn what seemed admirable in the eyes of those for whom alone the discourse was intended."

The practical implications for aesthetic appreciation are very different, then, depending upon which of these two theses one embraces. According to the romantic thesis you are far better off the way you are than, say, a contemporary listener to Beethoven. Expressed in intentionalist terms, the intentional object of the contemporary listener's Beethoven experience is, at least in a significant number of cases, as the quotations from the *Lexicon* suggest, one of a tediously long, dissonant, and eccentric work, lacking in comprehensible pattern or organization. Whereas the modern concertgoer's object is of quite manageable, even modest length, harmonically well formed and familiar, and the very paradigm of musical order and reason, the highest attainment of symphonic organization and logic. So who in her right senses would think it advantageous, then, to, for example, replace her present-day intentional object of musical appreciation, when listening to what August von Kotzebue called the *Fidelio* Overture, with *his*, which was of an "incoherent, shrill, chaotic and ear-splitting" composition, exhibiting "piercing dissonances," "a really atrocious harmony," and consisting of "a few puny ideas"?[11] The passage of time and the natural process of musical acculturation have allowed

[10] Hume, "Of the Standard of Taste," in *Essays*, pp. 244–45.
[11] What we now know as the *Fidelio* Overture was composed for the 1814 revision of the opera. In 1806, when von Kotzebue filed his report, it was to one of the *Leonore* Overtures that he was obviously referring, the opera at that time called, after its heroine, *Leonore*.

The Authority of Sound

posterity to come to a full appreciation of music that, in its time, was shocking and incomprehensible. It is a process repeated over and again, as even the slightest acquaintance with the history of music or any of the other arts will amply demonstrate.

But against the romantic thesis and increasingly so stands the historicist thesis, which also has a message that seems both commonsensical and appealing. A work of art is, after all, a cultural artifact. And one can, it seems reasonable to assume, no more comprehend and appreciate such an artifact without knowing what function it performed or what place it occupied in its culture than one could comprehend or appreciate a screwdriver without knowing that it flourished in an environment of screws.

Hume is obviously motivated by these kinds of considerations in the passage quoted earlier, for the very example that he chooses to illustrate the cultural and temporal "provincialism" of art, the art of oratory, is an art form we would think of as peripheral just because of its prominent "utilitarian" aspect. An oration is meant by the orator to persuade an audience to some purpose or end—"to govern their resolutions, and influence their affections." But to do so the orator must know his audience, "must have a regard to their particular genius, interests, opinions, passions and prejudices," or else he cannot persuade. And if *we*, living two thousand years later in a different cultural milieu, wish to evaluate the ancient orator's performance, how can we do so unless we too know not only what the orator aimed to convince his audience of but what the nature was of the audience he meant to convince? We must know if the party of the second part is a nail or a screw before we can know if the screwdriver is well or ill contrived to do the driving. It is here that Hume's argument becomes ambiguous and that ambiguity must be briefly explored.

We are told by Hume that "a critic of a different age or nation . . . must place himself in the same situation as the audience, in order to form a true judgment of the oration." If he does not do this, remaining "full of the manners of his own age or country," then in all likelihood he "rashly condemns what seemed admirable in the eyes of those for whom alone the discourse was calculated." But two constructions can be put on this demand that we place ourselves in the same situation as an earlier audience in order to evaluate an oration properly, devolving on two constructions that can be put on both what it might mean to *place ourselves* in a situation other than our own *and* what it might mean to *evaluate*.

One possible way to construe the notion of putting oneself in someone else's place is simply as coming to know things about that person—his circumstances, his beliefs, his emotions, his weaknesses, his motives. On the basis of knowing these things, I can then form an educated opinion as to whether something he did was morally reprehensible or not; that is to say, I am able to evaluate his action morally. In like manner, once I get to know what the circumstances, beliefs, emotions, weaknesses, and motives of Cicero's audiences were, I am then in a position to make an informed, rational evaluation of his orations against Catiline, because I am able to judge whether what Cicero wrote (and spoke) is well or ill calculated to have the effect he wanted on those particular audiences. We might call this the "cerebral" interpretation of Hume because it involves, both in the putting of oneself in the place of the other and in the evaluation, merely knowledge that, knowledge of, and "cool calculation"— nothing that might be described as an "aesthetic experience" of the work.

But another, more intriguing if more problematical construction lurks here in Hume's tantalizing suggestions that no "work of art" can "produce its due effect on the mind" or "be fully relished by persons whose situation, real or imaginary, is not conformable to that which is required by the performance." Now, Hume cannot be talking *here* about putting oneself in the place of the other as merely coming to know things about the other, because the dichotomy, "real or imaginary," would simply make no sense relative to it. What he must be contrasting here is the person who *really* is in the position of the other, that is, the other herself, and someone who tries, by an imaginative leap, virtually to be the other for a while. I shall call this the "imaginative" or "sympathetic" interpretation of Hume on this point. (That this is a quite Humean thing to claim can readily be concluded by recalling the prominent role that the concept of "sympathy"—which is the very concept we are talking about here— plays in Hume's moral psychology.)

But, now, if the concept of putting oneself in the place of the other is cashed out in terms of "sympathy for" and "feeling with" the other, then the evaluation of the "performance" clearly is not going to be of the "cool calculation" variety; and what Hume says in relation to it bears this out.

The Authority of Sound

For the point of this imaginative leap into the other is so that the work can "produce its full effect on the mind" and "be fully relished" by the perceiver, all of which sounds like "aesthetic experience" of the artwork, not critical evaluation of it. Or, rather, the evaluation consists in either the "leaper" being affected by the work with pleasure and in the manner in which the work was intended, in which case the evaluation is positive, or not being affected with pleasure, not being affected in the manner intended, in which case the evaluation is negative. It is this construction and this one alone, put on Hume's remarks, that yields what I have been calling the historicist thesis. For the historicist thesis is about aesthetic experience of artworks, not their cool, critical evaluation; and it is only in the "imaginative leap," it would at first appear, that a full-blooded notion of aesthetic experience emerges.

Nevertheless, there is a notion of aesthetic experience to be extracted from what I called the "cerebral" interpretation of Hume. And in order fully to understand the contrast between the romantic and historicist theses as well as to avoid a possible misunderstanding of the latter, we must see what this more pallid notion of aesthetic experience might be.

.   .   .

I remarked at the outset of my discussion of Hume that his choice of oratory as an illustrative example was somewhat eccentric, from a twentieth-century perspective, and certainly skewed toward the view he wished to defend. For it was easy to see, in the case of an oration, that the artwork had a purpose, namely, persuading an audience to the orator's views and imperatives to action, and that its success depended upon accurately gauging the audience, so as to adjust the instrument to its intended object. But it is not easy or uncontroversial to discern such purposes in the more central cases of the fine arts as we conceive of them, particularly so in the case of absolute music, where it is generally assumed that propositional content is entirely lacking. It behooves us, therefore, to consider examples more to the present purpose. So let me try my luck with what I take to be a musical exemplification of the phenomenon Hume is talking about. It is an illustration I have adduced before.

I presume that Beethoven's First Symphony, unlike Cicero's orations against Catiline, does not have a clear, statable purpose apart from the obvious one of affording musical audiences the kind of satisfaction, however you want to describe that elusive thing, that musical audiences seek and have found to a very high degree in Beethoven's compositions. Nevertheless, we can certainly identify, quite readily, all sorts of effects that Beethoven intended his First Symphony to have, just as we can in the case of Cicero's orations. And one such effect is that of surprise, or perhaps even mild shock, at the rather startling opening on an active chord of the "wrong" key. Clearly Beethoven wanted to "shake up" his audience with the very first notes of his First Symphony, and, by all accounts, he succeeded (perhaps beyond his original intention).

Now, this startling effect of the introductory measures to Beethoven's Symphony no. 1 is a genuine aesthetic feature of the work that the passage of time and the history of music have rendered inoperable. Modern audiences simply are not startled or shocked by the opening of Beethoven's First. Indeed, it seems to them quite calm and sedate. And if we could recapture that startling effect, we would be increasing our appreciation. Here is a case in which *we* are missing something that Beethoven's audience could enjoy.

Transferred from oratory to this musical example, the Humean suggestion would be that we can recapture this startling effect of Beethoven's First Symphony by *being*, "imaginatively," of course, Beethoven's original audience. If we could do that, then, like they, we too could be surprised, startled, perhaps even a little bit shocked by this daring departure from classical style in symphonic slow introductions. This is a case in point of the historicist thesis; it exemplifies what I shall call "historicist listening."

But now I want to distinguish historicist listening from another kind with which it might be confused, called previously "historical listening." And I can highlight this distinction by drawing it out of the distinction we have already made between the two possible interpretations of Hume on putting oneself in place of the other: what I called the "cerebral" interpretation and the "imaginative" or "sympathetic" one. Historicist listening, as I have just described it, is what results from putting oneself in the place of the other, if that notion is given the imaginative interpretation. If, however, one gives it the cerebral interpretation, then we are not "becoming" the other but merely finding out about the other. In the context of this example, when I put myself in the place of the other, under the imaginative interpretation, I imaginatively become the other and am genuinely surprised and shocked by the opening measures of Beethoven's First Symphony, this aesthetic surprise or shock becoming part of my enjoyment of

The Authority of Sound

the work. On the cerebral interpretation, however, when I put myself in the place of the other, that means merely that I come to know that the other was surprised and shocked by the opening of Beethoven's First, that Beethoven intended to produce that effect, that he produced it by departing from the usual manner of Haydn and Mozart of strongly declaiming the tonic in the opening measures of slow introductions, that the departure consisted in starting on an active chord of the "wrong" key, and so on. Now, none of this knowledge facilitates my actually or "imaginatively" being surprised or shocked by Beethoven's stroke. But it can facilitate appreciation of *what* Beethoven was trying to do and *how* he was trying to do it. And *that* appreciation, I want to claim, is a kind of *aesthetic* appreciation of the work that is by no means contemptible. Nevertheless, it is the result not of historicist listening, as recommended by the historicist thesis, but of historical listening. And whatever else may be said for or against historical listening—and more of that anon—it is distinctly not authentic listening, in the sense of sensible authenticity—of restoring the contemporary intentional object of appreciation. For historical listening in general is mostly a twentieth-century development and hardly to be expected of earlier audiences.

It is, thus, the historicist thesis and historicist listening that we are concerned with, in evaluating the argument for sensible authenticity. To that evaluation I now shall turn.

·   ·   ·

For a long time the music lover and the public at large have been very comfortable with what I have denominated the romantic thesis. It is, one might almost say, a mind-set that we all have brought not just to the concert hall but to all our encounters with the fine arts. "The artist has to be dead before he or she is appreciated" is a cliché generally accepted, if at times railed against for its injustice by contemporary artists and their supporters. It used to be the inevitable theme of program notes; and images of Mozart thrown in a pauper's grave, Beethoven the object of outrage and raillery, and Schubert dying in obscurity and neglect were constantly thrown up to us as a prelude to the testament to their genius and immortality and our own enlightenment that we were about to experience in the performance of their works.

What I think is most amazing about the institution of historical musicology, of which the authentic performance movement is such a visible part, is that the romantic thesis is being called into question, not merely as a mistaken historical generalization, in its wholesale depiction of the composer as neglected genius, but as a mistake as well in its emphasis on the advantage of posterity over the composer's contemporaries in understanding and appreciating musical works of the past.

That Handel, Haydn, Beethoven, and Verdi, to name just a few, died national heroes, not obscurities starving in garrets, is evidence enough that in *this* regard the romantic thesis, as a historical generalization, is a hopeless caricature. But there is a serious question, nevertheless, of whether we may not now be on the verge or in the process of throwing out the proverbial baby with its proverbial bathwater. For it is one thing to claim that all great composers die in obscurity and neglect, their genius unsung by their contemporaries, which is demonstrably false, and quite another to claim that, in the nature of the case, no great composer's music can be fully or even adequately appreciated and enjoyed by his contemporaries, which is the baby we don't want to throw out, at least not before carefully examining it for signs of life. It is this latter claim, the "baby," that I will take to be the viable content of the romantic thesis, against which the historicist thesis now seems pitted. In what directly follows I shall be claiming that performance authenticity construed as sensible authenticity implies a denial of the romantic thesis. And to the extent that the romantic thesis is true, performance authenticity construed as sensible authenticity is not a desirable goal of musical performance, even if it is a possible one (which, indeed, it may not be).

Were I to make the intentional objects of my musical appreciation as like as is possible the ones that must have been present to the consciousness of Beethoven's contemporaries, when they listened to, say, Beethoven's symphonies and overtures, then I would be experiencing those works as incoherent, eccentric, dissonant, noisy, tedious, and prolix, if indeed the quotations from Slonimsky are to be credited. To recapture those ways of experiencing Beethoven's works obviously seems the opposite of desirable, and such a conclusion simply strengthens our confidence in the romantic thesis.

But *are* Slonimsky's Beethoven invectives to be credited? A recent scholar, Robin Wallace, warns us against doing so. Slonimsky, he writes, "deliberately gives the impression that these quotes are typical. They are not. Beethoven was almost at once, and universally, recognized as a composer of genius, and this recognition is reflected in practically everything that was written about him during his lifetime."[12] So it would appear that, contrary to popular opinion, they *didn't* laugh at Beethoven: "No myth can have been so obstinately preserved as the claim that Beethoven's music was not well received by the press."

Who is to be credited, then—Slonimsky or Wallace? Well, what exactly is the question? To begin with, the question for Wallace is Beethoven; the question for me, the romantic thesis. The question for Wallace is how Beethoven was received by the *press*; the issue for me, how Beethoven was received by the *audiences*—not merely the people who go to concerts for "professional" reasons but those who go merely to enjoy music as well. What implications Wallace's conclusions may have for the romantic thesis is my subject; and that remains yet to be seen. But for me Beethoven's reception by his contemporaries is not, of course, the major concern—rather, a useful example among others, chosen just because Beethoven is a symbol of the "difficult" artist who must struggle, posthumously, to ultimate appreciation.

It may perhaps be doing something of an injustice to Slonimsky to suggest, as Wallace does, that he deliberately represents the Beethoven invective (or any other in his book) as "typical." What Slonimsky actually says of his collection is as follows: "This is an anthology of critical assaults upon composers since the time of Beethoven. The criterion of selection is the exact opposite to that of a press agent. Instead of picking a quotable flattering phrase out of context from an otherwise tepid review, the *Lexicon of Musical Invective* cites biased, unfair, ill-tempered, and singularly unprophetic judgments."[13] As is clear from this statement of intent, Slonimsky is well aware that his sample is biased, *purposely so*, in the direction of the violently negative and, of course, the humorous. Obviously, if he has purposely skewed his collection toward the negative, and says so, he cannot be fairly represented as putting forward the negative as typical, if by "typical" one means anything like an overall consensus.

The humorous notwithstanding, however, Slonimsky does have a serious thesis that his *Lexicon* is supposed to support: "Its animating purpose is to demonstrate that music is an art in progress, and that objections

[12] Wallace, *Beethoven's Critics*, p. 1.
[13] Slonimsky, *Lexicon of Musical Invective*, p. 3.

The Authority of Sound

leveled at every musical innovator are all derived from the same psychological inhibition which may be described as Non-Acceptance of the Unfamiliar."[14] That *all* objections to musical innovation are motivated by what Slonimsky calls Non-Acceptance of the Unfamiliar, or, for that matter, any other *single* psychological mechanism, I sincerely doubt. Nevertheless, the spirit of Slonimsky's thesis, and his *Lexicon*, which I take to include the notion that new music is frequently difficult for its first audiences to grasp and appreciate fully, I wholeheartedly endorse. It is, in fact, the romantic thesis.

To what extent have Wallace's conclusions with regard to Beethoven's reception by the contemporary press, taken merely as a typical (though excellent) example of such research, made inroads into the romantic thesis? Certainly, to start with, it is a healthy antidote to the *Lexicon of Musical Invective* to know that a substantial number of Beethoven's contemporary critics were not musical troglodytes but musical prophets and seers. But with that happily acknowledged, we had better not be overhasty in rushing on to the conclusion, so contrary to long-established common sense in these matters, that Beethoven's contemporaries were in a better position than we to appreciate his music. Such research as Wallace has undertaken shows no such thing. What, then, does it show?

To begin with, it shows that a group of musically elite and well-educated professionals—namely what we would call the musical "press corps"—as well as musical analysts and writers "at once, and universally, recognized [Beethoven] as a composer of genius" in Beethoven's day. But we must be careful to distinguish between recognizing Beethoven's musical genius and fully appreciating or enjoying his music. My unsystematic but devoted reading of the Bach literature suggests to me that Bach's musical genius was recognized by those of his contemporaries who knew or knew of him. But it was not *our* Bach whose genius they were recognizing. Unsurpassed in playing and improvising on the organ, master of "archaic" forms, the most learned contrapuntist of his day, perhaps more accomplished than any in the "musical science"—such might have been what his contemporaries had in mind in calling him a great musical genius. But even if they *could* have formulated the notion of *musical* genius in terms of the survival of musical masterpieces over generations, which I doubt, it would not have been Bach whom they would have

[14] Ibid.

The   Authority   of   Sound

209

marked out for that destiny. Recall: third choice at Leipzig, with Telemann leading the pack!

There is no doubt that Beethoven's *genius* was recognized by many of
his musically sophisticated and trained contemporaries. The sheer power
of his musical intellect, including, of course, his prodigious powers of improvisation at the keyboard, was by all accounts unmistakable. And even
though most listeners could neither fully enjoy nor fully comprehend and
evaluate his musical works, they recognized these works, in all their difficulty, as of a power, complexity, and daring that only genius could have
produced, albeit perhaps a genius "out of control." But we must not allow
this kind of recognition of genius, even where it has its source in perception of the music itself, to pass muster for truly appreciating the genius of
Beethoven, the composer of beloved musical masterpieces, equal in perfection to the now accepted ones of Mozart and (especially) Haydn. I
daresay Schoenberg's musical *genius* is universally recognized by those
who have heard about him and know what he did. Yet as of this writing,
there are still few people who truly appreciate and enjoy his musical
works. Whether this is to be Schoenberg's permanent fate remains, of
course, a disputed question for our times. However that may be, we must,
in all these cases, distinguish between the recognition of transcendent
musical genius, which Bach, Beethoven, and Schoenberg all enjoyed in
their lifetimes, and full, rich appreciation and enjoyment of their music,
which none of them experienced, and which the romantic thesis tells us
can only happen, if it ever does, in the passage of time and the development of musical sensibility.

But Wallace is not merely claiming that Beethoven's genius was recognized by writers and members of the press. He presents, in addition, substantial evidence, extensive documentation to the effect that these (albeit
musically elite) listeners both enjoyed their encounters with this new and
(to them) difficult music and offered it their approval. Yet even here we
must be careful in what we conclude from this about the romantic thesis.
For two relevant questions immediately arise. What was the quality of
this musical appreciation, and how was the music understood by its
appreciators?

What I mean by the *quality* of musical appreciation is this. It seems clear
that for Beethoven's contemporaries, the appreciation of his music was a
struggle, not an easy and familiar enjoyment as it is for us. It was a strug-

gle even for the sophisticated listeners whom Wallace quotes, all the more so, one must assume, for the rest. It was, in a sense, a heroic feat. But it is not, I think, an experience of Beethoven I would like to substitute for my own comfortable and deep enjoyment, always there for me when I want and need it. It was their struggle that helped win my Beethoven for me. All credit to them for that. Having made this acknowledgment, however, why in the world should I want to recapitulate their struggle?

Furthermore, it is again clear, from Wallace's research, that when Beethoven's music was appreciated by his contemporaries it was frequently appreciated, by my lights, for some of the wrong reasons, as I suspect is the case of my appreciation of the ragas of South India. Even Wallace, who is obviously predisposed to find understanding rather than misunderstanding in Beethoven's early critics, is forced to concede, "What they do show is an acutely tuned sensitivity to musical fashion, *broken in rare instances by genuine insight and understanding.*"[15] Insight and understanding are *rare*, even among the musically elite, then, in Beethoven's day. And why should we be surprised by that? So far the romantic thesis, *properly construed*, stands up to the new scholarship.

But further, it is clear from Wallace's book that not only were genuine insights and understanding rare among Beethoven's contemporaries; understanding, in the form of (to modern ears) overblown poetic or programmatic interpretations was rife, which is perhaps to be expected both as a sign of the times and, significantly, as an obvious indication that an extramusical apparatus was required to help grasp an as yet little understood and unassimilated musical structure. Surely it would be folly to recapture, as I think some in the musicological community are indeed recommending, an understanding of Beethoven like that of E. T. A. Hoffmann's, as much as we (quite rightly) revere the man for his command of the language, his poetic inspiration, and his unstinting labors in the interest of Beethoven's musical reputation.

·   ·   ·

Let us see, now, if we can draw some general conclusions about the validity of the romantic thesis, as it might be affected by the kind of results Wallace has reported in his work on Beethoven's early reception. I will operate under the assumption that for those composers like Beethoven, who are generally seen as being scorned or ignored by their contemporaries,

[15] Wallace, *Beethoven's Critics*, p. 5; my italics.

The   Authority   of   Sound

such research as Wallace has done will either support the story of scorn
and neglect or refute it in much the same ways that Wallace has refuted
what he calls the "myth . . . that Beethoven's music was not well received
by the press."[16] This assumption may of course be false. But it is the most
reasonable assumption I have at this juncture, and so I shall rely on it for
what it is worth, namely, an assumption's worth.

Let me first say what we cannot conclude from Wallace's results. We
certainly cannot conclude, as Wallace seems to, that Beethoven's contemporaries knew best. Wallace writes, toward the end of his book, "The age
that produced Beethoven's Fifth Symphony was also capable of doing it
justice. . . ."[17] And I take it that this is not just a specific conclusion about
Beethoven's Fifth and its age but generalizable to all Beethoven's music.
Indeed, I shall expand it to a general claim about all music in all ages
within our own music history (although I do not attribute this "oceanic"
claim to Wallace). The claim that I want to examine, then, is that an age
that can produce any given musical work is also able to do it justice. I shall
discuss Wallace's specific claim about Beethoven's Fifth Symphony and its
age, but I mean my remarks to have the wider range just alluded to in the
preceding.

The first thing that must be settled, in discussing Wallace's claim, is
what he means by "doing justice." I take it he means to fully, or at least
adequately, understand and appreciate. If he doesn't mean that, the claim
is of no interest, for no one is naive enough to believe that Beethoven's age
had no understanding or appreciation *at all* of the Fifth Symphony. Furthermore, with direct reference to his claim about the Fifth and its age,
Wallace lets drop the (to me) staggering opinion that, as he puts it, "our
understanding of music has [not] advanced momentously in the interval"
between then and now.[18] It would seem to follow, then, that if Beethoven's age did "do justice" to the Fifth Symphony, and our understanding
of music has not increased to any large degree in the interval, then if we
have a rich and full understanding of the work—and I assume that we do,
which is to say, rich and full but never *complete*—Beethoven's contempo-

[16] Ibid., p. 1.
[17] Ibid., p. 143.
[18] Ibid. Wallace's full thought here is: "If the most sophisticated analyses of 150 years
ago have been reduced to textbook fodder, it is surely not because our understanding of
music has advanced momentously in the interval." I do not think I have misinterpreted
him on this regard; but the reader can decide.

The Authority of Sound

raries must have had also. In any event, at *whatever* level Beethoven's contemporaries appreciated his Fifth Symphony, on Wallace's view, we have not exceeded it. My own reading of Wallace is that what he was attributing to Beethoven's contemporaries was a rich, full appreciation and understanding of Beethoven's Fifth Symphony (which seems to me not to sit very well with his previously stated view that genuine insight and understanding of Beethoven, in his lifetime, was rare, unless, of course, the Fifth Symphony is a notable exception to that rule).

The second thing I want to point out about Wallace's claim is that it seems to be an *inference*. I take it that what Wallace is saying is this: if an age is capable of producing Beethoven's Fifth Symphony, it *follows* that it is capable of understanding and appreciating it. In point of fact, the inference is patently a bad one, an instance, to adopt a famous distinction of Gilbert Ryle's, of fallaciously arguing from "knowing how" to "knowing that."[19] It surely does not follow that if someone knows how to do something, then she also understands fully what it is she has done. And, pari passu, it surely does not follow that if an age is capable of producing something, it also understands fully or even adequately what exactly the nature or significance is of what it has produced. Thus, if Wallace means to *argue* from the capability of Beethoven's age of producing the Fifth Symphony to the capability of that age of fully or even adequately comprehending it, it is a bad argument and should be rejected out of hand.

But arguments aside, is it even the least bit plausible to think that Beethoven's age, which produced the Fifth Symphony, fully or even adequately comprehended it? Compare: Robespierre's age produced the French Revolution and fully comprehended it. Newton's age produced the *Principia Mathematica* and fully comprehended it. Prehistoric man produced fire and fully comprehended it. All three seem obviously false. How could Newton's age, for example, have known that Newtonian mechanics turns out to be a special case (so I am told by the physicists) of Einstein's theory of relativity? And how could Robespierre's age have even begun to comprehend the nature and implications of their revolution? Did the first fire builders understand combustion? Why in the world, then, should we think it any different with so complex and innovative an artwork as the mighty Beethoven Fifth?

[19] See Ryle, *The Concept of Mind*, pp. 27–32, for the distinction between "knowing how" and "knowing that."

The   Authority   of   Sound

Wallace makes the startling claim, as we have seen, in connection with his assertion that Beethoven's age fully comprehended the Fifth Symphony, that in general our understanding of music has not significantly increased in the interval since its premiere. That in itself is hard to credit. There is no branch of human knowledge or learning or science, one would have thought, that has not progressed *exponentially* since the Enlightenment. Is music alone excepted from this explosion in human knowledge? Have we really learned nothing of moment relevant to the appreciation, enjoyment, and understanding of Beethoven's Fifth in the last 150 years, from Hanslick, or Gurney, or Schenker, or Langer, or Meyer, or contemporary analysis and historical musicology, or half a hundred other persons or disciplines I could name?

I don't think I am mistaken in seeing in these remarks of Wallace's and others like them elsewhere in the literature, a spin-off of the "historically authentic performance" movement. What seems to be emerging is some kind of argument that goes from the now familiar notion that we cannot improve over contemporary performance practice to the parallel notion that we cannot improve over contemporary musical appreciation and understanding. But whatever might initially, or by way of subsequent argument, be plausible about the former claim, the latter seems to be so very eccentric as to be almost crackbrained. Are we really to say that with regard to works of music, or works of art across the board for that matter, human understanding is not susceptible of improvement? Improving everywhere else, apparently, but not improving here?

This of course is not to say that human knowledge of an artwork might not also *decline*. Alas, we do not understand music of the very distant past as well as its contemporaries did. Indeed, in some cases we do not appreciate or understand it at all. And it surely would be, therefore, a highly profitable outcome if we could just regain, for example, the knowledge and appreciation of ancient Greek music that was possessed by the most *unmusical* of Plato's contemporaries. But to grant the rather weak and uninteresting thesis that sometimes our musical appreciation and understanding is less than that of a past audience, is surely not to grant the stronger one that it cannot ever exceed that past appreciation and understanding. And for music currently within the performing repertory, even "early" music, I would urge that just because of our enhanced historical perspective and music-theoretical understanding, our grasp and appreciation exceeds that of the music's contemporaries, *so far as it is considered as an object of aesthetic appreciation.*

So, to repeat, what we *cannot* conclude from Wallace's research, and research like it, is that the romantic thesis is mistaken: we cannot conclude that contemporary audiences are as a rule in a favored position, over ourselves, to understand and appreciate the music of their times. Indeed, even for music in which a performing tradition has lapsed and has had to be recovered, as long as we are in full or substantial command of the notation, the romantic thesis is in place. It is no paradox, but merely the inexorable result of time and historical perspective, that we understand and appreciate Josquin more fully even than those of his contemporaries who acclaimed him the Prince of Music.

So much, then, for what we cannot conclude from current musical research into the reception of composers by their contemporaries. What *can* we conclude, relevant to our purposes here?

Nothing very much, indeed; but that is hardly to say that such research is either useless or inherently uninteresting. At least, apart from its intrinsic interest as a form of historical knowledge, it is a healthy antidote to the romantic thesis in its more naive and unacceptable form. That all composers are unknown and unsung in their lifetimes, starving in garrets, is the version of the romantic thesis that research such as Wallace's lays to rest forever. That great composers are frequently appreciated and even lionized in their own times, their music received with a considerable degree of praise and some understanding, must *not*, however, shake us loose from the romantic thesis in its mature, sensible formulation, which is that the music we most revere and glory in—the musical masterworks that we now enjoy so deeply as old and familiar friends and feel we understand, if not completely (for great works of art always hold promise of future enlightenment) then at least fully and richly—cannot have been so enjoyed, appreciated, understood in this way and to this degree by those who initially experienced them. To be sure, Beethoven and many other composers of similar stature must have been clearly recognizable to their contemporaries as musical intellects of the highest order. And their music, even where it met incomprehension, must have been recognizable as the product of musical intellect at its highest level, just because of the musical difficulties it presented to comprehension. All this is to be granted and is the kind of thing that Wallace's study, at least as I read it, reveals. But what it

The   Authority   of   Sound

does not reveal, and what the romantic thesis maintains it cannot, is the kind of rich, full, totally fulfilling musical appreciation and understanding described earlier, which only time and history and the evolution of musical sensibility can accomplish, and which (therefore) a great composer's contemporaries cannot possibly possess.

Nevertheless, there are two responses that one might reasonably have, even to what I hope is a more sophisticated version of the romantic thesis than used to be the stock-in-trade of program annotators and the like, the first more anecdotal than deeply philosophical, the second coming from a philosophical "school." I must examine them now briefly in turn.

.   .   .

All of us have, I am sure, musical works in our listening repertories that we love and admire but that have grown stale with overexposure. My own prime candidate, not a very surprising one, is the work I have just been discussing, the mighty Beethoven Fifth. I am told by my mother (who may tend to exaggerate just a little) that I was already listening to it with rapt attention, and humming the tunes, when I was five. Be that as it may, I have memories of Beethoven's C-minor Symphony as far back as I have memories at all. And, having lived through the Second World War, I think I can say that through at least one extended period of time, I heard it as frequently as "The Star-Spangled Banner." So often have I wished, in my musical maturity, that I could experience that sublime work with "fresh ears," as if for the first time, so that I could hear it without all the accretions time and a lifetime of memories have laid upon it, obscuring, so I tend to believe, its true structure and expression. But is not that wish, and all it implies, in direct contradiction to the romantic thesis, which I have been so stubbornly defending? Am I not hankering here after just that tabula rasa, with regard to Op. 67, that its original auditors—and only they—could have, when it was fresh from the writing desk and new to the world? I think not.

I think, rather, that what I am after is this: the experience of hearing the Fifth Symphony as if for the first time, *knowing what I know now*. I don't want to hear Op. 67 in what I take to be the *unadvantageous* position of its first auditors. I want to hear it as a work of Beethoven's that *I* have never heard before, but with all my experience of Beethoven's other music, all my musical education and acculturation to date, as propaedeutic for the experience. It is not my twentieth-century knowledge, experience, and acculturation that is occluding my perception of this all-too-familiar masterpiece. On the contrary, it will, if given the chance, greatly enrich it. But if Leonard Meyer is at least partly right that musical expectations too reliably confirmed are destructive of musical enjoyment, then one of the things perturbing my full enjoyment of Beethoven's Fifth is just overfamiliarity. For, as Meyer quite rightly observes, "ordinary observation indicates that composers, performers, and listeners do in fact tire of music with which they become very familiar,"[20] overfamiliarity being spelled out, in Meyer's information-theoretic sense, in terms of lack of "information." Furthermore, I believe that, at least in my own case, and I doubt I am singular in this, it is not merely the sheer number of listenings that has affected me but the circumstances—in particular, listenings stretching back to early childhood—that have built up unconscious listening habits in me of a damaging kind: damaging, I think, because they are the result of immature, uninformed attention to and overemphasis of the "wrong" things. In other words, in ways I cannot now put my finger on, I am unconsciously listening to Beethoven's Fifth as a five-year-old.

Thus, it is a combination of sheer overfamiliarity, in Meyer's information-theoretic sense, and bad habits of listening formed at a tender and uninformed age that is poisoning the well of appreciation when I listen to Beethoven's Fifth Symphony, *not* my twentieth-century ears. It is not the ears of Beethoven's contemporaries I am hankering after when I long for a "fresh" experience of Beethoven's Fifth Symphony. On the contrary, I am hankering for *my own ears*, but unencumbered by fifty years of listening, some of which have given me "bad habits." This longing for a "fresh" Beethoven Fifth—a particular example of a common artistic phenomenon—is not in conflict with the romantic thesis but, rather, completely consistent with it. I move on, therefore, to the "historicist" reaction.

.   .   .

I have argued, on the basis of the romantic thesis, that it would be folly to want to recover the consciousness of those who first received the great musical works of the past. For they were ill prepared to appreciate them fully. How could it be otherwise? Only time, familiarity, the education of

[20] Meyer, "On Rehearing Music," in *Music, the Arts, and Ideas*, p. 49.

The   Authority   of   Sound

musical sensibility that these works themselves would eventually contribute to, and their eventual working out of their place in musical history could gradually bring them to full, rich, and complete appreciation.

But there is another form the historicist thesis may take, which marks out as the contemporary consciousness to be recovered and "lived through" not the contemporary audience but indeed the contemporary artist himself, who, after all, *is* the first "audience" to his work. And who, after all, can be better qualified or better situated to understand the work of art than its very creator?

Benedetto Croce writes of what we must *lose*, through the passage of time, of our appreciation and understanding of artworks and how (at least in part) this loss can be made good. Of the loss he remarks: "Cimabue's Madonna is always in Santa Maria Novella; but does it speak to the contemporary visitor as it did to the Florentines of the thirteenth century?"[21] And of the recovery: "To restore in us the psychological conditions that have changed during history is the work of historical interpretation, which revives the dead, completes the fragmentary, gives us a way of seeing a work of art (the physical object) as the author saw it in the act of creation."[22]

Croce, needless to say, has a specific philosophical ax to grind in the passages from *Aesthetic as the Science of Expression* that I have just quoted; that ax would seem to be the historicist thesis in its full-blown form. It certainly is in *one* of its full-blown forms. But it is crucial to remark that it isn't the form in which I, and most others, understand that thesis.

The way in which the historicist thesis is usually stated by historians of the arts, and usually accepted by those of the laity who do, is in terms of recapturing the attitude of the contemporary *audience*. Croce, it is apparent from the preceding quotation, expresses it in terms rather of recapturing the attitude of the artist himself "in flagrante," as it were: "as the author saw it in the act of creation" is the phrase he uses. Those who are familiar with the so-called expression theory of art will recognize this as following from a doctrine characteristic of that theory, derived by Croce (no doubt) from Schopenhauer, and passed on by him (no doubt) to Collingwood et al., that in appreciating a work of art, when it is done correctly or successfully, the appreciator is recapitulating in his or her mind,

[21] Croce, *The Aesthetic as the Science of Expression and of the Linguistic in General*, p. 138.
[22] Ibid., pp. 139–40.

The Authority of Sound

with the help of the "physical work of art," just what went on in the creator's mind when he or she produced the work. What went on in the creator's mind was "expression," which *is* the work of art properly so called, and what goes on in the audience's mind, in the best case, is a duplication of that creative, expressive act.

I do not intend to refute but neither to adopt the very shaky metaphysics of the expression theory of art. Cleansed of that metaphysics and other of its philosophical baggage, however, what Croce suggests here can be evaluated as an alternative version of the historicist thesis that has at least some prima facie plausibility and demands our consideration. Most of us would agree, I presume, that art-historical research into the circumstances surrounding a work of art's production has, as at least one of its goals, the enhancement of artistic appreciation. To advert to Croce's example, if I come to know what Cimabue's Florentine contemporaries knew, I will be able more fully to understand and enjoy the Madonna in Santa Maria Novella. How will such knowledge help me? It cannot do so merely by being known. "One who is simply erudite will never succeed in putting himself into direct communication with great spirits. . . ."[23] That is to say, art-historical knowledge must be translated into aesthetic or (if you prefer) artistic experience. On what I called, previously, the imaginative or sympathetic version of the historicist thesis (in connection with Hume), that aesthetic or artistic experience was taken to be the experience had by putting oneself imaginatively in the place of the contemporary audience to the work. With regard to what we normally take the word "audience" to connote, that kind of experience turned out, on examination, to be far from obviously desirable; and I shall not now rehearse my reasons for saying so, except to remind the reader that in general it was concluded that the contemporary audience was in a far poorer position than we ourselves are to appreciate and understand the work.

But what if the "audience" is construed, rather, as the one responsible for the very existence of the work and, therefore, its truly first "spectator"; what if, as Croce puts the role of art-historical research, "We encircle, by memory, the physical object with all the circumstances in which it arose, and so we make it possible for it to work anew on us as it once worked on its producer"?[24] Two things may seem to have been accomplished by this

---

[23] Ibid., p. 143.
[24] Ibid., p. 140.

The   Authority   of   Sound

move: the successful transformation of art-historical knowledge into aesthetic experience, and the blunting of the objection to the standard version of the historicist thesis to the effect that the contemporary audience is hardly in an advantageous position to appreciate and understand the work of art. For as to the first, who would deny that a Beethoven, in the very throes of musical creation, is not gripped by the most powerful aesthetic experience possible? And as to the second, who could possibly understand better than the creator himself the nature and workings of the composition he himself has brought into being? May I suggest that the historicist thesis, so construed, is mistaken on both counts?

It seems, to begin with, doubtful that somehow, by "sympathy" (or whatever), achieving the consciousness of a Bach or a Beethoven in the throes of creation, or even merely contemplating his completed work in tranquility, is a possible project for a musical audience, unless it is an audience of composers of genius or at least talent. Sympathetic or imaginative identification with *anyone* is a possibility that is bound to be contentious. But "identifying" with musical genius is for most, I would think, beyond the merely contentious and well into the mind-bending. Thus the aesthetic or artistic payoff of art-historical knowledge, as Croce construes it, seems a failed enterprise.

This, however, is not the objection I really want to rest on. Doubtful though it may be, there are ways of tinkering with the concept of "becoming in the imagination" the creator of the work that can at least partially ameliorate its prima facie impossibility. Rather, I want to go after what may appear to be the far more plausible, seductive claim that the most favored appreciator and knower of the musical work *must* be, *of course*, its composer. Who can, after all, have more *intimate* and detailed knowledge of the work than its creator? This seems to be a special case of the Cartesian precept that I am in a privileged position to know *myself*, coupled with the motto of Montaigne's that "who touches this book touches me." I think it is false, and the more dangerous because of its seductiveness.

I have written elsewhere about the mistake of thinking that the composer, of necessity, must be the greatest expert on his or her work.[25] Some of that bears repeating here. As we have seen, the belief has an intuitive pull on us. After all, the greatest musical intellects are agreed on all hands to be the great composers. And if they are the greatest musical intellects,

[25] Kivy, *Music Alone*, pp. 103–5 and 118–23.

The Authority of Sound

then they must (it would seem to follow) be the ones who best understand music in general and, a fortiori, their own works in particular.

But this turns out to be yet another case of confusing (or ignoring) the
distinction between knowing how and knowing that, as well as of assuming the false premise that we cannot come to know more about the author's "text" than the author herself could know, whether that "text" be
a musical composition or a treatise on metaphysics. As regards the first
error, it merely needs to be pointed out that no one exceeds Beethoven's
or Bach's or Josquin's musical knowledge when it is clearly understood to
be *knowledge how* to create musical works; and it is *that* knowledge we are
enshrining in our beliefs that Beethoven, Bach, and Josquin are some of
the greatest musical intellects the world has yet seen. However, this in no
way implies that Beethoven, or Bach, or Josquin had, even for their own
times, the keenest awareness of what exactly they had done: the most adequate knowledge of their works (from the analytic or appreciative point
of view). It is frequently said nowadays that "textbook" analysis of sonata
form cannot truly be valid for music written before the "textbooks" because the analysis, coming after the fact, could not possibly have been on
the minds of the composers or part of what they were doing in composing
their works. But this is plainly nonsense. In many ways they *didn't* know
what they were doing. This is no paradox but the timeless truth of Plato's
Ion. What they did know supremely well was *how* to do what the analysts
later came to understand the "whatness" of.

Nor does it seem that appreciation and enjoyment are best achieved by
taking the attitude (if that were possible) of the creator to his or her artistic creation. For there is much about the relationship of the composer to
the work that defeats spectatorship. "He is too close to his work to really
be able to appreciate it" is a saying that scarcely needs to be defended.
(Remember that Mendelssohn wished the manuscript of his "Italian"
Symphony destroyed because, apparently, he thought it unworthy of
him; and yet we now value it as one of his most perfect works!) Furthermore, even *if*, which is not necessarily so in every case but might be in individual cases, a composer of a particular work *is* the one among his contemporaries who best understands or appreciates it, that understanding
and appreciation are as susceptible of improvement, emendation, and expansion over the course of time as the understanding and appreciation of
any of the composer's contemporaries. The composer of a work is in no

The Authority of Sound

better position than they to give a *final* judgment on its true and ultimate significance or nature. His sensibility as well as theirs is time-bound and far from infallible.

That being said, however, as a perfectly general point, it may still be the case that in some instances authorial authority may be indefeasible. It is always perennially arguable, in questions of either semantic or work meaning in the literary arts, that the author has at least veto power over meaning ("I did *not* mean *that*") even though he or she may not have what might be called positive legislative power over meaning ("I *meant that*") if, for example, the words she wrote simply *cannot* mean what she says they do, as where Humpty Dumpty insists that "glory" *means* "there's a nice knock-down argument for you!" Although there is certainly contention over the matter, *I* believe that when A. E. Housman insisted the last lines of his poem "1887" were not ironic but "straight," that settled the matter once and for all.

Now, where *meaning* cannot be the issue, as in absolute music, the cases may be less clear. But I do want to hold out the possibility that, as in Housman's poem, the composer may at times, in certain instances, have veto power over interpretation. That being said, I also want to adduce some fairly important instances where it would be tempting, but quite mistaken, to accept the composer's veto. If I should perceive motto *A* to be thematically related to motto *B*, as if "derived" from it, and if the composer had insisted that he did not derive *A* from *B*, what should I conclude? If, indeed, on reconsidering the matter, I still find it absolutely compelling, aesthetically, to hear *B* as deriving from *A*, I can, I think, safely override the composer's veto in this wise: "Of course the composer was not aware, *in this particular case*, that *B* came from *A*, any more than Ion was aware of how he got his wonderful ideas about Homer. *In this particular case*, talent and instinct were operating below the level of conscious awareness." Sheer talent, unabashed genius, just does these sorts of things without quite realizing it.

With these important qualifications read into the record, let us now make a general conclusion about the Crocean project for utilizing art-historical research to enter into, as it were, the artist's consciousness. It is misconceived, as is the more usual historicist project of entering into the consciousness of the contemporary audience, and for many of the same reasons, which can all be summed up in simply invoking the romantic thesis: great works of art can only slenderly, if at all, be understood by their first audiences. Time and history must give us the perspective fully to grasp, appreciate, and enjoy them.

But we are now in something of a dilemma. What I have called the sympathetic or imaginative interpretation of the historicist thesis, which in either its ordinary or its Crocean form tells us we must "become" the contemporary of the work to appreciate it, turns out to offer us a distinctly undesirable goal, all things considered. For although I may be in a position to gain or regain some valuable perceptions in hearing, say, Beethoven's First Symphony the way its first audience heard it (the shock and surprise of the opening, for example), I will lose far more than I will gain, by virtue of the fact that the first audience was hearing a new, unfamiliar, difficult, and innovative work that they were unprepared to appreciate fully.

However, this leaves us with a problem. For we all do agree with Croce's insistence that a full appreciation of an artistic work requires the recapturing of a great deal of factual information about it. We all, in other words, agree that the histories of art, literature, and music have a vital contribution to make to our appreciation of the artworks of the past. *How* can they help us? That is the problem. How can historical knowledge of artworks be transformed into rich, aesthetic experience of them? The imaginative or sympathetic interpretation of the historicist thesis offers us an answer. In the event, that interpretation turns out to be unacceptable, and so the answer it proffers as regards aesthetic experience unavailable to us. What remains is the "cerebral" interpretation. But the answer *it* proffers seems rather pallid. It offers "understanding" of a kind that seems only distantly and weakly "aesthetic." That is the dilemma. Let me illustrate it with an example.

In his introduction to *The Complete Plays of Aristophanes*, Moses Hadas makes the wise and witty remark that:

> allusions to contemporary persons, events and usages, special
> connotations of words, and, in a more general view, the intellectual
> bent of Aristophanic wit sometimes leaves us in the dark—just as
> reflections of contemporary life in our comedy would be lost on a
> Greek audience. An old movie has Groucho Marx's secretary say

The   Authority   of   Sound

when two men are waiting to see him, "Epstein is waxing wroth," and Groucho replies, "Tell Roth to wax Epstein." How many volumes of commentary would a Greek require to understand all of the joke, and how unfunny it would be after he had studied the commentary.[26]

One thing, straightaway, that Hadas makes clear in his unphilosophical but colorful way is that recapturing information the first audiences of an artwork possessed does not of itself recapture *their*, or any other, aesthetic appreciation of the work. I can come to understand and appreciate *why* Aristophanes' audience found something funny; it is doubtful, though, that this knowledge will succeed in making it funny *to me*. And it is the funniness as such, not the knowledge that such and such was funny to so and so, and why, that is the aesthetic experience, the artistic enjoyment. Nor, of course, is humor a singular case, although it is a *particularly* perishable commodity. It is a stand-in for any aesthetic experience that relies on knowledge or awareness that we no longer possess but must *repossess* through art-historical research. How can this knowledge pass from "knowledge that" to artistic appreciation? That is our dilemma.

It is a dilemma I cannot resolve here. For that, another book would be required, of a very different kind from this one. I will merely assume, as I think most of us now do, that historical research does have an aesthetic payoff even if we do not fully understand how it works. I will assume, further, that it has two kinds of payoff. One kind, in the case of music, is what I have called historical listening. Here we have what might be called cerebral appreciation of various aspects of the work, based on historical knowledge of what the composer was trying to do, but we are not able to "internalize" the intended effect. This is what is happening when we are recognizing that the opening of Beethoven's First Symphony is "surprising" but are not ourselves surprised. It is the musical analogue of understanding a joke in Aristophanes but not being amused.

But it is possible also, I think, sometimes to internalize art-historical knowledge in such wise as to be actually affected the way those were who originally possessed that knowledge as part of their contemporary outlook. I probably cannot experience, with my secular outlook, nor do I

[26]Hadas, *The Complete Plays of Aristophanes*, pp. 2–3. Actually, Professor Hadas had the joke a bit mixed up. Groucho was the president of Darwin College, and it was the dean that was doing the waxing. But no matter.

The Authority of Sound

really want to, the religious ecstasy of Palestrina's audience, no matter how much I learn of their religious beliefs and attitudes. But I think I can come to experience some of their appreciation of the way post-Tridentine polyphony succeeded (as I hear it) in capturing the essence of human utterance in music, under the discipline of the Council of Trent, by learning what these composers were trying to do in response to the demands and directives of the Council and so being drawn to those aspects of their music in which they were trying to do it and that I was either missing or mishearing.

I want to emphasize, however, in no uncertain terms that even here we are listening historically, not in the manner of the sympathetic or imaginative version of the historicist thesis. I have not "become," even imaginatively, a sixteenth-century listener. I am very much a twentieth-century listener who, through historical awareness, is able to recapture the appreciation of a work's aspect, otherwise unremarked. But I am fully aware of what I have done, and this awareness makes my experience self-conscious and historically situated in a way that is completely alien to the sixteenth-century musical mind. I am not having a sixteenth-century experience; I am having a twentieth-century one. I have not relived a sixteenth-century experience, I have merely revived one.

More, I think, I cannot say, nor need I in this place. But it is time now to take some kind of accounting, after this rather lengthy excursus into the romantic and historicist theses, of what the ledger might show, in profit and loss, *if* imaginative or sympathetic historicist listening could really be achieved—if, that is, we could really achieve sensible authenticity.

. . .

I think I can be brief here. The question I wish to pose, and that I have been alluding to more or less throughout the present chapter, is this: what would I gain, aesthetically, through achieving sensible authenticity, and what would I lose—and would I come out ahead or behind in the final aesthetic sum?

A thorough answer to this question cannot, I think, be given a priori or in complete generality. The question must be answered case by case. What would I gain and lose achieving sensible authenticity in listening to Beethoven's First Symphony, or Bach's *St. Matthew Passion*, or a motet by Josquin, or a canzona of Giovanni Gabrieli's? The pros and cons of each

The Authority of Sound

might be very different, the accounting in detail interesting and rewarding to have in hand. But I can undertake no such "empirical" investigation here. Rather, I rely on the romantic thesis, in its mature, sophisticated form, to convince the reader that where we do have a firm grasp of a notation and performing practice—where, that is, we can perform and hear a believable version of the work—we must lose far more in musical enjoyment and appreciation than we can ever gain, in hearing the work as the original audiences heard it.

Where we are not in full or satisfactory command of notation and performance practice, as I gather we are not with regard to, say, pre–Notre Dame polyphony and chant, we cannot, needless to say, have any believable musical experience at all. And in such cases achieving sensible authenticity would be an obvious desideratum. *Something*, after all, is better than nothing; and a contemporary experience of even a notoriously difficult work is considerably more than "something." But if the romantic thesis applies even here, then an even more desirable goal is to hear this music, if that were possible, just as we hear the music of Beethoven and Bach, of Gabrieli and Josquin, of Ockeghem and even Leonin, as part of *our* repertory, enriched and vivified by *our* culture and *our* history.

Perhaps, though, the romantic thesis does *not* apply everywhere. I am inclined to believe that it does not. And when it does not apply, perhaps indeed music *cannot* survive its own time at all. If, that is to say, there is a music that time, history, and experience do not make more enjoyable but less, do not render more fully understood but less, that is a music that time, history, and experience will destroy, *unless* we can somehow achieve sensible authenticity in listening to it. That would be an ephemeral music (in the nonpejorative sense).

But where either tradition or musicological research, or both, has made music part of our listening repertoire—a repertoire that now stretches back, thanks to historical musicology, to the twelfth century—it is my view that the romantic thesis does apply: that more would be lost to us in achieving, if it were possible, sensible authenticity than ever would be gained. That is the conclusion in which I want to rest.

But desirability aside, *is* it possible to achieve something like sensible authenticity—and (of special concern to us here) is sonic authenticity the way to do it? These are the questions we must consider in closing.

•   •   •

The Authority of Sound

I have not said much about the *possibility* of achieving sensible authenticity—of imaginatively or sympathetically "becoming" a contemporary listener—because it is such a can of worms as makes me loath to lift the lid. The perplexing thing is this. My wish to experience something "through someone else's eyes," as the saying goes, raises the annoying question of just *who* would be doing the experiencing if the wish were granted, and leads from there to the suspicion—perhaps justified and perhaps not—that the wish might be an idle one and really, in the event, not just impossible (like the wish to levitate at will) but quite unintelligible.

What would I be wishing, for example, if I wished to hear a performance of the *St. Matthew Passion* "through the ears of" a contemporary listener? Am I wishing to *become* that listener temporarily? And if my wish were granted, would I really get what I wished? Would *I* be having the experience? If I really were to become the contemporary listener, even if only "imaginatively" or "sympathetically" and not, *per impossibile*, by time travel, it appears as if I would lose my personal identity. "I" would not be "I" but "he." So in that case I would not be getting my wish; for my wish is that *I* have a certain experience, but *I* wouldn't be having the experience at all: *he* would be having it.[27] That cannot be what I am wishing, then. It would seem to be a *reductio ad absurdum* of sensible authenticity.

A more intelligible way of putting my wish for sensible authenticity is that I am wishing to hear the *St. Matthew Passion* "from the contemporary's point of view." Here I am not asking to become someone else—an idle wish, anyway—but asking to "get his angle on things." But how is this different from listening historically, which is a distinctly *inauthentic* way of listening to most of the music of the past, peculiar to the twentieth-century audience? This *is* a possible way of listening. We do it all the time, particularly when we listen to "historically authentic" performance. It just is not achieving sensible authenticity but, rather, something like its opposite in most cases.

There is an ontological gap, then, between the perfectly possible task of hearing the *St. Matthew Passion* "from a contemporary point of view" and the completely self-defeating task of "hearing it through contemporary ears." The former is not sensible authenticity, although quite achievable; the latter *is* sensible authenticity but turns out to be unintelligible. And

[27] I have discussed this perplexing eventuality previously in "On the Concept of the 'Historically Authentic Performance,'" in *The Fine Art of Repetition*.

The Authority of Sound

the question is, Is there a listening stance, in that ontological gap, that is *both* intelligible and a bona fide example of sensible authenticity?

Presumably, when someone envisions hearing the *St. Matthew Passion* "through contemporary ears," she is not envisioning the loss of her personal identity. She has some vague idea of either "being" *both* the contemporary listener *and* herself at the same time or else, in the listening experience, sort of switching back and forth between the two. In either case, she is both being the other and being herself; she is hearing through someone else's ears but, at the same time, *she*, not someone else, is having the experience.

I do not know whether this double-aspect notion of sensible authenticity, in either form, is unintelligible. But I am certainly wary of declaring it so. I daresay it is no *more* problematic than self-deception or weakness of will, two well-known psychological phenomena also seeming to involve incompatible mental states, that have both undergone considerable philosophical scrutiny, proved stubbornly recalcitrant to analysis, and yet survived pretty much intact, without having been declared nonsense by the philosophical community or having fallen into disuse in ordinary discourse. So I shall pass no final judgment either way about whether sensible authenticity is a *possible* goal of the musical listener. Rather, assuming that it is, I shall conclude by raising the more tractable question of whether sonic authenticity is an infallible or reliable means toward that end. The answer, as was beginning to become clear in Chapter 3, is in the negative.

.   .   .

There are, as we have seen, all manner of particular ways in which achieving sonic authenticity might work against rather than for the achievement of sensible authenticity. And to review the previously examined examples or produce new ones would simply be otiose. What I would like to bring forward, rather, are two more general, overarching ways in which sonic authenticity, as pursued by the "historically authentic" performance movement, runs against the grain of sensible authenticity. They are endemic to sonic authenticity and, I suspect, not fully appreciated as yet.

First, as I have had occasion to point out in Chapter 3, sonic authenticity, as exemplified in the authentic performance movement, represents historical listening in its most fully developed "public" form. The listener

The   Authority   of   Sound

who now, quite consciously and with purposeful intent, insists on listening to each composer on "period" instruments, with careful adherence to the performance style of the composer's period, is pursuing historical listening in its most "out-front" (if not its most sophisticated) form. And because, further, historical listening is a distinctly twentieth-century phenomenon, the historical listener is, ipso facto, a listener who in a deep sense experiences music in a sensibly inauthentic way.

Compare, in this regard, the audience who attended Baron van Swieten's performances of Handel oratorios, orchestrated by Mozart, with an audience today, hearing the works on original instruments and the rest. The modern audience, with its elaborately developed historical sensibility, hears not only a work in its historical period but a *performance* in *its* historical period. The eighteenth-century Viennese audience, on the other hand, whatever historical awareness they may have had, heard the *performance* as part of their contemporary musical culture, not as an archeological dig. Or, to put it in the current musical jargon, *all* performance, in eighteenth-century Vienna, was *mainstream* performance. And to the extent that we are hearing any music in "historical" rather than "mainstream" performance style, we are hearing it in a sensibly inauthentic manner, whether it be Viennese classical music or the music of *any* period prior to the advent, in our own century, of musical historicism.[28]

My second point has to do with a recurring defense of the authentic performance movement I have been encountering with increasing frequency these days. It is that the *novelty* of hearing music on "period" instruments, in "period" style, refreshes these works for the jaded listener. It helps renew them. Thus, so goes the defense, "if you think you can't possibly hear anything new in Beethoven's Fifth Symphony, try hearing it rendered with sonic authenticity; the performance will shake you up by the strangeness of the sounds and the novelty of the interpretation." There is, of course, nothing new in such a rationale for innovative performance. What is strange, as we will see in a moment, is its new use in defense of *authenticity*.

One way of looking at the physical sounds of a performance is as a *medium* by which the music is projected. In this we might compare them to the medium by which a representation is conveyed in painting. A point

[28] Ibid.

The Authority of Sound

made by Arthur Danto, in regard to the medium of representational painting, is relevant here. He writes that

> ways of seeing are perhaps transparent to those whose ways of seeing they are, and these may turn, so to speak, opaque when they no longer *are* their ways of seeing. The history of art is filled with such examples. I have little doubt that the contemporaries of Giotto, astounded at the realism of his paintings, should just have seen men and women and angels in those paintings and *not* a way of seeing men and women and angels. Giotto's mode of vision has become a kind of cultural artifact.[29]

Danto's point, I take it, is that a painter's contemporaries—the contemporaries of Giotto, for example—may find the painter's medium so "transparent" that they "see through" it right to the subject matter: the men, women, angels. Whereas a later generation finds that same medium thick and opaque: an object of attention, and thus not "seeing," *sans phrase*, but "a way of seeing."

Later on in his discussion of these matters, Danto does indeed draw an analogy to music, where he writes: "Music is not generally regarded as an imitative art. . . . But from the perspective of the concept of medium, the intermediate substance and avenue of transmission from subject to spectator, music shares crucial features with painting and sculpture and drama."[30] The example he gives, however, to illustrate this claim, is not in the direction I wish to go and is somewhat puzzling into the bargain. "And again in the performance of music," Danto remarks, "it is the goal of certain players to evacuate themselves from the space between audience and sound; to the extent that the audience is conscious of the musicians it is distracted from the music."[31] Danto does not get any more specific than this; and so what he may have in mind by "the goal of certain players" is pure conjecture on my part. But one can reasonably suppose he may be thinking of opera, where the orchestra is partially hidden away in the pit (and, in Bayreuth, indeed hidden completely to make the music of the orchestral accompaniment somehow a disembodied part of the fictional world). Or it may perhaps be that Danto means to suggest a kind of

[29] Danto, *The Transfiguration of the Commonplace*, pp. 42–43.
[30] Ibid., p. 152.
[31] Ibid.

The Authority of Sound

230

attitude toward musical performance in which the performer tries, as much as possible, to efface herself as a performer, while placing the music in the foreground. One might view the performer as medium, the musical work as what is "represented," with the flamboyant, Liszt-like performer as a thick, opaque medium, the submerged, laid-back performer as the transparent one.[32]

Be that as it may, it is not the visible aspect of music making that I have in mind in making an analogy between the visible medium of representational painting and the "medium" of musical presentation. Rather, I have in mind precisely the "audible" medium. What I want to suggest is that in much the same way that Giotto's contemporaries found his representational medium "transparent" to perception, we may conjecture that a late eighteenth-century Viennese audience, completely at home with its musical instruments and musical practice, would experience them as a relatively transparent medium through which music was made present to them. But reproduce that medium in a twentieth-century context and it becomes as opaque, as much a "cultural artifact" (to use Danto's phrase), as Giotto's medium of representation has become for us. To generalize, an "authentic" performance continually and persistently draws attention to itself, to the medium: relatively transparent to its contemporaries, relatively opaque to us. Thus, the defense of authentic performance to the effect that its novelty may renew our interest in overfamiliar works is a defense rooted not in sensible authenticity but in its very opposite. The *very same* defense could appropriately be made for the performance of music of the past on weird electronic instruments or any other unfamiliar, novel kinds. It is the novelty, not the authenticity, that makes the difference.

In two very important general respects, then, "historically authentic" performance is directly in conflict with sensible authenticity, and productive of its opposite. It encourages historical listening, and it calls direct attention to, makes a primary object of attention, the medium of sound production. In both instances, the result is sensible inauthenticity. On the

[32] Let me add here that in the quotations concerning music that I have adduced in the preceding, Danto is in the process of constructing an argument *against* the view that the goal of art is to render the medium completely transparent, which is not just an "empirical" impossibility but a "metaphysical" one. I am grateful to Lauren Oppenheim for suggesting the second interpretation of what Danto is saying here about music and medium, although I may have changed the emphasis of her suggestion somewhat.

The Authority of Sound

other hand, "mainstream" performance practice encourages ahistorical listening and presents a far more transparent medium to a twentieth-century audience. "Mainstream" performance, then, in these two important respects, is more sensibly authentic than is "authentic" performance practice.

This, of course, is not to deny by any means that there are other aspects in which "authentic" performance might be more conducive to sensible authenticity than "mainstream" performance. It *is* to say that the authority of sonic authenticity does not lie in its sole command over the means to sensible authenticity. Whatever *other* attractions mainstream performance may have, it also has the attraction, if it is one, of sensible authenticity *in certain respects*. And, as we have just seen, sonic authenticity has the distinctly *inauthentic* attractions—and *attractions* indeed I take them to be—of providing a most highly developed form of historical listening, and the refreshing quality of novelty, that opacity of medium lends to even the most overworked warhorses in the concert repertory. Not surprisingly, we are again confronted with the stubborn truth that there is no single road to sensible authenticity and that sensible authenticity may not be the road to deep musical understanding and appreciation. It behooves us, in any case, to leave all roads open.

⊙

The Authority of Practice

As we saw in Chapter 4, there seem to be two obvious ways in which to understand the concept of historically authentic performance practice: as a means or as an end in itself. As a means, performance practice can be construed either as our pathway to the realizing of the composer's performing intentions or as our pathway to the realizing of contemporary sound. In the former case, its authority lies in the authority of intention; in the latter, in the authority of sound. And these two claims on our obedience have already been canvassed.

As an end in itself performance practice must be construed, then, not as a sonic feature of music at all. Of course a practice is not, strictly speaking, "heard" in any case. But if performance practice were cashed out either as a means to realizing the composer's performing intentions *or* as a means to realizing contemporary sound, we might, loosely speaking, call it a "sonic feature," at least as short for "relevant to the sound of a musical work." As an end in itself, however, it is no more a sonic feature of music, even loosely speaking, than the actions and mise en scène of an opera. And, indeed, it is opera that initially served as our introduction, in Chapter 4, to this distinctively *nonsonic* aspect of musical performance.

I shall construe musical practice here, as I did in Chapter 4, as an end in itself, therefore a nonsonic, mainly visible feature of musical performance. And the question to be raised about it is what value, if any, there might be in restoring to the performance of music of the past the performance practice of its particular period and circumstances.

To make this question clearer, I will, as a first step, distinguish two aspects of performance practice, so construed: what I shall call its choreography, and what I shall call its setting or mise en scène. Thus, for example, the choreography of a Bach church cantata is the Lutheran service in which it functioned as an integral part; its setting or mise en scène, during the Leipzig period, the *Thomaskirche*, or, generally, the Lutheran place of worship. And the question to which we shall direct our attention presently is, What, if any, might the justification be for performing, for example, a Bach cantata not, as we now do it, "in concert," and in the concert hall—which are, respectively, *our* choreography and setting—but with its original choreography and setting?

But we shall never get a purchase on this question without first understanding what the raison d'être of the modern concert and concert hall are. And for that purpose we must examine, from the point of view of the philosophy of art, the historical origins of both.

·   ·   ·

The public concert and concert hall, as we saw in Chapter 4, came into being in the eighteenth century and fall on our side of what I called there the "great divide" between musical practice in a variety of social and institutional settings, and musical practice as it, for the most part, currently manifests itself, in a single social and institutional monolith. The crossing of the great divide might be understood from more than one point of view. But as I view it, in the context of this book, it reflects and is a part of a philosophical revolution in our attitude toward the arts in general and music in particular.

The revolution I refer to might justly be termed the "aesthetic revolution," for it brought into common use the word "aesthetics" itself, erected the modern philosophical discipline called by that name, and inspired, as well, a cluster of related theories, all adumbrating in one way or another what was finally to be called the "aesthetic attitude" and that brought to the fore the general view that our basic attitude toward all the arts is, or should be, the same: an attitude of rapt *contemplation*. The hallmark of that attitude of contemplation was "disinterestedness," which, in Kant's third *Critique*, achieved the status of an elaborately worked-out philosophical doctrine, very much favoring, although not in fact implying, an aesthetic formalism of one kind or another.

The rise of the aesthetic in the eighteenth century, its consequences and attendant circumstances, is a more-than-twice–told tale. There is no point in rehearsing it yet again here. There definitely is a point, however, for our purposes, in understanding what some of the implications of the eighteenth-century "aesthetic revolution" were both for the musical listener and for music's social setting. It is those implications that I wish to discuss briefly now.

Let us begin not at the beginning but at the end of what I have been calling the "aesthetic revolution." Very near the outset of the *Critique of Judgment* Kant famously presents and illustrates the central claim of the Analytic of the Beautiful—indeed, the central claim of his aesthetic theory *tout court*—that "the satisfaction which determines the judgment of taste is disinterested":

> The satisfaction which we combine with the representation of the existence of an object is called "interest." Such satisfaction always has reference to the faculty of desire, either as its determining ground or as necessarily connected with its determining ground. Now when the question is if a thing is beautiful, we do not want to know whether anything depends or can depend on the existence of the thing, either for myself or for anyone else, but how we judge it by mere observation (intuition or reflection). If anyone asks me if I find that palace beautiful which I see before me, I may answer: I do not like things of that kind which are made merely to be stared at. Or I can answer like the Iroquois Sachem, who was pleased in Paris by nothing more than by the cook shops. Or again, after the manner of Rousseau, I may rebuke the vanity of the great who waste the sweat of the people on such superfluous things. In fine, I could easily convince myself that if I found myself on an uninhabited island without the hope of ever again coming among men, and could conjure up just such a splendid building by my mere wish, I should not even give myself the trouble if I had a sufficiently comfortable hut. This may all be admitted and approved, but we are

The   Authority   of   Practice

235

not now talking of this. We wish only to know if this mere representation of the object is accompanied in me with satisfaction, however indifferent I may be as regards the existence of the object of this representation. We easily see that, in saying it is *beautiful* and in showing that I have taste, I am concerned, not with that in which I depend on the existence of the object, but with that which I make out of this representation in myself. Everyone must admit that a judgment about beauty, in which the least interest mingles, is very partial and is not a pure judgment of taste. We must not be in the least prejudiced in favor of such things, but be quite indifferent in this respect, in order to play the judge in things of taste.[1]

The stringent Kantian requirement that even considerations of existence, let alone utility or sensible agreeableness, must be distilled out of a judgment if it is to be a pure judgment of taste, a bona fide judgment of the beautiful, is the logical summing up—the culmination, if you will—of what I described earlier as the "aesthetic revolution," in which, one might say, all interactions with a work of art, except that of pure *contemplation*, became extraneous as well as destructive of the now favored "aesthetic attitude." For no more powerful check can be put on any latent tendency we may have to depart from the purity of "mere" contemplation than the stipulation that we must not even entertain the least inclination toward belief in the existence of what is presented to us in perception. Where existence is ruled out, what *else* but contemplation can remain—contemplation, that is, of whatever in the perceptual presentation one's aesthetic theory will allow, in Kant's case the purely *formal*?

The famous example of the palace gives Kant, of course, a fairly crude device for his initial purposes—all the more useful, in these preliminary stages of the inquiry, because of its crudeness—in introducing the concept of existence. For it is easy to bludgeon one into submission here by appealing to the surface intuition that denying "beauty" to a palace or other such "utilitarian" physical object on the basis of one's aversion to the politics of people who build them or the lack of usefulness of these structures on an uninhabited island is to confuse the judgment of taste with some other, and that such a confusion, in the present case, could be infallibly avoided by being sure that what you judge would be judged the

[1] Kant, *Critique of Judgment*, pp. 38–39 (§2).

The Authority of Practice

same even though it did not exist at all—was a mere "castle in the air," so to say, and what you were judging was only what was present to your imagination as visual fantasy, or to your perception as visual hallucination. For where would your politics or practical comfort be then? And what would be left to "judge" beautiful or not but the *form* or *appearance* of an "image"?

Such a crude instrument, however, may seem of little use in considering the more abstract and fine arts, absolute music in particular. For what, one wonders, would the opposite be of "disinterested" perception when attending to a sonata or a symphony? It has no content; it has no "use"; and it is difficult to see what exactly one could be doing, in this case, in following or not following the Kantian precept to abjure concern "with that in which I depend on the existence of the object." Indeed, absolute music might seem to be the art, par excellence, where nothing *but* a pure judgment of taste is even possible.

Let me hasten to add, straightaway, that it is a gross caricature of Kant to suggest, as I seem to be doing, that he thought proper appreciation of *any* of the arts, even absolute music, was a case of pure, disinterested perception. Kant fully acknowledged the "content" of the fine arts other than absolute music; and the (to me) murky doctrine of the "aesthetic ideas" was meant to accommodate that content to the Kantian pure judgment of taste. Furthermore, even in the limiting case of content, absolute music, Kant recognized an emotive dimension (as did his entire century) and tried to connect it with the selfsame doctrine of aesthetic ideas, with not particularly happy results.[2]

Consider, therefore, not the letter of Kantian aesthetics, which I make no claim to be elucidating here, but its spirit: the culmination of a century in which—and I mean this not at all pejoratively—the arts were steadily moving from the arena of social interaction to the pedestal of public (or private) *contemplation*, a contemplation increasingly construed by philosophers and critics in some kind of technical, "aesthetic" way, frequently emphasizing formal properties. And consider now music, in particular absolute music, in this historically developing context.

It is, I daresay, no accident that the aesthetic revolution—the revolution that, among other things, brought music from the arena of social inter-

[2] On this see Kivy, "Kant and the *Affektenlehre*: What He Said and What I Wish He Had Said," in *The Fine Art of Repetition*.

The Authority of Practice

action to the pedestal of public contemplation—was coeval with the revolution that brought the art of pure instrumental music from the status of a secondary concern to the position of equality, even dominance, in Viennese classical style. For absolute music, as we begin to know it in late Haydn and Mozart and early Beethoven, is the very epitome of Kantian free beauty, as Kant himself makes clear.[3] It is made for contemplation and contemplation alone; and its increasing complexity not only makes greater and greater demands on our contemplative powers but, in that very process, draws our attention inexorably to the act of contemplation itself, making its crucial role in what has now come to be called the "aesthetic experience" unmistakably clear. In a sense, then, the triumph of absolute music in the late eighteenth century is the *artistic* culmination of the aesthetic revolution. And because the aesthetic revolution is supposed to be a revolution in our attitude toward all of the arts, Walter Pater's oft-quoted remark becomes true that *all the arts aspire to the condition of music.*

But it is just this attitude of rapt contemplation, "aesthetic disinterestedness," toward music that requires for its setting something other than the assortment of social arenas where music, both texted and instrumental, had traditionally been displayed. For in these arenas, whether the church or the palace, the private estate, or the public square, music was not the only attraction or (usually) the center of attraction. It was part of a social choreography, a "mixed-media event," in a complex mise en scène. It was the advent of the concert hall and the public concert that plucked music from this three-ring circus and put it at the point of focus. Indeed, it is just the very structure and purpose of the concert hall to frame music and constrain the audience to concentrate there and nowhere else. The lights go out, silence descends, and there remains but one thing to do except sleep: *listen*, with, the musicians hope, concentrated attention to the only noises emanating from the only illuminated place in the audience's perceptual field.

Thus, the aesthetic revolution, the ascent to prominence of absolute music, and the advent of the public concert hall seem three completely integrated historical processes, the latter two unthinkable without each other and without the former, it the completely understandable precondition, if not sufficient condition, for them. But as we observed in Chapter 4, the fact that the concert hall and public concert were historically devel-

[3] *Critique of Judgement*, §16.

The Authority of Practice

oped as the altogether appropriate choreography and mise en scène for the "new" absolute music by no means precluded music written for the various social settings prior to the "great divide" from being made part of the modern concert repertory. And the questions before us now are whether it might not be a good idea to remove these pre–concert hall works from the concert hall and restore them to their original settings (insofar as that is possible); conversely, whether there is a convincing reason for leaving them where they are and, indeed, furthering the process of transference through the discovery, restoration, and adaptation of even more "early" music to the modern concert repertory. These are the questions with which we shall, from now on, be mainly concerned.

· · ·

Let us consider, to start with, an argument coming from the camp of the "historical purist" *against* the barbarous and insensitive vandalism (as she sees it) of appropriating "objects" made for particular social uses before the aesthetic revolution had given us such notions as "disinterested perception," or, indeed, the concept of the "aesthetic" itself. "These things were not made for 'aesthetic' contemplation, or any 'contemplation' at all," we can hear this particular kind of purist saying, "any more than a totem pole was, or a magical mask, or a Greek pot. They were made to be used; and listening to them with rapt attention for their so-called aesthetic qualities is an exercise in self-deception. You are reading into them, anachronistically, what could not possibly be there."

In response to the "historical purist" one feels compelled to point out that we just *do* find, even in artifacts from the remotest past, features of structure and form, color, representation, abstraction, and willful distortion remarkably like those that, in artworks of the modern era, we call "aesthetic" and gain "aesthetic satisfaction" from; and it would, surely, be more than an acceptable coincidence or accident to find such "aesthetic-like" qualities present without there having been some intention or other that they be there and that they be admired or contemplated in just the ways we feel compelled to do.[4] In saying this, there is no need for us to attribute, anachronistically, a modern conceptual apparatus, replete with a post-Kantian notion of aesthetic contemplation, to a Renais-

[4] I am greatly influenced in my argument here by conversations I have had with my colleague Jerry Fodor, and by his essay "*Déjà vu* All Over Again: How Danto's Aesthetics Recapitulates the Philosophy of Mind," in Rollins, *Danto and His Critics*.

The Authority of Practice

sance composer or a pre-Columbian sculptor. Nevertheless, their "objects" speak to us across centuries in ways that it is hard not to describe as "aesthetic." And it is merely arguing to the best explanation to suggest that the intentions behind these objects, however different they were from those of a modern sensibility in numerous respects, must have been intentions to view aspects of these works in ways rewarding of what *we* call aesthetic contemplation, and what they must have been at least dimly aware of as well, under *something* like that description. In lieu of such an assumption, the world becomes subject to a degree of "aesthetic luck" repugnant to reason and suggestive of monkeys typing the works of Shakespeare in an unacceptably short period of time.

Perhaps this is overkill. It is not, after all, very outlandish to maintain that at least as far back as our polyphonic repertory goes, as far back even as the *Magnus liber*, among the many different compositional intents present we can justifiably recognize one that clearly is "aesthetic" in spirit. Whatever other intentions of social use composers prior to the aesthetic revolution and the great divide may have had for their works, surely one of their intentions has always been to have aspects of these works—structure, sensuous surface, expression—admired, contemplated, enjoyed for their own musical sake as "fine," "beautiful," "sumptuous," "impressive" qualities. Whether the word was in place or not, the concept of aesthetic appreciation certainly was, at least in some recognizable form. It had, after all, to come from somewhere; it could not have sprung, fully armed, from the heads of the eighteenth-century philosophers and critics.[5]

I think we can conclude with confidence, then, that a historical argument, based on the absence of a full-blown concept of the aesthetic prior to the great divide, fails to show, a priori, that music predating the advent of the concert hall and composed specifically for "social use" lacks the "aesthetic features" necessary for public display as an object of "aesthetic contemplation." But it behooves us nevertheless, I think, to go beyond this negative conclusion to a positive account of what happens when a work is transferred from an earlier social context to the public concert and its setting. We should have at least a little musical chapter and verse. What's in it for us?

·   ·   ·

[5]On the origins of aesthetics and the aesthetic, see Summers, *The Judgment of Sense*.

The   Authority   of   Practice

Example 4. Johannes Brahms, Concerto in D for Violin, Op. 77 (Adagio)

Two very simple examples will, I think, convey an idea, initially, of what the positive justification is for putting music of "earlier times"—the music of "social practice," as it were—into the place of aesthetic contemplation—the sonic museum. My first example, from the very core of the nineteenth-century concert repertoire, will serve to introduce the point I wish to make.

In the slow movement of his Violin Concerto, Op. 77, Brahms has written one of the most exquisite oboe solos in the orchestral literature. In the midst of this stunningly beautiful passage, however, the composer seems to recall that there is also a *second* oboe and gives that humble personage, in mm. 14–15, a lick that should bring tears to the eyes of anyone who hears it. Of course not everyone *is* going to hear it. It is one of those wonderful details that great composers lavish on their work with perhaps the ideal listener in mind. But it is just that kind of concentrated scrutiny that the sonic museum facilitates, and that such works as Op. 77 were meant to elicit and sustain, that makes these structural details perceivable and, therefore, musically meaningful.

But such details have been lavished upon the music of the Western classical tradition since long before the aesthetic revolution, the sonic museum, and the advent of the modern aesthetic sensibility. I shall not go far back for my examples, though; rather, I return to the series of woodwind divertimentos that I mentioned in Chapter 4, written by Mozart in the Salzburg years, 1775–77 (K. 213, K. 240, K. 252, K. 253, K. 270, K. 289). Public concerts and something like the modern concert hall were already a going concern, then, in the major capitals of Europe. However, the great divide had not yet been decisively traversed; and the modern way of making music in the sonic museum continued to exist alongside the older social practices and places, soon to be but a memory, and then a history.

The Authority of Practice

We do not know for what specific occasions these woodwind sextets of Mozart's were created. But we can readily surmise. They were not "chamber music" for the drawing room, as were the string serenades, but, writes Alfred Einstein, "truly 'open air music' . . . that lack marches for the entrance and exit of the players; for they were written, not for chamber-music performers, whom one invites into the salon and then dismisses with respect, but for pipers who have to remain outside, beneath the window." He adds: "They are true garden music; . . . and it is from afar that they sound most beautiful."[6]

Imagine, now, the murmur of conversation, the clink of glasses, and the music of a Mozart wind sextet wafted through an open window on a summer evening in Salzburg, and you have a pretty good idea, one supposes, of the choreography and mise en scène of this kind of music. Meant, as Einstein suggests, to be heard from "afar," "the sonata-like movements are as simple as possible, . . ." and "the voices usually proceed in pairs, in thirds or sixths. . . ."[7]

But yet, to one who has ever performed these works, or looked closely at the scores, Einstein's description does not *quite* ring true: true perhaps of the many Bohemian composers of woodwind music from whom Mozart learned, no doubt, how to write idiomatically for these instruments; not, however, true for Mozart, even in Salzburg, even with the Köchel numbers in the 200s still. The second oboe parts, for example, are far from merely moving in thirds and sixths with the first. On the contrary, the oboes exhibit, in numerous places, the most exquisite part writing, in true counterpoint with one another. I could cover pages with examples. Two will have to suffice.

Now, the point is that these touches are every bit as subtle as the one quoted earlier from the Brahms violin concerto, and every bit as difficult to hear—indeed, quite impossible to hear in their social setting, wafted through an open window from a garden below, during a *conversazione*. (They would have been lost on the wind.) Why did Mozart put these passages there in the first place? To please himself, no doubt; and to please the musicians, who were the only ones likely to be able to hear them in performance. Indeed, for all the effect these strokes of contrapuntal ge-

[6] Einstein, *Mozart*, pp. 201–2.
[7] Ibid., p. 202.

The Authority of Practice

Example 5. W. A. Mozart, Divertimento in F, K. 253 (first movement);
Divertimento in B♭, K. 270 (second movement)

nius in the second oboe would have had on a Salzburg audience, through
an open window, they might just as well have been listening to Myslive-
czek or Triebensee or Wenth, who really did write in parallel thirds and
sixths and really do sound more beautiful from far away.

But transferred from their original choreography and setting to the
sonic museum, these sextets will be able to yield up their contrapuntal
treasures to the rapt aesthetic attention that the modern musical scene
and practice are expressly intended to foster. And that, of course, is justi-

The Authority of Practice

243

fication for taking them from their original surroundings to this new and seemingly alien one. For it is in the new place that these aesthetic refinements can best be heard, and scarcely so in their old, albeit elegant, social setting.

. . .

Another example, this time from the vast literature of liturgical music, may help to strengthen the argument. It is one of the richest legacies of historical musicology that it has made available to the modern concert repertory the entire corpus of Bach's surviving church cantatas and, indeed, made it as much a part of our musical life as such standard choral works as Handel's *Messiah*, Mendelssohn's *Elijah*, or the Brahms Requiem. But unlike the last-named works, all of which were written with the public concert in view, the Bach cantatas were of course intended as part of the Lutheran service; and the larger ones, in two parts, were indeed not heard as self-contained entities but were, rather, interrupted between the parts by the sermon, to which the music essentially belonged, as part of the Sunday's "lesson." For whatever concertlike qualities the performance of a Bach cantata in situ may have had, it was seen by Bach's employers and, one can assume, by Bach himself as, horribile dictu, a musical "sermon." As Bach's contemporary Johann Mattheson expressed the vocation of the "complete Kapellmeister," in his influential book of the same name, it was "to present the virtues and vices in his music well, and to arouse skillfully in the feelings of the listener a love for the former and disgust for the latter. For it is in the true nature of music that it is above all a teacher of propriety."[8]

It would seem, then, a far greater dislocation to transfer a cantata by Bach from its liturgical setting to the modern concert hall than to transfer a wind divertimento by Mozart from garden to stage. For, after all, whatever the conditions under which Mozart's works of this kind were (or were not) attended to, they were meant for nothing more than musical enjoyment, when they *were* attended to; and musical enjoyment (if that is not too pallid a term for what, after all, its enthusiasts consider an exalted experience, at its best) is what the public concert and concert hall came into being to provide to a paying public. But it is hard to imagine that Bach's sacred cantatas, when removed from the religious service and transferred to the sonic museum, could adequately fulfill *their* primary in-

[8] Mattheson, *Der vollkommene Capellmeister*, p. 105 (Part 1, chap. 3, §54).

The Authority of Practice

tended function, if it is indeed, as Mattheson avers and their setting strongly argues, to teach a moral and religious lesson. For without the sermon and the rest of the homiletic support system of the church, the sacred cantata alone, in a concert setting, is but a weak conveyer of moral or religious precepts, written, rather, in poetic and musical parable as an illustration of the lesson rather than the vehicle itself.

Needless to say, anyone with an ounce of musicality is going to be put off at the thought of treating Bach's church cantatas, one of the pinnacles of Western musical culture, as not *even* sermons and moral lessons but, indeed, merely adjuncts to them. To the modern aesthetic sensibility, moralizing and sermonizing are just about as damning charges as could possibly be brought against a work of art. The fact nevertheless remains that that is just what Bach was employed to do every Sunday, as a composer, by the church fathers of Leipzig. And ultimately we do have to come to terms with that fact in appreciating these remarkable works—perhaps all the *more* remarkable when one understands the intellectually enervating purpose they were created to fulfill. (The texts, indeed, display forth this baleful, mind-deadening influence in all their sometimes dreary, sometimes garish rhetoric.)

I fully believe—the evidence seems conclusive on this point—that Bach did really see himself as doing in the church cantatas pretty much what Mattheson said the complete church musician ought to do: teach religious and moral rectitude. But that this overarching intention, so repugnant to our aesthetic sensibilities and incompatible with the purposes of the sonic museum, motivated the composition of these works in no way precludes the presence of other intentions and other qualities, compatible with and indeed superlatively well (if not ideally) suited to the public concert and its setting. If a Greek vase, created two centuries before the aesthetic revolution, should nevertheless still repay the kind of contemplation that revolution enfranchised, it should come as no surprise that the cantatas of Bach, created on the verge, do so as well. "Concert qualities" the cantatas possess in abundance (particularly those influenced by operatic music). And that these qualities were intended for just the purposes of aesthetic contemplation the sonic museum opens them to cannot be doubted, if the argument to the best explanation carries any weight.

It would, I daresay, be a waste of time to point out in detail to a musical

The Authority of Practice

245

readership all the eminently musical qualities that Bach's church cantatas possess in such depth, richness, and abundance: the harmonic, contrapuntal, formal, expressive, and representational features that reward aesthetic contemplation as fully as any in the repertory of Western art music. Indeed, even though the church was the center of musical life in Bach's Leipzig and these features intended to be heard therein, anyone who has made music or listened to it in churches knows full well that, by and large, these spaces are ill suited to close musical listening, compared to a good hall; so we are forced to admit, I think, that whatever may be lost in transferring Bach's vocal music from church to sonic museum, the "concert" features of this music will come off better in the latter place, even though the church is also a setting that tends to encourage and facilitate musical listening. (We all recall Pope's couplet: ". . . as some to Church repair, / Not for the doctrine but the music there."[9])

But as pointless as it would be to argue the obvious, preach to the converted that Bach's church cantatas possess an abundance of musical qualities that pay off far more handsomely in the concert hall than in the Lutheran service, there may be some point in calling the reader's attention to one major structural feature of just those cantatas that seem most fully integrated into the liturgical choreography—the large, two-part ones in which the sermon is heard between the parts.

What distinguishes the two-part cantatas from the others is, of course, that they are not experienced as autonomous musical entities. They are to be viewed either as, so to speak, mixed-media events, the middle part being the spoken sermon, *or* as simply two separate musical works, one performed before and one after the sermon. How, one wonders, did Bach think of them?

I rather strongly suspect that Bach must have wanted the two-part cantatas, at least the majority of them, to be heard as unified works. They are, to begin with, constructed with an unusually strong sense of unity of key, not common in the baroque. Half the approximately twenty extant two-part cantatas begin and end in the same key or its tonic major; six end in the relative major or minor. (Of the remaining, four end in the dominant, one in the subdominant, and one in the relative major of the minor dominant.) In the case of those works (half of them all) that return to a close

[9] *An Essay on Criticism.*

The Authority of Practice

246

in the tonic key, there is no reason to think Bach did not intend this return as a unifying feature—a musical resolution that the "ideal" listener was expected to hear and respond to; and the same may be said for the one cantata (BWV 75) that ends in the relative major. Needless to say, even the "ideal" listener is going to be hard put to it to *hear*, after ten or eleven numbers, interrupted by a sermon, the "return" to the relative minor that occurs in five of the works under discussion. It would take the "perfect" listener to hear *that*.[10] Nonetheless, this "intellectual" return to the home key signature, if I may so put it, whether heard or not, gives unmistakable evidence of Bach's intention that these works be perceived not as two cantatas with a sermon in between but as one unified whole.

This intention of Bach's that these cantatas be heard as integral wholes, not fragmented parts, is even more apparent where he reuses a movement from the first part as a conclusion to the second, which he does on five occasions, in other words, in one-quarter of the extant works. In BWV 20 the simply harmonized chorale that concludes part 1 also concludes part 2; in BWV 75, BWV 76, BWV 147, and BWV 186, the same accompanied chorale concludes both parts; and in BWV 30 the chorus that opens the work also concludes it.

I think it a near certainty that the comparatively large number of two-part cantatas in which a movement is reprised as conclusion to the work indicates an attempt by Bach to bridge the musical gap made by the sermon, and to knit the two halves together by something stronger than mere tonality, which is to say, *thematic* binding as well. And in this regard it is interesting to note that in three of the five cantatas where the finale is a reprise of a movement in the first part, the key relationship of finale to opening movement fails to be the tonic, and the finales are all repetitions of the movement that ends the first part. So it appears that at least some of the time Bach is substituting thematic unity for key unity, as structural glue.

Without pushing this analysis any further, I think we can conclude with confidence that Bach made special efforts to bind together the parts

[10] There is, indeed, some interesting experimental evidence to show that even musically trained listeners do not hear the return of the original key and fail to hear it even in short pieces. On this see Cook, *Music, Imagination, and Culture,* pp. 43–59. This, of course, says nothing about the importance to composers of key structure in the composing of tonal music, which is indisputable.

The   Authority   of   Practice

of cantatas that were separated by the sermon (or in some cases the communion). It seems clear that he must have seen these liturgical interruptions as a threat to the musical continuity—hence the aesthetic integrity—of these large-scale works and bent every effort, within his stylistic parameters, to make sure this continuity and integrity were maintained and felt by the listener. I am not for a moment suggesting that Bach resented or did not take seriously his spiritual role, as Mattheson described it, of teaching in his music love of virtue and hatred of vice. But to the extent that this didactic role was at cross-purposes with his musical and aesthetic sensibility, as it must have been where the cantatas were performed not as self-contained "concerts" but as musical "frames" for the sermon, Bach, as we have seen, took special care to counteract the damage to musical unity that the didactic, unmusical break in the musical fabric was bound to make.

Bach's attempt at aesthetic damage control could not, I think it is clear, entirely succeed; the interruption of the musical fabric of the two-part cantatas by the sermon or other liturgical business could not fail to fragment drastically the musical continuity and integrity, in spite of unity of key or even the thematic unity that a musical reprise could accomplish. But the palpable presence of these unifying features surely indicates, in no uncertain terms, an intention on Bach's part for these works to be heard as autonomous, unified musical works, in spite of the ceremonial interruption. And in the sonic museum and public concert, unlike the church service, that unity can be fully perceived and appreciated. We are, therefore, fulfilling one of Bach's deepest, and necessarily frustrated, musical intentions for these works in experiencing them under the conditions that render aesthetic contemplation of them feasible. That is, in part, our justification for taking them from the place of worship, for which they were designed, to the place of musical display, for which they are, by nature, so well suited.

.   .   .

I have, up to this point, been putting forward by way of example the justification for transferring musical works from their original, prerevolution settings to the public concert and concert hall. It is now time to ask what the justification might be for restoring them to their original social settings—what, in other words, the justification might be for achieving, with regard to them, a historically authentic performance practice.

The Authority of Practice

248

In order to give this question an adequate answer within the framework of the present inquiry, we must remain perfectly clear about what *kind* of a justification we are looking for. It is, broadly speaking, an *aesthetic* one. This needs some spelling out.

It will be recalled that musical performance, before the great divide, took place in a variety of social settings, in which it served, naturally, a variety of social functions. Now, where the function of a musical work in its particular social setting was other than merely the function of being listening to for something like "aesthetic" enjoyment—and surely we must assume that "aesthetic" contemplation and enjoyment together were always one intended function of music—that special function would obviously be sacrificed in the sonic museum, as would the corresponding audience interaction with the music. If the function in the *Redoutensaal* of a set of minuets by Mozart, to take an obvious example, was to be danced to as well as to be listened to, then the former function, in the sonic museum, is completely short-circuited in favor of the latter one, and intentionally so. Indeed, the whole point of taking these dances out of the ballroom and into the concert room just is to obliterate all functions but that of aesthetic contemplation, so that whatever aesthetic qualities the works may have can be appreciated to the fullest. You can't fully appreciate the aesthetic qualities of Mozart's or Beethoven's minuets while dancing to them or fully appreciate the aesthetic qualities of Bach's church cantatas while engaging in the complex emotional and intellectual act of Christian worship.

I make this obvious point to avoid answering a justification for restoration of musical works to their original, pre–concert hall settings, based on the argument that only there can they fulfill their original, and richly rewarding *social* functions. I have no intention, in this chapter or in this book, of defending the aesthetic contemplation of music or the institution of the public concert and concert hall. There are, I know, those with moral, aesthetic, and even political agendas somehow involving the devaluation of the whole concert institution as we know it and the so-called "aesthetic attitude" that goes along with it. There may be something to these various agendas, and there may not. That is the subject for an inquiry other than this one. I operate under the assumption that the aesthetic contemplation and enjoyment of music is an intrinsic good, among others, and in no need of defense. Music written after the great divide and for the sonic museum was written if not *only* for that purpose then at least always *importantly* for that purpose. And the sole question I am asking is whether there is justification of an *aesthetic* kind for performing music written before the great divide and not, therefore, for the sonic museum, in its original setting—whether, that is to say, as objects of aesthetic contemplation and sources of aesthetic satisfaction, works written prior to the great divide fare better in their original settings or in the setting and choreography of the public concert.

Here it may well be objected that I have really begged the question right from the start in confining myself merely to the *aesthetic* justification of returning preconcert music to its original social settings. For framing the question in terms of the concept of the "aesthetic" assures us, ipso facto, that there can be no such justification. After all, the sonic museum is part of the very "aesthetic revolution" that enfranchised the so-called aesthetic attitude as the favored state of aesthetic contemplation and enfranchised the formal properties associated, since Kant, with that attitude as the proper objects of that contemplative state. So, *of course* it is bound to turn out that the best place and the best routine for facilitating that selfsame aesthetic attitude of contemplation and the appreciation of those selfsame qualities are the concert hall and public concert, which were conceptually bound up with the attitude and qualities: designed to show them up. *Of course* the glove fits the hand better than the foot.

But that objection would place undue historical and philosophical significance on my use of phrases like "*aesthetic* appreciation," "*aesthetic* features," "*aesthetic* attitude," and the like. For, to begin with, I am no formalist in the philosophy of art; I recognize *expressive* qualities even in absolute music, which card-carrying musical formalists do not, and I recognize *representational* qualities, in a full-blooded sense of "representational," wherever they seem to occur in texted or program music, which in the Bach church cantatas, for example, is quite frequently (and, on my view, quite significantly). So I construe "aesthetic quality" more broadly, certainly, than the objection suggests; and I mean no more by "aesthetic qualities" than what might better be denominated simply "*artistic* qualities," which is to say, just those qualities one thinks appropriately enjoyed in a work of art *qua* work of art.

Furthermore, I place no special significance—psychological, philo-

The Authority of Practice

sophical, or any other—on the notion of aesthetic or artistic "contemplation," least of all that it is "disinterested," in any of the various ways *that* much belabored concept has been construed by philosophers since Kant. I think we all pretty much know what it is like to look intently at a painting, listen closely to a symphony, become engrossed in reading a novel—each for the purpose of deriving therefrom aesthetic or artistic enjoyment. And I shall say no more about it than that.[11]

•   •   •

If I have not, it may be replied to all of this, begged the question in favor of a formalist aesthetics and a technical notion of "aesthetic contemplation," I have indeed begged a far deeper question in talking exclusively, even though not in any special philosophical sense, of aesthetic "contemplation." For who is to say, the question may well be put, that *contemplation* is the only true source of aesthetic or artistic satisfaction? The great divide, after all, separates music written exclusively for the sonic museum, where *pure aesthetic contemplation* is the *sole* intended activity, from music written for a variety of social settings, where aesthetic contemplation is just one intended activity among others. And why should we believe that the only *aesthetic* or *artistic* satisfaction (properly so called) that we obtain from these pre–concert hall works, *in their original settings*, is by way of *contemplation*? What of the other activities going on in these pre–concert hall arenas? Are they to be ruled out as sources of aesthetic or artistic satisfaction merely because they are not "contemplation"? That surely would beg the question in favor of a mind-set that we have as a result of the aesthetic revolution and immediately, unfairly force a negative answer straightaway to the question of whether restoring pre–concert hall music to its original settings and practices might sweeten its *aesthetic* payoff.

But *are* there real examples of activities vis-à-vis the music, other than contemplation, that can plausibly be seen as yielding *aesthetic* satisfaction—and, furthermore, satisfaction that can rightly be described as having its source *in* the music and not just "accidently" occasioned by it? Here are two examples that I think might fill the bill.

A fairly obvious case is that of genuine dance music—that is to say, mu-

[11]For the basic (implicit) argument behind my remarks here see Dickie, "The Myth of the Aesthetic Attitude."

The Authority of Practice

sic written for the avowed purpose of being danced to in a social setting.[12] It seems beyond question that persons dancing to such music are deriving from the activity multiple satisfactions, not all of them "aesthetic." But it also seems beyond question that they are experiencing an aesthetic satisfaction both from attending to the music and from dancing to it. And, furthermore, it seems to me altogether appropriate to say that the aesthetic satisfaction they are experiencing in dancing to that music is derived from the music not by contemplation but by the activity of dancing. Here is, then, I think, a straightforward case of an activity that is not contemplation, has music for its "object," and yields up artistic satisfaction, properly *musical*, fostered in the dance hall, foiled in the concert hall; it is one *aesthetic* justification for returning such music to its original social setting and practice.

Another example, even less problematical (if indeed one finds the first problematical at all) is the case of what Paul Hindemith called *Gebrauchmusik*—music written not so much to be listened to as to be *played*; that is to say, music for "amateurs" to enjoy by performing it for themselves, not music to be performed by professionals for an audience to contemplate and enjoy.

Now much of the instrumental music that there was before the great divide was written for people to play in their own houses (or palaces) and for their own pleasure as performers: *Gebrauchmusik* in Hindemith's sense. This of course is not to say that such music was not meant to be listened to also, to be contemplated by such audience as it would find in a social gathering as well as by the performers themselves. There would, clearly, be no point to the playing, even if the music were written *only* to be played, if it did not reward listening into the bargain; for to reward *playing* it would have, at least, to reward the listening of the players; failing that, the playing could hardly make sense as an aesthetic activity.

But it would certainly be a mistake to think that, from the players' point of view, such music as was written for domestic or aristocratic music making can simply be reduced to a means-end thing, in which the playing is a

[12] *Not*, that is to say, "stylized" dances, as in Bach's suites, or the minuet and trio of the classical symphony, which *were* designed for audition only, or ballet and other "theatrical" dance music that was intended, indeed, for dancing, but dancing, of course, as part of a "mixed-media" artwork, to be merely contemplated aesthetically although not merely heard.

The Authority of Practice

means to the performers, while playing, for gaining aesthetic satisfaction from the simultaneous *contemplation* of their collective product. Anyone who plays chamber music knows that that is not the way things are. The aesthetic or artistic satisfaction is a complex, interactive one, stemming from *both* contemplation of the product *and* the activity of producing it. Thus here again one is forced to concede an aesthetic satisfaction gained from music, properly belonging to the music itself, that is not a satisfaction of aesthetic *contemplation* but of aesthetic *activity*, in this case, *playing*.

Here, then, I think, are two straightforward cases of aesthetic satisfaction derived from music not through pure contemplation but through other activities—dancing or playing—in which contemplating, that is, listening, plays an essential role to be sure but is not the sole source of the satisfaction. These are enough (although there may well be more) to show, beyond question, that offering a justification for the return of music to its pre–concert hall settings and practice, in terms of aesthetic *contemplation* alone, does not exhaust the *aesthetic* possibilities, and the failure to justify, on those grounds alone, does not imply failure to justify altogether.

Nevertheless, I do intend to confine my considerations here to pure aesthetic contemplation of music, to the exclusion of any other activities, like dancing or playing, that might fairly be construed as deriving aesthetic satisfaction from the music. In doing so I am not begging the question in favor of contemplation against those or other activities; for I am openly acknowledging that such other activities exist and exert bona fide aesthetic claims. I am simply limiting the universe of discourse to the *contemplation* of music; and there is, so far as I know, nothing logically naughty in that.

But I do think the reader is entitled to some justification for so limiting the discussion to contemplation and nothing beyond. Why, it might well be asked, should such a discussion, which concentrates on this single activity to the exclusion of all other interactions with music, be worth one's while to consider? It is a reasonable question, to which, I think, I can give a brief, yet reasonable answer.

•   •   •

It is a historical fact, as I have emphasized on a number of occasions, that during the eighteenth century, Western art music transmigrated from a variety of social settings to the venue of the concert hall. In the process

The Authority of Practice

this music, and the music to follow in the concert hall tradition, became exclusively a music to be listened to and to be aesthetically enjoyed in the contemplation. It became, indeed, the very paradigm of "listening" music: music to be seriously, deeply, and concentratedly contemplated. The concert and concert hall were, at the same time, both the effects and the partial causes of the "cult of listening," if I may so call it, a special case of the "cult of aesthetic contemplation" and, arguably, the paradigm case.

At present, listening to classical music in the concert hall and in recorded form is a major recreational activity of a significant number of people who share my and my readers' cultural heritage; and, indeed, so serious an enterprise is it for many of these that something deeper than "recreation" would be required to satisfy them as a proper description of what they are doing. For most of these people, the *only* aesthetic satisfaction they derive from classical music is through listening: in particular, few of them are musical performers, partly, I suppose, because the phonograph has put classical music in the home and thus made it unnecessary to do so by performing it oneself, it obviously being easier to play a recording than to play a piano or flute.

Like many others, I deplore the decline of amateur music making, both because it is intrinsically satisfying to a very high degree and because it enhances the satisfaction of listening.[13] Be that as it may, listening to classical music in the concert hall, or in the home on recordings, stands in no need of any defense whatever. It is an intrinsic human good—a source of the deepest satisfaction to those who pursue the activity.

The aesthetic contemplation of music, through listening, is a major artistic institution in our culture: the sole way in which most musical enthusiasts relate to the object of their enthusiasm. And that in itself is my justification for wishing to concentrate solely here on the aesthetic contemplation of music to the exclusion of all other ways of interacting with it. It is just *that* important in our lives. Whether it *should* be, to the exclusion of all other ways, I will not attempt to determine.

Our question, then, is this. For music written before the great divide, and for social settings other than the sonic museum, would the aesthetic payoff of *contemplation* be greater if that music were performed in its original settings and choreographies, or in the sonic museum and public concert? If *listening* is the only form that the aesthetic contemplation takes,

[13] On this see Kivy, "Music and the Liberal Education," in *The Fine Art of Repetition.*

The Authority of Practice

the answer is clear. The concert hall and public concert were designed specifically to facilitate listening; the preconcert arenas were not. The concert hall wins hands down. Therefore, the only way this question can hold any interest for us and escape triviality is if we include in our understanding of *musical* contemplation sense modalities other than that of hearing. With that in mind, we can get on with the business at hand.

What should, I think, be obvious from the start is that the only significant contribution to be made to our aesthetic appreciation of pre–concert hall music, if performed in its original settings rather than in the sonic museum, must be *visual*: its visual mise en scène and choreography. I suppose a braver ecumenist of the senses than I might claim for the smell of incense during the performance of a Palestrina mass in the Catholic service, or for the taste of champagne at a social gathering in Salzburg with a Mozart wind sextet for accompaniment, the status of aesthetic quality: part of the "musical fabric." Whoever wants to make out such a difficult case is welcome to try. I shall not, but would be glad to welcome a positive result as entirely consistent with my view.

How, then, are we to characterize "visually enhanced" music, in its pre–concert hall settings, as an object of aesthetic contemplation? Perhaps what best captures my thought on the matter is something like: an audiovisual spectacle. I say "spectacle" because those musical settings that naturally seem to hold out promise of aesthetic satisfaction beyond the aural, in substantial quantity, are just those meant to be the places for the magnificent, glittering ceremonies of earlier times in which other arts and other aesthetic paraphernalia played so prominent a role, along with the ceremonial music: in short, the "big events," what amounted to multimedia aesthetic "productions," in which music performed a significant function.

It should not, however, be surmised from this that it is merely the magnificent setting and ceremony that do the business. Just playing music in a visually attractive context does not, on the view I am trying to develop here, enhance the aesthetic qualities of *the music*. That is not what I am talking about. It no more increases my aesthetic satisfaction in a Haydn symphony to hear the work in the beautiful surroundings of Esterházy castle rather than in some dreary (but acoustically equivalent) concert space than it would increase my aesthetic satisfaction in *Pride and Preju-*

dice to read it in Buckingham Palace rather than in a Holiday Inn. All that I can say, in either instance, is that my surroundings are more pleasant.

What is needed, to make our aesthetic satisfaction in the visual surroundings, setting, and choreography an aesthetic satisfaction *in the music* is that the music, setting, and choreography be, to use a nice, old-fashioned word, "organically" related: an integrated whole. Or, expressed in a slightly different way, there must be an aesthetic *interpretation* of the music that works into it the setting and choreography, an interpretation that makes them one "aesthetic," one "musical" work.

Examples are not far to seek; and the most obvious as well as the most plausible ones come from the literature of liturgical music. The reason, of course, that the liturgy is such a rich fund is that, to begin with, the service itself—and I am speaking particularly here of the kind of luxuriant one to be found prior to the "puritanical" inroads of the Counter-Reformation, and, later, German Pietism—is such an artfully crafted procedure, so resplendent in costumes, "props," and visual symbols, as to constitute an "aesthetic object" in its own right. And it is performed in a setting—the cathedral or church—that also, clearly, is an artwork, or collection of artworks, of the most impressive kind. But it is also a setting and choreography in which music is not merely an extraneous "accompaniment" but a "written-to-order" part. Thus there is every reason to think of the liturgical service, in this "luxuriant" period, as a multimedia event, a *Gesamtkunstwerk*, in which visual setting, costume, property, choreography, and music are all integrated into one aesthetic object, which can be "framed" by the spectator and appreciated as such.

With this example in hand, although we could have looked at others as well, such as state ceremonies, we can now put our question more specifically. Where is the aesthetic payoff of musical contemplation going to be higher—in the luxuriant Christian service or in the public concert? But here, as before, the answer cannot be a general one. Which musical work? It obviously is going to make a difference. The question can only be answered on a case-by-case basis. It might be instructive, however, in conclusion, to see how the answer would come out on one side or the other in practice and not just in principle. I adduce two works to illustrate.

Take, first, a mass by Johannes Ockeghem, at the apex of fifteenth-century Flemish polyphony, in the luxuriant setting and choreography

The Authority of Practice

256

for which it was written. Compare this spectacle, this glittering audiovisual "work of art" with a concert performance of the mass in the comparatively austere, even drab setting of the sonic museum. Which has the richer aesthetic payoff?

It seems only natural to answer immediately that the performance of the Ockeghem mass in its original setting and choreography is just obviously, nolo contendere, a richer aesthetic experience of the music than what one could possibly derive from a stripped-down concert performance in the sonic museum. The latter would be to the former as a concert version of an opera to a staged production. But we must be careful here. The obvious answer is not, I would urge, the correct one.

Let us remind ourselves, first, that we are talking here about the aesthetic payoff of a *musical* work, even though I have described the mass, in its liturgical setting and choreography, as an audiovisual, multimedia event. One does not in fact have to look at the liturgical event as a basically musical one. It could, for example, be viewed by a more visually oriented spectator as basically a dance pantomime, with the music a more subsidiary element, like ballet music, or the musical sound track of a film. But *we* are music lovers; and *we* are "framing" this multimedia event as basically a musical one, like an opera, perhaps, with the Ockeghem music as the centerpiece of our attention. And Ockeghem's music is some of the most complex, rich, and dense polyphony ever written: a musical structure rivaling in intellectual challenge Bach's most complex fugues, or Beethoven's late quartets. That being the case, we can now see directly why the richest aesthetic payoff of the Ockeghem mass, *from the music lover's point of view*, is to be had not in its original setting and choreography but in the sonic museum. The reason is simply that the sonic museum optimizes just those "viewing" conditions that make this kind of musical complexity perceivable to the fullest extent, whereas the opulent setting and choreography of the liturgical "pantomime" present a distraction to concentrated aural contemplation that must either be overcome or partially defeat pure musical perception.

Indeed, it is just this "dilemma of concentration" that the Counter-Reformation and the Council of Trent wished to resolve in favor of religion as against music, by simplifying musical practice in the interest of the text. For the musically inclined, music like Ockeghem's, with all its intriguing structural and "sensual" complexity, was a temptation too great

The Authority of Practice

257

to resist; and so attention was torn from matters spiritual to matters musical. But in any event, attention, in the liturgical setting, was strained to such a degree as to defeat optimal *musical listening*. And optimal listening conditions were just what the sonic museum was designed to provide.

But, of course, if the aural object is not of the complexity of an Ockeghem mass or (later) a Bach cantata, the story can be entirely different. Thus, to retrieve an example adduced previously in Chapter 4, the sacred music of Michael Haydn, in its original setting and choreography, is, I should think, enhanced rather than compromised, as over a concert performance in the sonic museum. For all their musically attractive qualities, these works are cosmetic: all surface. It is a wonderful, glittering surface; but it will not greatly reward *close* musical scrutiny in the sonic museum. In fact, unlike an Ockeghem mass in *its* liturgical setting and choreography, all that there is to a Gradual or Vespers of Michael Haydn can be taken in while attending as well to the rest of the ceremonial goings on. The visual aesthetic only enhances the whole; it does not detract in the least from the aural part. The original setting and choreography (or similar ones) are, therefore, the ideal vehicles for the aesthetic appreciation of these works. And although they will survive transferral to the public concert and concert hall, they *thrive*, rather, where they were originally meant to be: in the opulent Austrian Catholic service of the late eighteenth century.

.   .   .

A plausible conclusion from all this might appear then, to be that in general, works of sonic simplicity fare better in their original, pre–concert hall setting and choreography, sonically complex ones being more comfortable in the sonic museum. That is an acceptable approximation. But it is not entirely true.

Complicated music is not necessarily great or even very good music; and uncomplicated music can be good or even great. And whether or not a piece of music demands and rewards close scrutiny, entices perception, is a matter not merely of its complexity but of its goodness or greatness (in the spectator's eyes). Thus with regard to complexity there is nothing to choose, between Michael Haydn's music and the music of Gluck. But Gluck is generally rated with the masters and is firmly within the canon, whereas Michael Haydn is generally rated a *Kleinmeister* and is on the peripheries of the canon at best. So for all its transparent simplicity, Gluck's

De Profundis, for instance, is going to demand and reward just the kind of aesthetic contemplation that the concert hall is meant to facilitate and will have just the same problems, being part of the liturgical pantomime, as an Ockeghem mass, competing for the spectator's full attention with its compelling musical attractions, while the setting and choreography beckon it away. The place for the *De Profundis*, then, musically uncomplicated though it is, is in the sonic museum.[14]

Thus it would appear to be a complex function of musical complexity and just plain musical "goodness" that is going to be the major factor in determining whether a musical work composed before the great divide is to fare better transferred to the sonic museum or performed and choreographed in its original setting. Beyond that conclusion I do not think philosophy can take us. The rest is for the musicians, theoreticians, and musicologists to work out in actual practice. And that, perhaps, is where it will be best to leave the argument.

---

[14] Alfred Einstein, on apparently no evidence (at least none is adduced), assumes that the *De Profundis* was in fact written not for the liturgy at all but for concert performance. He describes it as "a piece of so-called church music" and goes on to say that "one must suppose that he composed it for the Concert Spirituel in Paris." My own suspicion is that he perceives, as I do, that the work would come off much better in concert than in church. But that is true of so much sacred music that *was* indeed written for the church that it hardly constitutes a believable argument for Gluck's intention to have the work performed in concert. See Einstein, *Gluck*, p. 184.

The Authority of Practice

⊙

The Other Authority

The authority of personal authenticity might seem to be so obvious as to require neither explanation nor defense. For, as I argued in Chapter 5, performing is a species of composing, and performances therefore works of art; and I argued, further, that personal authenticity is to be cashed out in style and originality. But if, as it does indeed seem, style and originality are agreed on all hands to be always highly desirable qualities for works of art to have, then there can hardly be much point in "defending" them to anyone. So to expatiate on the authority of personal authenticity in musical performance is, apparently, as pointless as praising profit to a capitalist.

I believe that the authority of personal authenticity in musical performance as I have just stated it is, indeed, all there is to say. If *you* believe that performing is a kind of composing and performances versions of the work in the sense that arrangements are, as I do, then you *must* believe, too, as I do, that personal authenticity in performance is an indefeasible desideratum. And there is nothing further for me to say to you in its justification.

But there *is* a normative question here. The problem is to formulate it.

For it cannot be the question of whether personal authenticity in musical performance is or is not a good thing, and why. *That* question answers itself: "yes," and "self-evidently."

To put the normative question of personal authenticity in tractable form I shall begin with what amounts to a truism of such triviality that it will hardly seem to the reader worth stating or of any use whatever in the circumstances. To the contrary, I hope to show that it is of the essence and that its recognition makes the normative question transparent although not necessarily easy to answer. The truism is this: what we call "classical" music has always been, as far back as we have listenable examples and until certain recent developments in the twentieth century, *a performing art.*

The logical and ontological characteristics of music, as I see it, if it is to be construed as a performing art, are as follows.

1. There has to be some viable distinction between the performance (object) and what it is a performance of: that is to say, there must be a performance and some at least vaguely autonomous, identifiable entity that "survives" performances and endures through time— what has, since the modern era, been called the "work."

2. The performance (object) is a work of art itself, an arrangement or version of the musical work that has been performed, and, as such, a subject of the kind of evaluation and aesthetic satisfaction that artworks support and provide.

3. The performer is an artist, somewhat akin to a composer or, better, "arranger" of musical works.

Now the distinction between performance and work, item 1 in the list, is a much-disputed one, for both ontological and (more recently) historical reasons. And although I insist that it must be in place if music is properly to be thought of, as it has been, as a performing art, I want to keep that distinction informal enough so that I will not run afoul of either metaphysical or historical scruples.

With regard to ontology, let me just say that although I have defended, in the past, a Platonistic account of the work/performance distinction, in which works are conceived of as universals and performances as instantiations of them, I make no such Platonistic commitment here.[1] Most people, Platonist or not, allow a logical distinction of some kind between work and performance; and that is all that I insist upon. The historical question may be a bit more troublesome (but not, I think, unmanageable). Lydia Goehr has argued at length that the concept of the ironbound, ontologically firm musical work is of fairly recent coinage, not completely in place until as late as the nineteenth century.[2] And it might appear as if I am saying that a concept of *the work* is necessary for the work/performance distinction to be in place. If that is the case, however, then it seems to follow that Western art music cannot have been a performing art, in my sense, until the nineteenth century. That is an intolerable conclusion.

But there is no need, I think, to impose upon pre-nineteenth-century music a strict concept of *the work* that is completely anachronistic. There is no doubt that we can establish *the text* of Brahms's First Symphony, for example, in a way that we cannot of even such relatively recent works as a Handel opera, let alone music from the earliest periods of musical notation. Handel was a working "theater man" and his operas in a continual state of flux. What *the* work is, as determined by establishing *the* text, might be an impossible question to answer not just in practice but in logic as well. And where a notation does not indicate determinate pitch or rhythm, the notion of work and text becomes even more obviously problematic and inappropriate, drawing our attention, as Leo Treitler puts it, to "the narrow historicality of the work concept and its satellites," to wit, "closure, unity and not least autonomy. . . ."[3]

Nevertheless, we can, I think, settle for a weak notion of text and work that possesses enough of the logic of these concepts to allow a performance/work distinction for at least as much of the music of the Western tradition as will ever be accessible to us as listeners. For we obviously cannot realize in sound any music that has not been notated at all. And where there is a notation *determinate enough* for *us* to derive therefrom a

[1] For my previously expressed views on this regard, see Kivy, "Platonism in Music: A Kind of Defense," "Platonism in Music: Another Kind of Defense," and "Orchestrating Platonism," all in *The Fine Art of Repetition*.
[2] Goehr, *The Imaginary Museum of Musical Works*.
[3] Treitler, "The 'Unwritten' and 'Written Transmission' of Medieval Chant and the Start-Up of Musical Notation," pp. 132–33.

The Other Authority

believable, viable sound experience, there is, in virtue of that, both a performance and a "what" that has been performed.

There is another way, perhaps, of making this clear. The Western musical tradition has, as far back as our performable music goes, placed a high value on "improvisation" as a musical attainment of the composer-performer. As opposed to a tradition in which there is no notation and *all* performance is "improvisation," the Western musical tradition *requires* for improvisation the standard case of performance from notation as a foil. The value of and satisfaction in musical improvisation, in the Western musical tradition, is derived in large measure from the knowledge that what is being done is being done neither from notation nor from memory of a notated, previously existing work but spontaneously. That is why the crowning glory of the improvisational art, for a long time, was the improvisation of fugue and other "strict" contrapuntal forms. For it is just those intellectually demanding forms that require the most premeditation, the most revising and reworking: they are the least spontaneous. And so to be able to produce them on the spot, on demand, spontaneously is the feat of improvisation most to be wondered at.

The point I am making is that *improvisation*, which flourished in the Western art music tradition most resplendently well *before* the development of the ironbound "work" concept in the nineteenth century, was a species of improvisation that required for its enjoyment the concept of a preplanned, preformed, and enduring kind of music as the standard against which it could be measured. (That Bach or Mozart could improvise a fugue as complicated as one that would *ordinarily* require weeks of laborious "working out" was what made the feat almost magical.) And although that concept may fall far short of the ontologically firm "opus," it possesses enough of the work / performance logic to sustain my argument.

It is not, indeed, the work / performance distinction, however, that is uppermost in my mind here. Of far more importance to the argument are items 2 and 3 in the list: the performance as artwork and the performer as artist. I shall turn to those now.

. . .

I want to begin with R. G. Collingwood's brief discussion of musical performance in *The Principles of Art*. To us, at the floodtide of the historical performance movement, Collingwood's remarks have, perhaps, a quaint, prelapsarian naïveté about them.[4] But we can learn a good deal from them for present purposes, just because they are as yet "untainted" by current concerns with "authenticity"; and, furthermore, they have embedded in them, at least as I see it, an important truth, philosophically sophisticated, in a Collingwoodian way, and yet at the same time musically "commonsensical":

Collingwood writes:

> Authors and performers have found themselves driven into a state
> of mutual suspicion and hostility. Performers have been told that
> they must not claim the status of collaborators, and must accept the
> sacred text just as they find it; authors have tried to guard against
> any danger of collaboration from performers by making their book
> or their text fool-proof. The result has been not to stop performers
> from collaborating (that is impossible), but to breed up a generation
> of performers who are not qualified to collaborate boldly and
> competently. . . . Authors who try to produce a fool-proof text are
> choosing fools as their collaborators.[5]

There are reasons of philosophical doctrine, unnecessary to go into here, why Collingwood believed that, as he put it, "Every performer is co-author of the work he performs"[6]—the composer's "collaborator." For Collingwood, the composer has not completed the artwork after having written down the notes: "He recognizes that what he is putting on paper is not a . . . symphony, or even complete directions for performing one, but only a rough outline of such directions, where the performers, with the help, no doubt, of . . . [the] conductor, are not only permitted but required to fill in the details."[7]

It might be useful, at the present juncture, to contrast Collingwood's view, on this regard, with mine. According to Collingwood, the composer and performer collaborate to create the musical work of art that, technically speaking, in the language of Collingwood's "expression theory of

---

[4] Whether Collingwood was aware of it or not, musicians in his own country had already put the so-called early music movement in gear in his own time. For a well-told history of the historical performance movement, see Haskell, *The Early Music Revival*.
[5] Collingwood, *The Principles of Art*, p. 321.
[6] Ibid.
[7] Ibid., pp. 320–21.

The Other Authority

art," does not preexist the performance of it. The performer and composer, therefore, are "collaborators" on the work. On my view, however, the composer is sole author of the work and the performer an "arranger," who produces a "version" of the work. Unlike Collingwood, I hold that the work does indeed preexist its performance, just as Beethoven's Septet, Op. 20, must precede his later version of it for piano trio, Op. 38.

But Collingwood and I, in our disagreement, do indeed agree on two crucial points: that performances are works of art and that performers are artists. Because, on Collingwood's view, the performer is a collaborator with the composer in creating, in the performance (object), what we call *the* work of art, it of course follows that the performance is a work of art. And as the performer is the composer's collaborator in creating the work of art, he or she is an artist. (*Both* Beaumont *and* Fletcher were playwrights!) But on my view too the performance is an artwork, namely, an "arrangement" of the musical composition, and the performer therefore an artist, namely, someone akin to an arranger. So even though Collingwood and I differ on a number of points regarding what kind of artwork a performance is and what kind of artist the performer, we do agree on these two essential points: that the performance *is* indeed an artwork and that the performer is its "composer."

.   .   .

I began with the truism that music as we have known it since the invention of musical notation has been a *performing* art. What the performer "performs" is given him or her in a "text." And where it is acknowledged, as Collingwood did and as many others besides myself have done, that the performance is an artwork and the performer an artist, it is usually thought that the "artistry" of the performer is exerted in some sort of "gap" between the "text" and its execution. That is to say, when the text "fails" to determine execution, the performer is "free" to do it this way, or that way, or the other way. Freedom makes creativity; creativity makes art. Collingwood puts the point in the traditional manner:

> But the book of a play or the score of a symphony, however cumbered with stage-directions, expression-marks, metronome figures, and so forth, cannot possibly indicate in every detail how the work is to be performed. Tell the performer that he must

The Other Authority

265

perform the thing exactly as it is written, and he knows you are talking nonsense. He knows that however much he tries to obey you, there are still countless points he must decide for himself.[8]

Igor Stravinsky, who was well known for his wish to "control" performance strictly, makes a point strikingly similar to Collingwood's but, characteristically, cannot bring himself to refer to the performer as exercising "art" in the space between score and performance, only "talent."

> But no matter how scrupulously a piece of music may be notated, no matter how carefully it may be insured against every possible ambiguity through the indications of *tempo*, shading, phrasing, accentuation, and so on, it always contains hidden elements that defy definition because verbal dialectic is powerless to define musical dialectic in its totality. The realization of these elements is thus a matter of experience and intuition, in a word, of the talent of the person who is called upon to present the music.[9]

What is as interesting as the striking similarity between these statements of Collingwood's and Stravinsky's in letter is their glaring dissimilarity in spirit. For the impression we get from what Collingwood says about the gap between notation and execution is that it is altogether desirable and intended. The composer both knows of the gap and "reckons on it";[10] and one cannot help feeling that the strength of "reckons on it" is positive, particularly as the alternative on offer is represented as a text being "cumbered" with performance directions, which is to say, the alternative is the opposite of creativity, namely, clumsiness and pedantry. The composer wants this gap because he wants the performer to be his "collaborator," to be an artist in his own right. (As Collingwood has said earlier, the performer is "not only permitted but *required* to fill in the details.") Whereas Stravinsky leaves us with quite the opposite impression—that the gap between score and performance, composer and performer, is far from desirable but, on the contrary, a necessary evil. And although it is never quite stated outright, it can be read between the lines in such remarks as "The sin against the spirit of the work always begins with a sin against its letter. . . ."[11]

[8] Ibid., p. 320.
[9] Stravinsky, *Poetics of Music in the Form of Six Lessons*, pp. 127–28.
[10] Collingwood, *The Principles of Art*, p. 320.
[11] Stravinsky, *Poetics of Music in the Form of Six Lessons*, p. 129.

The Other Authority

Furthermore, the attitude toward the gap between score and execution that Stravinsky is expressing is amply demonstrated not only by what composers have *said* since the late nineteenth century but by what they have *done*; which is to say, it is demonstrated by the attempt to fashion a score that, as Collingwood puts it, is "fool-proof"—that *fixes* more and more precisely what would have been in former times the variables under the performer's judgment, discretion and "artistry." The performer was in the process of becoming "the composer's machine," as someone put it some years ago, or, as Collingwood was essentially putting it in a passage quoted earlier, "the composer's fool." The ultimate step in this movement toward the composer's absolute power over sound production is where "the composer's machine" quite *literally* becomes the composer's *machine*—when, that is, the "performance" becomes the playing of a tape or other electronic event, the "work," depending upon your ontology, the electronic signal, in whatever form it is encoded, or the "performances" themselves, which, of course, are no longer performances as I understand that concept. I shall return to this crucial point in a moment. But before I do I want to discuss the composer's "text" briefly.

.   .   .

In the musical tradition with which we are concerned, the performer requires a "text" from which to perform. The concern of the performer with the accuracy of his or her text has, of course, increased exponentially in recent years, because of the very movement toward "historically authentic performance" with which this book is concerned. And what is meant by the term "accuracy" itself has undergone considerable change. But presumably in any period in our tradition, as far back as we have notation that can be realized in a believable performance, and not just a purely conjectural one, we have a right to assume as a matter of aesthetic "logic" and "ontology" that the performer used a written notation that established *what* it was that he or she was performing, and that this notation prescribed some things, proscribed other things, and left many things to the artistic discretion of the player. To evade many, or too many of the prescriptions and proscriptions would be to abrogate one's role as performer *of* the piece—to, in other words, not give a performance. To make poor choices among the "variables" left to the performer would be to give a poor performance. All this seems obvious enough.

Since the great musical publication projects of the nineteenth cen-

The Other Authority

tury—Chrysander's Handel edition, the *Bachgesellschaft*, and others—we have become used to the notion that the performer is served, in his or her task as transmitter of the composer's creations to the public, by a middle-man, the "editor" of musical "texts," more and more frequently these days in the person of the academically trained historical musicologist: an "expert" in these matters. But whether or not we think of "establishing the text" in this modern, institutional form, we can, as a matter of simple logic, distinguish at any time between the establishing of the text, and its performance.

It is, I suppose, natural to think of "establishing the text" as a rather "physical" sort of thing, like restoring a building or piecing together the skeleton of a dinosaur. The "text" is, after all, physical markings on paper; and the question before the editor is whether some particular mark is this shape or that, as where a recent practitioner of the art has established that the English horn part in m. 208 of Rossini's *William Tell* Overture[12] reads

rather than the familiar

But of course the "black marks" are not, on anyone's account, alone "the text." For they must be interpreted under a set of conventions for so doing; and, as historical musicology has made increasingly clear, these conventions of musical practice are in flux. Thus, to take the most ob-vious of examples, the grace note

---

[12] See Percival R. Kirby's edition of the overture, pp. iv, vi, 30, and frontispiece.

The Other Authority

would be being played as written if it were played thus

and if it were played thus

if the former occurrence were in a sonata by Handel and the latter in one by Haydn. So merely establishing that there was a black mark, ♪, in a score does not wholly establish "the text" in that regard. We want to know how that black mark "sounds." And just how serious that question can be becomes quite apparent if our "black marks" are, say, from the Middle Ages. For if it is a "performing text" we want—and that really is what we are talking about here—the editor's task, having established the "black marks," has only just begun. For what the performer needs is not the black marks shown in Example 6 but, rather, those in Example 7.[13]

But to return to more mundane examples, let us observe that, even in the extraordinarily trivial case of the grace notes, something rather crucial has taken place. The knowledge that the dissonant appoggiatura, in the baroque period, was played "slow," as much as half the value of the principal note, has now become so widely disseminated, the practice so widely accepted, that all performers, whether "mainstream" or "authentic," play them that way. It was not always thus. What used to be at the performer's discretion now has become de rigueur. Or, in other words, *something that used to be in the gap between text and performance has now become part of the text.*

Let me adduce one further example to establish this point. If a musicologist were to find that an A♭ in a composition by Bach had really been intended as an A♮, we would say, as in the case of the *William Tell* Overture cited previously, that he was, to use the terms of literary scholars, in the business of "establishing the text." If, on the other hand, a violinist were

[13] From Apel, *The Notation of Polyphonic Music, 900–1600*, p. 235.

The Other Authority

Example 6. *Wolfenbüttel* Manuscript (*W₁*, p. 22, third brace)

Example 7. *W₁*, p. 22, third brace (transcribed by Willi Apel)

to play a Bach partita for unaccompanied violin with a good romantic dollop of vibrato, most people prior to the historical performance movement would have said that she was performing the work in a certain style, different from, say, the style of a less romantic performer who was more sparing with vibrato. Both these folks, we would say, were in the business of "performing the text."

Suppose, now, that the historically authentic performance movement establishes that vibrato is not *echt* here—that Bach's performance practice did not include it; that Bach did not intend it. We might say that, from the point of view of the historical performance movement, vibratoless sound has now become part of Bach's "text." And from that point of view, in using vibrato a violinist would be just as much departing from the text, "playing the wrong notes," as if she played A♭ instead of A♮. What used to be thought of as a variable parameter of performance has become a fixed parameter of *the* text.

My point can be generalized. If the establishing of historically authentic performance were carried to its ultimate (and presumably desired) con-

The Other Authority

clusion, performance would collapse into text, and what we used to call "performances" would now have the logical status of prints (if you like) rather than true performances. Such a "performance" of a Bach partita would have the personal authenticity of Bach but not of a performer. All differences in performance, as all differences in prints, would be either aesthetically irrelevant or aesthetic defects.

I make no value judgments (so far). But I can, I think, now frame the normative question with more clarity than heretofore. The question of personal authenticity in performance versus historically authentic performance, when they are incompatible, is the question of whether or not, in any given instance, you want a parameter to remain a variable one of performance or become an inalterable one of text and, in general, whether you want the art music of the Western historical tradition to remain a *performing* art or to cease to be one.

But I have rushed on to this somewhat startling conclusion rather quickly. We had best step back, take a breath, and consider this matter with more circumspection.

·   ·   ·

I have argued that in establishing certain performance practices as "historically authentic"—for example, playing the dissonant appoggiatura as half the value of the adjoining note, or playing violins without vibrato—and adopting them as, therefore, required rather than optional, one is for all intents and purposes extending the concept of the musical "text" to include those things. Furthermore, I am arguing that if one were to carry this aesthetic of performance to its ultimate conclusion, performance would essentially collapse into "text"; in other words, the gap between performance and "text," in which the "art" of performance is to take place in the form of personal authenticity, is closed, and the concept of performance, at least as we know it, vanishes. Let me dilate on this.

It should be perfectly clear that in practice the gap between "text" and performance can never be completely closed. For no matter how much historical knowledge we gain of "period" sound or the performing wishes and intentions of composers, our knowledge will never be complete (which is simply a special case of the general precept that no knowledge will ever be complete). Thus the performer who adopts as his or her goal the "historically authentic performance," in either the sense of authentic-

The Other Authority

ity of sound or that of authenticity of intention, or both, will always have "space" in which to make performing decisions that are "free," not determined by the "text."

But what I argued in Chapter 5, and want now to reemphasize, is that there is a deep matter of principle here, apart from the facts of actual practice, important for us to recognize and consider. The "logic" of music as a performing art, if I may so call it, is a logic in which the gap between "text" and performance is not merely a necessary evil but at the same time a *desired, intended* and logically *required* ontological fact. It is in that gap that the work of art is produced that we call the "performance," and that I have likened to an "arrangement" of the work. It is in that gap that personal authenticity can either be or not be.

The quest for the historically authentic performance is a quest for closure—for absolute control of sound production, whether or not that can, in practice, ever be achieved. And the "gap" between "text" and production—I purposely refrain from calling it "performance"—under this discipline is of an entirely different "logical" or "ontological" nature from that of the gap between "text" and "performance" properly so called. It is a gap to be closed, not to be cherished: it is a "defect" in the sound-production "machinery."

Imagine a print maker who has a press with mechanical troubles. Each time it makes an impression, it produces a print with a perceivable difference from its other impressions. The prints are all different from one another in some grossly perceivable respect. But the print maker does not value these differences. On the contrary, she bends every effort to make her press produce a uniform impression. Her "art" lies elsewhere. It is just such a "gap" between her plate and her prints that exists between "text" and sound production in the historically authentic performance. Only the gap is caused not by mechanical malfunction but by incompleteness of knowledge: "knowledge malfunction," if you will. The "logic" of the gap is identical. The historically authentic performer and his musicological support team have as their goal the amplification of knowledge of authorial intentions or period sound or both to the end of determining, more and more fully, the production of musical sound as a matter of "textual authority," not artistic choice. As the print maker seeks to exorcise the gremlins from her machine, so the historical performer et alii seek to exorcise the gremlins from theirs; but their machine is far more complex,

The Other Authority

and its infections more evasive, their complete elimination of course for all practical purposes impossible. But the "logic" is the same: the historically authentic performance is to its "text" as print to plate, *not* as performance to work, in the traditional sense of the performing arts.

I have, of course, painted in very broad strokes: overstated the case for purposes of quick and graphic exposition. In particular, I have avoided so far the complication that arises when the composer's wishes or intentions *include* the exercise of personal authenticity. In that case, the quest for historical authenticity becomes very confusing to make out and perplexingly self-defeating, in the sense that the quest for personal authenticity seems at cross-purposes with so much of what is laid upon the historically authentic performer and yet, if mandated by the composer, itself constitutes historical authenticity in one of its recognizable forms. The point can be brought out with particular vividness in the question of the cadenza of the classical concerto. This warrants a brief detour.

. . .

Collingwood uses the example of the cadenzas in Mozart's concertos to underscore the performer's role as the composer's "collaborator": "When Mozart leaves it to his soloist to improvise the cadenza of a concerto, he is in effect insisting that the soloist shall be more than a mere executant; he is to be something of a composer, and therefore trained to collaborate intelligently."[14]

Mozart, as is well known, also wrote out his own cadenzas to a number of the piano concertos, for the benefit, one presumes, of players who were not talented enough to compose their own.[15] But for those who were gifted performers, in the way Collingwood characterizes them, there seems little doubt that Mozart's intentions for *them* was that they should compose or improvise their own. And although I do not suggest that Mozart put it to himself in so many words, I presume that his intentions included the one to be personally authentic, if you could. (Such a concept was not foreign to his times or to his aesthetic.)

What is the "historically authentic" way of playing a Mozart cadenza? The most obvious answer—and the one, I should say, usually sanctioned by the "historical performance movement"—is to play Mozart's written-out cadenza, if there is one, or one patterned after it and in the style of

[14] Collingwood, *The Principles of Art*, p. 321.
[15] For some examples see Girdlestone, *Mozart and His Piano Concertos*, pp. 500–504.

The Other Authority

Mozart's own cadenzas, if there is not, in other words, an "archeological reconstruction." In either case the cadenza, which originally was left as a gap in the text, is now meant to become *a part of the text*. Clearly, what will be achieved, following such a regimen, is sonic authenticity—but only an authenticity of intention *excluding* the intention, if it is there, that the performer express herself, that she improvise or otherwise compose *her own* cadenza and achieve thereby personal authenticity.

It is now easy to see, in the specific case of the classical cadenza, how the admonition to be "historically authentic" turns self-destructively on itself. The cadenza is the most obvious instance, in the modern concert repertory, where the composer has mandated a completely empty space in which the performer is free to "do her own thing"; it is an *intended* gap in the "text." And intentional authenticity would lie in the performer, if she can, doing her own thing, not slavishly imitating the composer's style. For *that* is not what the composer intended.

Indeed, if a twentieth-century performer is to produce her own cadenza to a classical concerto, it should be, if she is to achieve the personal authenticity the composer intended, in her own personal, *twentieth-century style*. We have an example of something like what I have in mind here in a set of cadenzas to all three movements of Mozart's Oboe Concerto in C, K. 314, by the contemporary American composer George Rochberg. The cadenzas are in the style of Rochberg, not in the style of Mozart, although clearly they are meant to be "evocative" of Mozart's style. I quote in Example 8 from the opening of the first-movement cadenza to give an idea of how un-Mozartian the harmonic structure of this distinctive though "conservative" twentieth-century style of Rochberg's is.[16]

Of course a cadenza might be a bad cadenza for many reasons, including *inappropriateness of style*. Cadenzas for the Mozart Oboe Concerto in, say, the atonal style of late Schoenberg, Berg, and Webern would, no matter how well composed, perhaps be too far from the Mozart idiom to be anything but musical gargoyles: protuberant monstrosities. And one thing a genuine Mozart cadenza, or Mozart imitation, would certainly

[16] Rochberg, *Three Cadenzas for Mozart's Concerto for Oboe, K. 314, for Solo Oboe*, p. 3. Besides everything else, the sheer length of these cadenzas is well beyond anything the eighteenth-century wind player would have been expected to produce.

Example 8. George Rochberg, Three Cadenzas for
Mozart's Oboe Concerto, K. 314

not lack is congruity of style. That, however, is not enough to make it a
good cadenza, although it would be a step in the right direction.

Be that as it may, what I want strongly to urge is that there are other
ways to make a cadenza "appropriate" to Mozart's (or anyone else's) style
besides making it in *the same style* or an "imitation" thereof. What Rochberg, for instance, has clearly tried to do—and done successfully, I
think—is, as I have suggested, to "evoke" Mozart in his cadenzas, in his
own Rochbergian style. In so doing he has made his cadenzas "original,"
"creative," "his own," and all those other good things that Mozart intended the cadenzas to be but that neither archeological reconstruction of
a Mozartian cadenza *nor* even playing Mozart's own cadenza can achieve.

Now, suppose I were a talented enough player on the oboe to be able to
improvise, in my own, personally authentic, twentieth-century style,
cadenzas for the Mozart Oboe Concerto like Rochberg's. Would doing so
be "historically authentic"? One's *first* reaction—and that the *only* reaction, generally, of the historically authentic performance movement—is
that it would surely be utterly bizarre to think a cadenza to an eighteenth-
century concerto in twentieth-century style could possibly be "historically authentic": it is, indeed, a stylistic anachronism if ever there was
one. But, after all, the place of the cadenza is not an accidental gap in the
text: it is an *intended* gap: and that intention includes, indeed mandates,
personal authenticity in the activity of filling it. Thus the classical cadenza
is a kind of showcase for the point in performance practice where per-

The Other Authority

sonal authenticity and historical authenticity, in the form of authenticity of intention, converge and come into direct conflict with that other major contender for historical authenticity, authenticity of sound.

Because, I suggest, the closing of the gap between text and sound production is such a dominant motivating force in the historical performance movement, the cadenza gap, so *obviously* an *intended* gap, paradoxically falls prey to the very same movement that stridently proclaims the authority of the composer's *intentions*. Why should the "freedom" of the cadenza, even to the point of a cadenza in a twentieth-century idiom for a concerto by Mozart, be rejected as historically *inauthentic*, given that it can be persuasively argued that, in a nonpedantic and generous construal of "intention," it is well within the ambit of the composer's wishes or intentions? Why should intentional authenticity be passed over here in favor of sonic authenticity, or an intention assumed to result from it? The answer, I think, must be as I have said: that the driving force behind the historical performance movement is the desire to collapse performance into text. The rejection of the personally authentic cadenza in favor of the sonically authentic one is only a special case. The point is a general one.

.   .   .

What we have learned from this brief discussion of the classical cadenza, I think, is that in general when intentional authenticity seems to mandate a gap between text and sound production, in which personal authenticity may, it is to be hoped, be achieved and in which sound authenticity, on the contrary, mandates that that gap be closed, by essentially making the "text" flow into the gap, in the form of "historical performance practice," the historical performance movement standardly opts for the latter. On theoretical grounds, the movement could perfectly well claim that it was being "historically authentic" in *maintaining* the gap between text and sound production for personal authenticity of the most diverse stylistic kinds, since so doing would be pursuing the spirit of the composer's intentions, which is to encourage, within the limits of stylistic coherence and good taste, performance as an art in its own right. But in practice it does not do so. It does not do so because it is basically a project in musical "archeology." And as such it sees the project of sound production as an attempt to reconstruct, as it were, an "object" of the past: the past *product* of a past event, the physical sound of a past performance. Thus although we are correct in seeing the quest for historical authenticity as, *theoretically,*

The Other Authority

complicated by the fact that it is in part a quest for the composer's intentions and those intentions may include the intention that the performer achieve, if possible, personal authenticity, *in practice* the movement is fairly uniform and uncomplicated in that respect, pursuing doggedly the reconstruction of historical sound and such intentions of the composer, narrowly conceived, that are to that same end.

The historically authentic performance movement, then, the way we have come to know it in practice, is pretty much as "overstated" earlier in this chapter: a project aimed at collapsing performance into text, in essence transforming the music of our past, as we have known it, from a "performance art," in the true sense of that concept, to an art in which sound production is completely determined by "notation," in an extended sense of that concept.

In that case we now have a very clear way of framing the normative question of personal authenticity. It is simply the question of whether or not it would be a good thing to so transform our historical musical tradition, in spirit if not, *per impossibile*, in letter, from one in which the performance is an artwork in its own right to one in which it is not, but is to the work as the print to the woodcut. And I say our *historical* musical tradition because, in certain particular instances—tape music, electronic music of various kinds—twentieth-century composers have indeed achieved the goal of dispensing with the performer altogether and made "performance" *performance* no longer but merely sound production pure (but perhaps not simple). Is that the goal we want to achieve for the music of the past? Do we want the *performance* to disappear as a work of art, a bearer of personal authenticity in its own right? Is all to be submerged into composer and work? It is the consideration of that question with which we shall conclude this chapter—and this book.

. . .

Now, it is bound to seem at first that I have stated my question so prejudicially as to be merely rhetorical. What other answer can there be to it except "Perish the thought that musical performance as an art form should cease to be practiced in our presentation of the music of the past. Who but a vandal, or a musical Savonarola would wish to accomplish such a bonfire of the musical vanities?"

I would like to emphasize as strongly as I can that, although I *do* think it an aesthetically undesirable goal to collapse performance into text and

The Other Authority

essentially phase out performance as an independent artwork, I do *not* by any means think that it is an *absurd* or *obviously* undesirable goal. Behind it is a very deep, understandable, and believable aesthetic ideology that is not just a pushover.

The ideology I have in mind might well be described as "composer worship," and it has its roots, it is obvious enough, in the nineteenth-century cult of genius. The status of the composer has risen steadily since the beginning of the eighteenth century, from artisan to artist; and the enshrinement of music by Schopenhauer and others as the romantic art above all the rest has tended to surround the composer with an aura of infallibility, symbolized in the nineteenth century by the stormy visage of "Beethoven the Creator," whose authority one questions at peril. I shall return to this point momentarily; but first let us get a general idea of what the defense of traditional performance is going to look like.

It seems clear enough that as the music of our historical past has traditionally been performed—if, that is, my analysis is right—we are in possession, always, of *two* artworks: the work of music, and, given an outstanding or high-quality performance, the performance (product) itself. Under the new dispensation, the goal, anyway, if never the fait accompli, is to have but *one* artwork, the sound production having been submerged into the text. So simple arithmetic says that the historically authentic performance has aesthetically shortchanged us by one-half. We used to have two works of art when we heard the "Goldberg" Variations, and now we have only one.

This *is*, I have no doubt, the correct way to defend personal authenticity in performance; but it is far too simplistic as it stands. For simple addition of artworks will yield the obviously absurd result that I would be aesthetically wise to trade Rembrandt's *Polish Rider* for two Utrillo watercolors. It is this vulnerability of the two-works defense that the historical performance advocate would undoubtedly exploit; and it is here that the ideology of the composer's hegemony would make its influence felt.

If it is to be shown that the program of historical performance, which, I have argued, in effect eliminates performance as a separate artwork in its own right, is justified in this elimination, then its advocate must convince us that the artwork left in its place, the "text" that completely determines sound production, is a far greater aesthetic object than the two artworks together, the musical work and the performance work, of traditional

The Other Authority

practice. He must convince us that the collapsing of performance into text will produce the *Polish Rider*, and traditional practice two Utrillos—that, in spirit, is the claim.

This claim has its basis, I suggest, in the ideology of the composer's infallibility or, perhaps, the "cult" of the composer as "superhuman," a "supermusician." In any event, not only the writing of the composer's performing intentions into the "text" but the writing of historically authentic period sound into the "text" as well is, both directly in the former case and indirectly in the latter, an attempt to put *all* parameters of sound production under the composer's discipline (under the assumption that historically authentic period sound is what the composer literally "had in mind"). There can be only *one* artist, or the work is spoiled. Here even *two* is a crowd.

What answer might the defender of music as a performing art bring against this powerful and proliferating ideology? It would be relevant, to begin with, to point out that the charge of being overly simplistic goes both ways. It is not merely that simple "work addition" is implausible, that two paintings are not necessarily a greater aesthetic quantity than one. It is not the case, either, that there being *two different works* rather than one is irrelevant—not the case that "aesthetic value" is a negotiable, uniform, common denominator. To lose the *Polish Rider* is to lose something of immeasurably greater aesthetic value than any painting by Utrillo. But to lose a painting of Utrillo's is not merely to lose something of less artistic value than the *Polish Rider*: it is to lose something uniquely different from the *Polish Rider* in ways that we value for their own sake. It is to lose a style.

Thus, even if it were the case that the collapse of performance into text would produce a single work greater by far than either of the two works of traditional practice, the musical work and the performance work, and even if these two works were to the other work as Utrillos to the *Polish Rider*, we *still* would have to consider the loss of the performance work not merely as the loss of some basic "aesthetic quantity" but as the loss of a *kind* of aesthetic quantity that performance uniquely gives. Ecologists mourn the disappearance not merely of individuals but, with far greater intensity, of the disappearance of *species*. To lose performance to work, no matter what the measure of value of the single performanceless work might be compared with the work-performance combination of our his-

The Other Authority

279

torical tradition, is to lose a *species* of artwork, not merely a collection of individual artworks. It is to lose a whole greater than the sum of its parts.

This, by the way, is not to go to the opposite extreme and claim that the collapse of performance into text, through the archeological reconstruction of period performance, should itself be rejected outright in favor of personally authentic performance. To the contrary, what the preceding argument sanctions is the maintaining of *both*. For some of the same considerations that lead to resisting the loss of one *kind* of artwork, namely the musical performance, also lead to resisting the loss of another *kind*, namely the single artwork that is the result of collapsing performance into text in the form of the historically authentic performance. This is a new kind of artwork, essentially discovered, or created, if you prefer, by historical musicology in our own times. It has turned out to be of great interest to musical listeners. And although we want to prevent, if we can, its driving into extinction the other authenticity in the interest of species variety, we likewise want it to survive itself in the interest of that selfsame variety. Wouldn't the ecologist just love to have *both* mammals and dinosaurs?

There is, incidentally, another way of looking at the historical "performance" that also imparts to it independent aesthetic value while still denying it the status of artwork. For as Bach's performance (product) of an organ fugue was a performance work of art, so a successful "reconstruction" of it, in the form of a historically accurate "performance," is a "reproduction" of a performance work of art, as my color slide is a reproduction of the *Mona Lisa*. And, it is generally agreed, reproductions possess at least some of the aesthetic values, to at least some degree, of the originals, which is why it is better to have a color slide of the *Mona Lisa* than no *Mona Lisa* at all. So again, in the interest of aesthetic variety, historically authentic performance is to be valued along with personally authentic performance: not instead of the latter, or the latter instead of the former.

But, furthermore, there is yet another answer to the argument that the one work achieved by historically authentic performance trumps the two works of traditional performance practice, with its emphasis on personal authenticity—that it is one Rembrandt to two Utrillos. For as this argument is motivated, at least so I suppose, by the "cult of the composer," its inner workings must in the end be founded upon what I called, in Chapter 6, the axiom that *the composer knows best* (CKB) and the related axiom

The Other Authority

of *the delicate balance* (DB). That is to say, the reason, ultimately, for collapsing performing parameters into the text is to take them out of the hands of the performer and put them under the total control of the composer. But *why* should we want total control of sound production to be in the composer's hands? Because, one must assume, of DB and CKB: because, in other words, the composer has put the work into that delicate balance that any change, no matter how apparently helpful or apparently trivial, is bound to upset, the performing parameters being part of that delicate balance, the composer knowing best how his or her work is to be realized in sound production.

But we have seen, in Chapter 6, good reason to doubt *both* these axioms. Or, rather, we have seen no good reason to accept either of them. There just is no evidence of any such delicate balance that will somehow be upset by a performance strategy departing either from the composer's wishes and intentions or from the practice and sound of his period. And, indeed, unless one simply begs the question from the start, there is good, believable evidence for the opposite—the conclusion that sometimes we have a better way than the composer's or the composer's times for performing some particular work.

Thus, our defense of personal authenticity in performance is, as was apparent at the outset, to point out that the alternative deprives us of a work of art, namely, the performance work. And our reply to the claim that the *one work* that historically authentic performance leaves us will be greater than the sum of the two works we originally had is twofold. We deny there is evidence to demonstrate that the one work is greater than the two; and, even granted that it were, we deny the conclusion of that claim. For the whole here is greater than the aesthetic sum of its parts. So it does not follow that if the one work is greater than the aesthetic sum of the two, it is *necessarily* greater than the whole. Or, put another way, to eliminate performance is to eliminate not merely a collection of works but a whole *kind*; and the kind has aesthetic value, artistic value of its own, as a kind. To lose performance is to lose a wonderful, richly rewarding kind of aesthetic experience that cannot be replaced by another kind of aesthetic experience, no matter if its quantity may exceed the quantity of the other (assuming these "quantities" can be measured in such a hedonic calculus).

·   ·   ·

The Other Authority

The very fact that a defense of personal authenticity and the existence of performance as an artwork was felt to be needed is itself strange, and to be wondered at, it appears to me. What I think must have seemed obvious to people in our musical tradition other than ourselves—that musical performance is an activity in which originality and personal authenticity are to be exercised with enthusiasm, even abandon—has ceased to be obvious to us, as Collingwood was already beginning to see. We seem to have lost faith in the performer, become suspicious of him or her, as somehow a source of *corruption du texte*, a "middleman" who at best inadvertently garbles the "message" and at worst intentionally or recklessly frustrates it.

Were this suspicion to emanate only from the composer, as it does so stridently from Stravinsky, for example, we might be inclined to put it down, in the modern manner, to musical "politics." Composers, we might claim, are an "interest group," after all, defending their turf, no more to be taken as expressing some ideological *Zeitgeist* than the tobacco lobby or the National Rifle Association, who will gladly make the worse cause appear the better to favor their own private agendas. Bad faith is taken for granted, and into account. But the fact is that this is not a composers' cabal. It emanated originally, of course, from the historical musicologists and is now a widely disseminated feeling among audiences. The historically authentic performance is not merely a scholar's hobby; it is now something of a "grass roots" movement.

Aside from anything else, this is an interesting social phenomenon in the musical world, worthy of study by the appropriate disciplines. But it is, as well, something for every music lover to ponder on. Why have we come to suspect, even reject outright, the flamboyant "performer-artist" of the past?

Usually, when aestheticians come to the end of their rope and can find no more "aesthetic" reasons to adduce, they conclude that the question must be an ethical one. Ethical considerations override aesthetic ones. It is an appeal to "higher authority."

I rather suspect that there *are* ethical considerations deeply at work here. But if so, they are, I believe, totally misplaced. For they are, I further believe, just those kinds of consideration discussed earlier, in Chapter 6, that have their origin in the mistaken notion that the musical work is the

The Other Authority

bearer of a "message" from the composer that the performer is *duty-bound* to deliver intact or be guilty, essentially, of lying. The flamboyant performer, the performer who puts personality into his or her performance—in a word, the personally authentic performer—is derelict of that duty. Much better, then, to eliminate the messenger altogether, before the message is garbled, either guiltily or inadvertently, by its bearer. With the historically authentic performance you are dialing direct.

But, as I have argued before, this is a false model of the composer-performer relationship. The music is not a message, at least where absolute music is concerned; and the performer is not the composer's messenger, thus not to be judged by the peculiar ethics of that profession. The performer is, rather, to be judged by the *aesthetics* of another profession—that, as we have seen, of the musical arranger.

Now, there is no doubt that the project of "archeologically restoring" a past performance is a thing of intrinsic interest itself and, as we have seen, produces something with the "aesthetic properties" of an artistic reproduction. It exercises a fascination, and understandably so, on scholars and musicians; and the result has its own attractions, both historical and artistic. One *does* want to know what an eighteenth- or fifteenth-century performance sounded like, in the sense of sonic authenticity, just as one would like to know what Pompeii looked like before the eruption. And just as restored Pompeii has its particular aesthetic qualities, so too does a restored performance of the *Play of Daniel* or the Brandenburg Concertos. Nor have I meant to suggest anywhere here that interest in such "musical archeology" is something to be shunned or denigrated. The question is not so much why the historically authentic performance *should* exist. Its credentials are in good order. The real question has become, for many, why the personally authentic performance *shouldn't* exist. Its credentials have been called into question by the historically authentic performance movement, which seems to be not merely a movement *for* but a movement *against*—for itself, of course, but also evangelically *against* what is called in the trade "mainstream" practice, and all that implies, including, at least as I see it, personal authenticity.

If I am correct in my diagnosis, the "negative thesis" of the historically authentic performance movement has its deepest motivation in a kind of musical puritanism: the performer is the composer's messenger; and the messenger is being killed because he or she is the bearer not (as is usual) of bad news but of false or distorted news. This realization leads us to a crucial juncture.

The crux of the matter I take to be that my defense of personal authenticity, and the performance as work of art depends upon rejecting a certain very basic assumption in the philosophy of music and embracing an entirely different one—something that, on quite different grounds, I have urged elsewhere.[17] (It is always gratifying to discover that, against all odds, one is actually being consistent.)

The notion that the musical performer is, as Susanne Langer aptly put it, the composer's "confidant and his mouthpiece,"[18] the music a message to be delivered untampered with, stems from the almost universal tendency since at least the eighteenth century to try to understand absolute music on a linguistic model of one kind or another. It is this that lays on the performer the moral straitjacket of the witness under oath, who must report the truth, the whole truth, and nothing but the truth, on pain of perjury.

The flamboyant, energized musical performer, like many other performers and entertainers, has tended to be seen as a kind of conjurer, a kind of charlatan who puts things over on an enthralled but willing audience. This image used to have attractive, positive connotations. But now, I suggest, at least in musical circles, the "charlatanism" is seen in an evil light, for it is seen as the corruption of the truth. And the remedy is to take from the musical performer the freedom to stray from the composer's message by placing, insofar as is possible, all sound production under the composer's discipline and authority: in a word, the historically authentic performance. As the composer of the past has become, in our times, a kind of musical oracle, his messenger has increasingly become not, as Collingwood would have it, his collaborator but merely his conduit, the instrument through which he speaks, like Ion of old.

The way out of this trap, the way to restore faith in the personally authentic performer, cannot be found without changing profoundly our philosophical model of the musical artwork itself. We must stop seeing it

[17] See Kivy, "The Fine Art of Repetition" and "Is Music an Art?" in *The Fine Art of Repetition*.

[18] Langer, *Philosophy in a New Key*, p. 215. Langer is no more sympathetic to this view of performance, for reasons of her own, than I am.

The   Other   Authority

as a linguistic entity and start seeing it, horribile dictu, for what it really is: a product of the arts of decoration. Then the performer is not, by consequence, the slave to the composer's message but one in whose hands lies the task of presenting, for his or her generation and in the best possible version, this decorative structure.

But in saying this—in saying that the role of the performer is to present music, as a decorative structure, in the best possible version for his or her times—I return yet again to what has been the basic, persistent theme of this book. No way of performing a work, from the most "dogmatic" historical authenticity to the most historically "careless," from playing in wigs to Stokowski's Bach, is either self-justifying or self-refuting, on ideological, theoretical, philosophical grounds. Every way of performing is, first, a hypothesis—a plan for execution. And a plan for execution can only, in the end, be evaluated by execution itself. It is a bad plan that cannot be revised in the light of execution, whether it is the composer's plan, the musicologist's, or anyone else's.

So this book is not, for all its critical comments on the *so-called* historically authentic performance, an attempt to "philosophically" refute it. That is not possible.

I am an enemy, to be sure, of "authenticity" in the *singular*. There is no such thing. I am a friend, however, of "authenticities" in the *plural*. Or, rather, I am a friend of any authenticity, or any mix of authenticities, that withstands the only relevant test there is: the test of listening.

The gush of enthusiasm for the historically authentic performance, in one or all of its versions, has quite naturally, as such things will, easily slipped from enthusiasm to orthodoxy. In attacking the orthodoxy, I by no means intend to cast a pall over the enthusiasm. The historical authenticity movement in musical performance has given us new and rewarding ways of listening to our musical repertory (as well as silly, vulgar, and unrewarding ones). And there is no reason why strands of historical authenticity should not be woven together with strands of personal authenticity to make a seamless and beautiful fabric.

Nor is there any reason to think that historical authenticity should not, on some occasions or by some performers, be pursued doggedly and single-mindedly to the end of collapsing performance into text. For as long as we live in a pluralistic musical society, there will be no danger of musical performance as we know it going up the spout. While pluralism

The Other Authority

in performance practice survives, the "extremes" of historically authentic performance will be just one kind of performance plan, among various others, to be tested and tasted by execution and ear. It is only when pursued as the single, solely justifiable ideology of musical performance that historical authenticity must in the ultimate, ideal case obliterate performance as we know it by emasculating personal authenticity and thus closing the gap between performance and work. It is that hegemony of the historically authentic that I fear and that has had the tendency to take "possession" of musicians' minds to the exclusion of all other performance goals—in particular, the goal of personal authenticity that the "performance heroes" of the recent and more distant past have embodied. It is the loss of that goal that I fear the most and that this chapter has been about.

But if we are to rekindle our faith in the personally authentic performer, rekindle our enthusiasm for the performance as artwork, we must escape the linguistic model of music, and the musical puritanism it spawns. When the performer departs from the historically authentic, she is analogous not to a messenger altering the message but, rather, to one who displays a decorative object to the best possible advantage, as she sees it, in the circumstances in which she finds herself. There is nothing of the liar in her work. If there is a kind of charlatanism about her, it is that of the conjurer and magician, not of the dealer in snake oil or the phony evangelist. The commitment of the musical performer has nothing to do with telling the truth, any more than does the commitment of the composer. That is not a misfortune. It is a liberation.

The Other Authority

Bibliography

Advertisement for the Roland C-50. *Early Music* 17 (1989): back cover.

Alperson, Philip. "On Musical Improvisation." *Journal of Aesthetics and Art Criticism* 63 (1984).

Anscombe, G. E. M. *Intention*. 2d ed. Ithaca: Cornell University Press, 1969.

Apel, Willi. *The Notation of Polyphonic Music, 900–1600*. 4th ed. Cambridge, Mass.: Medieval Academy of America, 1953.

Aristophanes. *The Complete Plays*. Edited by Moses Hadas. New York: Bantam, 1962.

Aristotle. *Poetics*. Translated by Richard Janko. Indianapolis: Hackett, 1987.

Aschenbrenner, Karl. *Analysis of Appraisive Characterization*. Dordrecht: D. Reidel, 1983.

Bradley, F. H. *Ethical Studies*. 2d ed. London: Oxford University Press, 1962.

Burney, Charles. *An Account of the Musical Performances in Westminster-Abbey*. With an introduction by Peter Kivy. New York: Da Capo, 1979.

——. *A General History of Music*. Edited by Frank Mercer. 2 vols. New York: Dover, 1957.

Carrier, David. "Art and Its Preservation." *Journal of Aesthetics and Art Criticism* 46 (1987).

Carroll, Noel. "Danto, Style, and Intention." *Journal of Aesthetics and Art Criticism* 53 (1995).

Collingwood, R. G. *The Principles of Art*. Oxford: Clarendon, 1938.

Cook, Nicholas. *Music, Imagination, and Culture*. Oxford: Clarendon, 1990.

Croce, Benedetto. *The Aesthetic as the Science of Expression and of the Linguistic in General*. Translated by Colin Lyas. Cambridge: Cambridge University Press, 1992.

Currie, Gregory. *An Ontology of Art*. New York: St. Martin's, 1989.

Danto, Arthur C. *The Transfiguration of the Commonplace: A Philosophy of Art*. Cambridge: Harvard University Press, 1981.

David, Hans T., and Arthur Mendel, eds. *The Bach Reader*. New York: Norton, 1945.

Davies, Stephen. "Authenticity in Musical Performance." *British Journal of Aesthetics* 27 (1987).

——. "Transcription, Authenticity, and Performance." *British Journal of Aesthetics* 28 (1988).

Dickie, George. "The Myth of the Aesthetic Attitude." *American Philosophical Quarterly* 1 (1964).

Dipert, Randall R. "The Composer's Intentions: An Evaluation of Their Relevance for Performance." *Musical Quarterly* 66 (1980).

Einstein, Alfred. *Gluck*. Translated by Eric Blom. London: J. M. Dent, 1954.

——. *Mozart: His Character, His Work*. Translated by Arthur Mendel and Nathan Broder. London: Oxford University Press, 1951.

French, Peter A., Theodore E. Uehling, Jr., and Howard K. Wettstein, eds. *Midwest Studies in Philosophy*, vol. 16: *Philosophy and the Arts*. Notre Dame, Ind.: University of Notre Dame Press, 1991.

Gann, Ernest K. *Island in the Sky*. New York: Popular Library, 1944.

Girdlestone, Cuthbert. *Mozart and His Piano Concertos*. New York: Dover, 1964.

Goehr, Lydia. *The Imaginary Museum of Musical Works: An Essay in the Philosophy of Music*. Oxford: Clarendon, 1992.

Goodman, Nelson. *Languages of Art: An Approach to a Theory of Symbols.* Indianapolis: Bobbs-Merrill, 1968.

Haskel, Harry. *The Early Music Revival: A History.* London: Thames and Hudson, 1988.

Higgins, Kathleen Marie. *The Music of Our Lives.* Philadelphia: Temple University Press, 1991.

Hume, David. *Essays: Moral, Political, and Literary.* Oxford: Oxford University Press, 1971.

Johnston, Gregory S. "Rhetorical Personification of the Dead in Seventeenth-Century German Funeral Music." *Journal of Musicology* 9 (1991).

Kant, Immanuel. *Critique of Judgment.* Translated by J. H. Bernard. New York: Hafner, 1951.

Kenyon, Nicholas, ed. *Authenticity and Early Music.* Oxford: Oxford University Press, 1988.

Kivy, Peter. *The Fine Art of Repetition: Essays in the Philosophy of Music.* Cambridge: Cambridge University Press, 1993.

———. "Mainwaring's *Handel*: Its Relation to English Aesthetics." *Journal of the American Musicological Society* 18 (1964).

———. *Music Alone: Reflections on the Purely Musical Experience.* Ithaca: Cornell University Press, 1990.

Langer, Susanne K. *Philosophy in a New Key: A Study in the Symbolism of Reason, Rite, and Art.* 3d ed. Cambridge, Mass.: Harvard University Press, 1978.

Le Huray, Peter. *Authenticity in Performance: Eighteenth-Century Case Studies.* Cambridge: Cambridge University Press, 1990.

Levinson, Jerrold. *Music, Art, and Metaphysics: Essays in Philosophical Aesthetics.* Ithaca: Cornell University Press, 1990.

Margolis, Joseph, ed. *Philosophy Looks at the Arts: Contemporary Readings in Aesthetics.* 3d ed. Philadelphia: Temple University Press, 1987.

Mark, Thomas Carson. "The Philosophy of Piano Playing: Reflections on the Concept of Performance." *Philosophy and Phenomenological Research* 41 (1981).

Marshall, Robert L. *The Music of Johann Sebastian Bach: The Sources, the Style, the Significance.* New York: Schirmer, 1989.

Mattheson, Johann. *Der vollkommene Capellmeister.* Translated by Ernest C. Harriss. Ann Arbor, Mich.: UMI Research Press, 1981.

Meyer, Leonard B. *Music, the Arts, and Ideas: Patterns and Practices in Twentieth-Century Culture*. Chicago: University of Chicago Press, 1967.

Planer, John H. "Sentimentality in the Performance of Absolute Music: Pablo Casals's Performance of the Saraband from Johann Sebastian Bach's Suite No. 2 in D Minor for Unaccompanied Cello, S. 1008." *Musical Quarterly* 73 (1989).

Power, Eileen. *Medieval People*. Garden City, N.Y.: Anchor, n.d.

Robbins Landon, H. C. *Haydn: A Documentary Study*. New York: Rizzoli, 1981.

Rochberg, George. *Three Cadenzas for Mozart's Concerto for Oboe, K. 314, for Solo Oboe*. Bryn Mawr, Pa.: Theodore Presser, 1989.

Rollins, Mark, ed. *Danto and His Critics*. Cambridge: Blackwell, 1993.

Rossini, G. *Overture to "William Tell."* Edited by Percival R. Kirby. London: Eulenberg, n.d.

Ryle, Gilbert. *The Concept of Mind*. New York: Barnes and Noble, 1949.

Saint-Foix, G. de. *The Symphonies of Mozart*. Translated by Leslie Orrey. London: Dennis Dobson, 1947.

Schmitz, Hans-Peter. *Die Kunst der Verzierung im 18. Jahrhundert: Instrumental und Vökale Muzierpraxis in Beispielen*. Kassel: Bärenreiter, 1955.

Sharpe, R. A. "Authenticity Again." *British Journal of Aesthetics* 31 (1991).

Slonimsky, Nicolas, ed. *The Lexicon of Musical Invective: Critical Assaults on Composers since Beethoven's Time*. 2d ed. Seattle: University of Washington Press, 1969.

Spade, Paul Vincent. "Do Composers Have to Be Performers Too?" *Journal of Aesthetics and Art Criticism* 49 (1991).

Spencer, Stewart. "Wagner's Nuremberg." *Cambridge Opera Journal* 4 (1992).

Spitta, Phillip. *Johann Sebastian Bach: His Work and Influence on the Music of Germany (1685–1750)*. Translated by Clara Bell and J. A. Fuller-Maitland. 3 vols. New York: Dover, 1951.

Stravinsky, Igor. *Poetics of Music in the Form of Six Lessons*. Translated by Arthur Knodel and Ingolf Dahl. New York: Vintage, 1959.

Summers, David. *The Judgment of Sense: Renaissance Naturalism and the Rise of Aesthetics*. Cambridge: Cambridge University Press, 1990.

Taruskin, Richard. "On Letting the Music Speak for Itself." *Journal of Musicology* 1 (1982).

——, et al. "The Limits of Authenticity: A Discussion." *Early Music* 12 (1984).

Thom, Paul. *For an Audience: A Philosophy of the Performing Arts.* Philadelphia: Temple University Press, 1993.

Tillman, Frank A., and Steven M. Cahn, eds. *Philosophy of Art and Aesthetics: From Plato to Wittgenstein.* New York: Harper and Row, 1969.

Treitler, Leo. "The 'Unwritten' and 'Written Transmission' of Medieval Chant and the Start-Up of Musical Notation." *Journal of Musicology* 10 (1992).

Wallace, Robin. *Beethoven's Critics: Aesthetic Dilemmas and Resolutions during the Composer's Lifetime.* Cambridge: Cambridge University Press, 1986.

Wilsmore, S. J. "Unmasking Skepticism about Restoration." *Journal of Aesthetics and Art Criticism* 46 (1987).

Young, James O. "The Concept of Authentic Performance." *British Journal of Aesthetics* 28 (1988).

Index

Beaumont, Francis, 265
Bechstein piano, 180
Beethoven, Ludwig van, 54–55, 65, 70–
    71, 77, 85, 96–97, 119, 131–32, 156,
    160–61, 164, 176–77, 180–83, 198–
    201, 204–17, 220–27, 238, 249, 257,
    265, 278
Bell, Clive, 56
Berg, Alban, 70, 274
Berlioz, Hector, 53, 69–70
Bernstein, Leonard, 123, 133
Bogart, Humphrey, 113
Bradley, F. H., 145–46, 190
Brahms, Johannes, 70, 93–94, 96, 100,
    116, 121–22, 132, 200, 241–42, 244,
    262
Brandenburg Concerto No. 2 (Bach), 43–
    45
Brandenburg Concerto No. 3 (Bach), 70
Brandenburg Concertos (Bach), 102–3,
    283
Burney, Charles, 49, 66–68
Byrd, William, 96–97

Cadenzas for Mozart's Oboe Concerto
    (Rochberg), 274–76
Cage, John, 51
Cahn, Steven M., 14n
Cantatas (Bach), 234, 244–49; No. 20,
    247; No. 30, 247; No. 75, 247; No. 76,
    247; No. 140, 29–39; No. 147, 247; No.
    186, 247
Carmina Burana (Orff), 53
Carrier, David, 193–95
Carroll, Noel, 61n, 62
Cartesian certainty, 163
Cartesianism, 220
Casals, Pablo, 32–33, 123, 132–34
Catiline, Lucius Sergius, 203–4
Cézanne, Paul, 56–57
Chopin, Frédéric, 6, 116, 164, 176–77,
    192
Choreography, of music, 234, 256–59
Chromatic Fantasy and Fugue (Bach), 77
Chrysander, Friedrich, 268
Cicero, Marcus Tullius, 203–5
Cimabue, Giovanni, 218–19
CKB. See Composer knows best

Clemenza di Tito, La (Mozart), 177
Collaboration, of composer and per-
    former, 264–65
Collingwood, R. G., 123, 218, 263–67,
    273, 282, 284
Commedia dell'arte, 165
Complex music, 258–59
Composer knows best (CKB), 162–71,
    173, 281
Composer worship, 278
Concert hall, 94–101, 234, 238, 241–59
Concerto for Violin in D (Brahms), 241–
    42
Concerto for Oboe in C (Mozart), 274–76
Cook, Nicholas, 55n, 247n
Corelli, Arcangelo, 129, 132–33, 167
Coronation Anthems (Handel), 91, 98
Coronation Mass (Mozart). See Mass in C
    (Mozart)
Council of Trent, 225, 257
Counter-Reformation, 256–57
Courtesy meaning, 124
Creatures of Prometheus Overture (Beetho-
    ven). See Overture to Creatures of Prome-
    theus (Beethoven)
Croce, Benedetto, 218–23
Crutchfield, Will, 3n
Cult of aesthetic contemplation, 254
Cult of listening, 254
Cult of the composer, 279
Culture of authorship, 186–87
Currie, Gregory, 59–60

Dance music, 251–52; of Mozart and Bee-
    thoven, 249
Dancing, and aesthetic satisfaction, 252–
    53
Danto, Arthur C., 51, 62–64, 95n, 230–
    31, 239n
David, Hans T., 35
Davies, Stephen, 9–10, 12, 19, 81–82, 85–
    88, 152n
DB. See Delicate balance
Death of the author, 187
Debussy, Claude, 156
Delicate balance (DB), 162–63, 166–73,
    281; Leibnizian version, 171–73
De Profundis (Gluck), 259

Index

294

I n d e x

Improvisation, 164–65, 263
Information theory, 217
Instrumental music, rise of, 238
Intention: artist's, 194–95; and authenticity, 21–22; author's, 222; composer's, 5, 9–21, 28–46, 78, 141–42, 145–55, 161–87, 189, 222, 273–77; concept of, 22–28, 34–35; inaccessibility of, 13–20
Interpretation, 102–6, 117–19, 136–38, 175–79, 182, 256
Ion the rhapsode, 40, 222, 284
"Italian" Symphony (Mendelssohn). *See* Symphony No. 4 (Mendelssohn)
Ives, Charles, 55

Janigro, Antonio, 123, 133
Josquin Des Prez, 76, 196, 221, 225

Kant, Immanuel, 200, 235–38, 250–51
Kenyon, Nicholas, 3n, 15n, 152n
Kirby, Percival R., 268n
Kivy, Peter, 72n, 101n, 121n, 137n, 151n, 167n, 181n, 198n, 220n, 227n, 237n, 254n, 262n, 284n
Kleine Nachtmusik, Eine (Mozart), 167–69
Kleinmeisters, 171
Knowing how, 213, 221
Knowing that, 213, 221
Kotzebue, August von, 199, 201
Kreisler, Fritz, 60
Kuhnau, Johann, 197

Landowska, Wanda, 127
Langer, Susanne K., 214, 284
Le Hurray, Peter, 152n–53n, 178–80
Leibniz, Gottfried Wilhelm, 169–73
Leonin, 40, 226
Leonore Overtures (Beethoven). *See* Overtures to *Leonore* (Beethoven)
Levinson, Jerrold, 61–62, 64–66, 81–88
Linguistic model, of music, 284–86
Listener. *See* Audience
Liszt, Franz, 164, 231
Literary model, of music, 121–22
Liturgical music, 90–93, 256–59
Live performance, 100–101
Logical positivism, ix

Magnus liber organi, 240
Mahler, Gustav, 70
Mainstream performance, 6, 33, 46, 70, 77, 79, 96, 198, 229, 232, 270, 283
Margolis, Joseph, 62
Mark, Thomas Carson, 115–22, 137
Marshall, Robert, 15–18
Marx, Groucho, 223–24
Marx, Karl, 154
Mass in B minor (Bach), 174
Mass in C (Mozart), 90–93, 101–2
Mattheson, Johann, 244–45
Meaning, 152–55, 222
Medium (artistic), 229–32
Meistersinger von Nürnberg, Die (Wagner), 92, 154–55
Melograph, 132–34
Mendel, Arthur, 35
Mendelssohn, Felix, 221, 244
Message (of music), 283–86
Messiah (Handel), 5, 10, 70, 174, 244
Meyer, Leonard, 214, 217
Michelangelo Buonarotti, 192
Mill, John Stuart, 175
Mise en scène, of music. *See* Setting
Montaigne, Michel Eyquem de, 220
Moore, G. E., xi
Mozart, Wolfgang Amadeus, 5–6, 69–70, 85, 87, 90–94, 97, 102–3, 131, 164, 167–69, 176–77, 179, 192, 206, 210, 229, 238, 242–44, 249, 255, 263, 273–76
Musical politics, 282–83
Music as decoration, 285–86
Musicology, 71–74, 80–81, 206–7, 244, 268, 280
Musikalische Exequien (Schütz), 93n

Napoleon Bonaparte, 40, 45
Neue Bach Ausgabe, 148
Newton, Isaac, 213
Newtonian mechanics, 213
Notation, 262–63
Notre Dame School of Polyphony, 40

Ockeghem, Johannes, 40, 226, 256–59
Opera, 89–93; Handel's, 262

Index

296

Index

Septet, Op. 20 (Beethoven), 131, 133–34, 136, 156, 160–61, 265
Serkin, Rudolf, 123, 133–34, 161
Sermon (in Bach cantatas), 246–48
Setting, of music, 85–89, 93–101, 234, 249–59
Shakespeare, William, 240
Sharpe, R. A., 74–78
Simple music, 258–59
Sincerity, in performance, 109–22
Sinfonia Concertante for Winds (Mozart), 192–93
Slonimsky, Nicolas, 199–200, 207–9
Socrates, 40, 186
Sonata for Violin in A minor (Albinoni), 129–31
Sonata for Piano, Op. 106 (Beethoven), 113–14, 161
Sonata for Piano, Op. 110 (Beethoven), 180–82
Sonata for Violin, Op. 5, No. 9 (Corelli), 129–30
Sonata for Piano in B♭ (Schubert), 167–69
Sonic authenticity, 48, 74–76, 79, 82–84, 138–41, 188–93, 195–98, 226–29, 232, 276
Sonic museum. *See* Concert hall
Spade, Paul Vincent, 136
Spencer, Stewart, 154n
Spitta, Phillip, 129n
"Star Spangled Banner, The," 216
Steinway piano, 180–81, 192
Stokowski, Leopold, 285
Story. *See* Interpretation
Strauss, Richard, 70
Stravinsky, Igor, 70, 156, 266–67, 282
Style, in performance, 123
Sublime, and beautiful, 167
Suite for Unaccompanied Cello in D minor (Bach), 32–33, 132–34
Summers, David, 240n
Swieten, Baron van, 70, 229
Sympathy, 203–6, 220, 223, 225, 227–28
Symphony No. 1 (Beethoven), 54–55, 71, 77, 198, 204–6, 223–24
Symphony No. 2 (Beethoven), 199

Symphony No. 3 (Beethoven), 47, 85, 191, 198
Symphony No. 5 (Beethoven), 212–14, 216–17, 229
Symphony No. 7 (Beethoven), 199–200
Symphony No. 9 (Beethoven), 96, 199
Symphony No. 1 (Brahms), 93–94, 122, 262
Symphony No. 4 (Brahms), 100
Symphony No. 45 (Haydn), 104–6
Symphony No. 4 (Mendelssohn), 221
Symphony No. 31 (Mozart), 168
Symphony No. 35 (Mozart), 94
Symphony No. 37 (Mozart/Michael Haydn), 131
Symphony No. 40 (Mozart), 131, 133, 135

Taruskin, Richard, 1–2, 13–14, 19–21, 30
Taste, 174–75, 183–84
Telemann, Georg Philipp, 170–71, 210
Text, musical, 267–73
Theory of relativity, 213
Thing, concept of, 124–28
Thom, Paul, 124–28
Tillman, Frank A., 14n
Titian, 194–95
Tomlinson, Gary, 15, 152n
Toscanini, Arturo, 123, 127, 133–34, 168
Traviata, La (Verdi), 127
Treitler, Leo, 262
Triebensee, Joseph, 243
Trio, Op. 1, No. 3 (Beethoven), 65
Trio, Op. 38 (Beethoven), 131, 133, 135, 156, 160–61, 265
Tristan und Isolde (Wagner), 114

Utilitarianism, 184
Utrillo, Maurice, 279–81

Verdi, Giuseppe, 47, 91, 207
Verklärte Nacht (Schoenberg), 55
Vibrato, 270–71
Viennese classical style, 238
Virgil, 167
Visible music, 89–107, 234, 255–59

Wagner, Richard, 91, 154
Wagner, Wieland, 154–55

Index